D1611734

# MAKING READING POSSIBLE THROUGH EFFECTIVE CLASSROOM MANAGEMENT

Edited by
Diane Lapp
San Diego State University
For the IRA Classroom Organization
and Reading Committee

International Reading Association
800 Barksdale Road    Newark, Delaware 19711

# INTERNATIONAL READING ASSOCIATION

Copyright 1980 by the
International Reading Association, Inc.

**Library of Congress Cataloging in Publication Data**
Main entry under title:

Making reading possible through effective classroom
    management.

    Bibliography:   p.
    1. Reading. 2. Classroom management. I.
Lapp, Diane.
LB1050.M345      428.4'07      80-10444
ISBN 0-87207-729-2

# Contents

iv

# Foreword

The topic of this book is one that is of extreme interest to teachers and everyone else who would like to see schools develop ever better readers. It focuses on an area in which increased teacher skill will almost certainly lead to improved reading achievement. Thus, *Making Reading Possible through Effective Classroom Management* ought to attract a large audience.

Teachers are continuously searching for practical and specific ideas concerning how to organize instruction in their classrooms. They search for this information so they can more easily and effectively manage a class which includes both eager and not-so-eager students. This book will certainly provide many of the answers for that search. It is significant that the book moves from chapters that depict good organization to the diagnostic assessment which directs it. It is a practical book, as its concern for the organization and use of the assessment data demonstrates. Yet it offers no panaceas and concludes on the continual assessment and improvement of the classroom implemented. The book should be a welcome source in both preservice and inservice teacher education programs.

It is the possibility of improved learning that makes classroom organization such as important topic, and teachers along with parents and all concerned citizens are interested in that. Good organization should mean improved learning because it should lead to more efficient and effective use of a teacher's time, increased attention to the most serious student problems, individual and group sessions for all students, and increased student/teacher interaction time.

With such potential, this book is a welcome addition to IRA's impressive list of publications on effective teaching.

Roger Farr, *President*
International Reading Association
1979-1980

# Preface

This book is designed for every teacher who has ever asked: Why am I unable to meet the needs of all of my children? Why do I feel inadequate?

The authors of this text have worked with many classroom teachers from all areas of the country who feel the frustrations inherent in similar questions. Through such interactions, these authors have found that the majority of classroom teachers experiencing similar frustrations have a good knowledge of current educational theories but are unable to implement these theories in a manner that provides for the individual differences of their students.

This inability to implement and facilitate personalized curriculum may be occurring because many teachers have not been adequately apprised of the *management procedures* needed to plan, implement, and maintain such a program. In attempting to eliminate this dichotomy between theory and practice by providing teachers with an understanding of the components and procedures inherent in an organized reading program, the International Reading Association, during the presidency of William Eller, initiated a committee to address the topic of classroom organization and reading. The appointed committee was charged with the task of preparing a manuscript that would provide the classroom teacher with a theoretical/practical step-by-step implementation of an organized reading program.

This volume addresses that charge. Throughout the text, *classroom management* is defined as a process which enables the teacher to provide a favorable atmosphere of organization in which individuals, either alone or in small groups, may apply their abilities and energies to the accomplishment of educational tasks. Through a managed system of classroom organization, the teacher is provided with a means of collectively meeting the individual needs of students. The key element to maintaining such a program is the teacher's ability to understand the relationships among individuals, groups composed of these individuals, and the organizational structure of the school and community.

Too often, the development of such a climate has been neglected because the term classroom management has been inappropriately associated with classroom discipline or student manipulation.

The contributors to this text address the issues which have hindered managed program implementation and they suggest ways teachers can help individuals or groups extend their basic skills through diagnostically planned learning tasks.

Lapp introduces the underlying constructs of classroom organization which are discussed in detail in later chapters. The author believes that, once these constructs are delineated, a definition of classroom organization will become a pragmatic realization.

## Chapter One   Overview: Classroom Management

Diane Lapp
*San Diego State University*

"I can't meet the reading needs of every child in my classroom and still have time to teach all of the other things that are required in the curriculum. I guess I'm just not cut out to be a teacher," said Melanson, the new second grade teacher. Hill, the fourth grade teacher, responded "It's only October; give yourself a chance. I felt the same way when I began teaching eight years ago."

Melanson continued, "I won't be in teaching eight years from now if I can't figure out a better teaching system. I don't think my students are gaining a thing. I'm bored, frustrated, and I don't know what to do. Can you give me some tips?"

Hill was able to offer advice such as the following.

## Educational Philosophy

In order to be a successful teacher, Hill believed there must be a direct correlation between a teacher's educational philosophy and the methods being implemented in the corresponding classroom. Through discussion, Melanson decided that the environment which would be the direct outgrowth of her philosophy would include provisions wherever possible for

1. individual student differences;
2. student awareness of their own strengths and needs;
3. student participation in planning general program goals and activities; and

4. student participation in the evaluation of self, goals, and activities.

Melanson also learned that her beliefs about education and educational settings could be implemented only if she viewed herself as a classroom manager—a facilitator of learning. She was slightly apprehensive because she realized that in her new role she would still design and control the program but would be using multiple materials and resources for implementation.

Hill cautioned Melanson to proceed gradually, since the skills of management needed by the teacher are a prime element in implementing an effectively organized reading curriculum, and to explore a working definition of classroom organization by addressing the following constructs or conditions inherent in implementing her educational philosophy.

## Philosophical Implementation

Teachers are often unable to implement their educational philosophies because of the dichotomy that may exist between prescribed educational theories and their knowledge of implementation strategies. Since Melanson defined classroom organization as a series of processes required to address the individual strengths and needs of students, Hill encouraged her to use the educational management system illustrated in Figure 1 as the schemata to correlate her educational philosophy and classroom practices.

## Management Systems

Throughout the 1950s and 1960s the use of educational management systems increased as steadily as the use of technology increased. Following a business management model, educational technologists designed curricula which relied on an interactional base. The interactional base, which has become more refined in the 1970s, integrates the efforts of parents, students, teachers, school boards, and community leaders. The success of such a program is dependent upon well-correlated goals.

Melanson compiled the following outline to further delineate the concept of educational management and provide the necessary procedures for implementation.

## Awareness of Existing Structures and Individuals

1. What are the daily influences in my classroom?
   societal influences
   budget allocations
   curricular requirements
   time schedules
   special services
   special teachers
   administrative philosophy
   community influences
   support of colleagues
   goals of parents
2. Who are the children with whom I am working?

As Melanson jotted down these questions, she realized that by addressing each she would better acquaint herself with existing program structures and the people who have decision-making powers regarding these structures.

## General Operational Themes

She continued to jot down notes as she further surveyed the management schemata of Figure 1.

1. What type of curricula can I manage?
   a classical setting
   a personalized, thematic setting
2. What themes are of interest to my students?
3. Can I integrate all of the designated reading, writing, and spelling skills into these themes?
4. Can I cover all of the content area skills through a thematic approach to teaching?

To answer these questions, it was necessary to compile charts of all of the reading, writing, spelling, and content area skills that were to be covered by the class. Once these skills were delineated, Melanson believed she would be more secure in planning integrated lessons within a thematic context.

## Assess Needs of Existing Program

1. What are the goals of the existing program?
2. Why do I believe there is a need to alter this program?

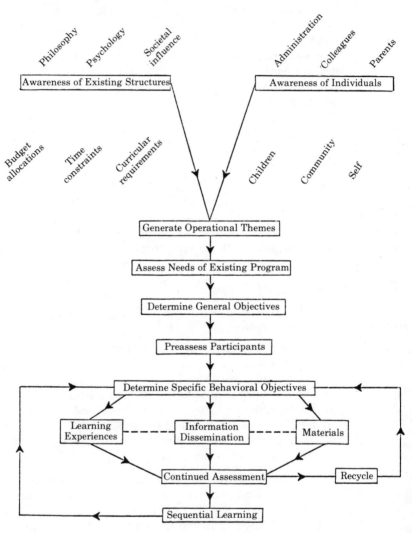

**Figure 1. Educational Management System**

Reprinted with permission from: D. Lapp and J. Flood. *Teaching Reading to Every Child*. New York: Macmillan, 1978.

3. Are the goals of my thematic program similar enough to accommodate the development of the designated curricular skills?
4. Am I covering areas that have been designated for another grade level?

After comparing the existing program with the intended program, Hill encouraged Melanson to begin more concrete program planning.

## Determine General Objectives

1. What are the general objectives for each thematic area?
2. Can I facilitate learning in all of the curriculum areas through a thematic approach?

Hill encouraged Melanson to delineate one theme and its corresponding general objectives. Melanson selected *Star Wars* because of high student interest.

| THEME | GENERAL OBJECTIVES |
|---|---|
| Star Wars | Develop an awareness of self. |
| | Identify various forms of life. |
| | Explore significant others. |
| | Identify geographical and cosmic boundaries. |
| | Identify cultural boundaries. |
| | Discuss the effects of social change. |
| | Explore the concept of time. |
| | Explore the concept of transportation. |
| | Discuss language etymology. |
| | Explore social boundaries of various cultures. |

As she explored the wide range of possible objectives that could be accomplished through this theme, Melanson became more confident that through a thematic approach she would be able to integrate the content areas and basic skill needs of each child. Within the theme of *Star Wars*, students could explore geography, history, astronomy, mathematics, and anthropology, as well as reading, writing, speaking, and listening. Through the integration of these areas, standard basic content skills could be explored within a context which was of interest to the student.

## Preassess Participants

John Dewey, philosopher and educator, has said (3):

The statement that individuals live in a world means, in the concrete, that they live in a series of situations. And when it is said that they live in these situations, the meaning of the word *in* is different from its meaning when it is said that pennies are "in" a can. It means, once more, that interaction is going on between an individual and objects and other persons. The conceptions of situation and of interaction are inseparable from each other. An experience is always what it is because of a transaction taking place between an individual and what, at the time, constitutes his environment, whether the latter consists of persons with whom he is talking about some topic or event, the talked-about being also a part of the situation; or the toys with which he is playing; the book he is reading (in which his environment conditions at the time may be England or ancient Greece or an imaginary region); or the materials of an experiment he is performing. The environment, in other words, is whatever conditions interact with the personal needs, desires, purposes, and capacities to create the experience which is had. Even when a person builds a castle in the air he is interacting with the objects which he constructs in fancy.

Melanson realized that in order to actualize Dewey's goal, it would be necessary to understand each child's strengths and needs. The following questions would aid her in future preassessment.

1. What standardized measures are employed by my system?
2. How are these measures beneficial to my program?
3. What informal evaluation techniques do I use?

Through a variety of techniques, Melanson attempted to determine each student's 1) sensory, perceptual, emotional, and social needs; 2) knowledge of oral reading; and 3) silent reading comprehension skills. She could then plan groups according to skill-development needs, achievement, and interest.

Hill reminded Melanson that grouping is a prime factor in successful classroom organization since the method used to group students determines flexibility in individualizing instruction, provides for economy of teacher effort, and increases student participation.

As Melanson was to learn through gradual program implementation, instruction is more efficiently provided for a

Lapp

group of children with similar strengths, needs, interests, and purposes than for a total classroom of separate individuals. Efficient grouping provides an opportunity to match learner with materials.

As shown in Figure 1, successful grouping practices are dependent upon the following steps:

1. Defining the objectives of the instructional program.
2. Determining appropriate methodology for teaching each objective.
3. Preassessing the reading behaviors of each student.
4. Forming initial groups according to preassessment.
5. Continuously evaluating student progress.

## Determine Specific Behavioral Objectives

After determining initial group composition, it is necessary to plan behavioral objectives for each group. Melanson asked the following questions:

1. What should each student accomplish?
2. What learning conditions must be operant for this accomplishment?
3. How will I know when the learner has acquired the new behavior?

A *behavioral objective* is simply a statement composed of three phrases.

1. *External conditions*, which describe the setting under which the specified learner behavior will occur.
2. *Terminal behavior*, which describes the desired type of learner behavior.
3. *Acceptable performance*, which defines that degree of learner competency that must be exhibited.

Behavioral objectives are important in conducting continuous program evaluation, and as teachers become skilled in using them an abbreviated system can be used.

To the charge that behavioral objectives or managed curricula dehumanize learning, Melanson said that if a student is in a classroom which in any way dehumanizes the student, it is the fault of the teacher/program manager rather than the curricula or materials since the planning is done by the manager.

## Learning Experiences, Information Dissemination, and Materials

After having determined group composition, needs, and objectives, Melanson began to determine the various *methods of instruction* for each group. She realized that while she would manage the entire program, she could not physically disseminate the instruction for each activity. At the suggestion of Hill, Melanson began to develop learning prescriptions (see Chapter Three).

## Continued Assessment, Recycling, and Sequential Learning

1. How successful is the child at completing the learning task?
2. How can I better motivate and reinforce successful completion of each task?
3. What type of materials are the most motivating?
4. How can learner independence be encouraged?
5. How can skill transfer be encouraged?
6. What procedures encourage the learner to synthesize and generalize information?
7. How can evaluative thinking and questioning techniques be conveyed?

The sequential next step in learning for each child can only be planned as a result of the learning acquired in each preceding lesson.

After making decisions related to the degree of successful learning, regrouping may occur and further instruction may be delineated. Mastery of learning may be affected by the 1) amount of instructional time utilized for the topical presentation, 2) background readiness of the student, 3) manner or method of presentation, 4) complexity of the material, and 5) student interest in the topic.

Hill reassured Melanson of the philosophical strengths of such a personalized program of learning and reminded her of the following conditions which influence a successful program.

1. Students are children. The degree of sophistication of program decision-making ability required must be

commensurate with the learner's ability and experience. The responsibility for program planning rests with the teacher/manager who must also guide each student's independence and initiative in learning situations. Students need to be provided with options and then taught how, what, when, and where to pursue the learning task.

2. As the teacher/program manager, it is important to design a manageable program. Begin with one lesson in one content area and expand your program once you have succeeded.

3. Build upon the materials which are currently housed within your classroom or school. Do not allow a lack of materials to impede program implementation.

4. As a teacher/program manager, you will be shifting a large portion of your time from instructional implementation to instructional planning.

5. You will need to encourage student participation in implementing and correcting portions of learning.

You, like Melanson, may feel that a dichotomy exists between your educational philosophy and practice. If your philosophy is similar to Melanson's, a well managed program may better enable you to personalize your curricula. The chapters which follow further articulate the procedures briefly discussed in this overview.

**References**
1, Anderson, Paul, and Diane Lapp. *Language Skills in the Elementary School*, Third Edition. New York: Macmillan, 1979.
2. Clymer, Ted, et al. *Ginn 720: Reading Management System*. Lexington, Maine: Ginn-Xerox, 1976.
3. Dewey, John. *Experience and Education*. New York: Macmillan, 1938, 43-44.
4. Lapp, Diane. "Behavioral Objectives Writing Skills Test," *Journal of Education*, 154 (February 1972), 13-24. (This text may be secured from Educational Testing Services, Princeton, New Jersey.)
5. Lapp, Diane. *The Use of Behavioral Objectives in Education*. Newark, Delaware: International Reading Association, 1972.
6. Lapp, Diane, et al. *Teaching and Learning: Philosophical, Psychological, and Curricular Applications*. New York: Macmillan, 1975.
7. Lapp, Diane, and James Flood. *Teaching Reading to Every Child*. New York: Macmillan, 1978.
8. Lapp, Diane. "Individualizing Made Easy for Teachers," *Early Years*, 7 (February 1977), 63-77.

Mangieri discusses six major factors believed to be operative in establishing and maintaining an effectively organized classroom and suggests that such a classroom provides the structure for the implementation of a personalized curriculum.

## Chapter Two  Characteristics of an Effectively Organized Classroom

John N. Mangieri
*University of South Carolina*

A commonly held belief among educators is that the teacher is the key element in a school's instructional program. It becomes easy to concur with this assertion since it is generally the teacher who determines a classroom's subject matter priorities, provides direct instruction to students, and evaluates their learning performances. Considering the significance of these tasks and the other activities for which the teacher is responsible, it is no wonder that the teacher is the key element in a school's instructional program.

This discussion does not deal specifically with the teacher but, instead, focuses upon the environment (the classroom) in which a teacher functions. By improving this area of the teaching/learning process, both teacher performance and student achievement will improve commensurately.

Information provided here may increase the effectiveness of a classroom although the author is acutely aware that the classrooms of those who read this chapter will vary greatly in stages of development. For some readers, the content of the chapter will serve as reinforcement for the organization of their classrooms. Others may view the ideas as innovative and perhaps the basis for major revisions.

## Organization for Reading Instruction

Is your classroom effectively organized for reading

instruction? Your initial, immediate reaction would probably be to respond affirmatively. Before you answer, however, reflect upon every aspect of your classroom. "Is it organized as efficiently as possible? Are my students achieving at a level congruent with their academic potential? Are my instructional procedures optimally effective?" If you answer "no" to one or more of these questions, then your classroom is not effectively organized for reading instruction.

What *are* the characteristics of a classroom effectively organized for reading instruction? An all-inclusive answer is impossible in a short chapter such as this one. The discussion must, therefore, include only the most pertinent information.

The remainder of this chapter is devoted to a discussion of the following six characteristics:

1. Individual differences of students are recognized and provision is made to accommodate these differences.
2. Comprehensive, continuous diagnosis occurs in order to ascertain student reading proficiencies and deficiencies.
3. Both immediate and long-range planning for reading instruction take place on a regular basis.
4. The nonteaching conditions of the educational situation are employed to their maximum usage.
5. Instructional procedures are utilized which will produce optimal reading achievement for *every child* in the classroom.
6. Evaluation of the instructional process relative to reading is conducted in a continuous and thorough manner.

1. *Individual differences of students are recognized and provision is made to accommodate these differences.*

Educators have long acknowledged that no two individuals are precisely the same in every respect. Individual differences exist in intellectual, physical, emotional, and educational traits; thus, it can be concluded that each person learns at a rate and in a manner congruent with the degree to which these traits enhance and/or hinder the acquisition of reading proficiency.

Although most teachers have accepted the concept of individual differences, this acceptance unfortunately is not generally reflected either in their pedagogical practices or in the structure of the reading programs in which they teach. Educators continue to spend the majority of the school day engaged in whole-class instruction. Reading programs frequently mandate activities which clearly conflict with the individual differences of children and adolescents. Some teachers and administrators impose behavioral and other disciplinary measures to which *every* student is expected to adhere.

If a reading program is to be truly effective, educators must close this gap between commitment and practice. Their reading programs must provide for the intellectual, physical, emotional, and educational differences of individual children and adolescents.

## A. Intellectual

In recent years, devices for measuring intelligence of individuals have been severely criticized. Generally speaking, these criticisms were quite warranted since many abuses were committed under the rubric of intelligence testing.

Although one may find fault with the devices employed to measure intelligence, Spache (*15*), Strang, McCullough, and Traxler (*18*), and Durkin (*14*) reaffirmed the relationship between intelligence and learning to read. The implication of the relationship between intelligence and one's ability to read is that individuals of superior intellectual development will *tend* to read at a comparable level; persons of limited intelligence will *tend* to be poor readers.

An effectively organized reading program will have estimates of the intellectual potential of each of its students. The measures used to determine these scores will not be haphazardly chosen. Careful study and much professional reading will serve as precursors to the selection of these assessment devices. Only by employing a meticulous process of selection and utilization of assessment devices will accurate information be procured about the intellectual capabilities of students.

The gathering of information on intelligence is not

meant to suggest a labeling of students into "haves" and "have nots." Instead, it should be viewed as a piece of salient information which the teacher can employ in gauging the degree to which a student is attaining potential in reading achievement. A year's growth in reading achievement may be reasonable for some students, but for others it may be an unrealistically high or low standard of attainment.

Thus, the effectiveness of the reading program and of a teacher's efforts would not be evaluated on the basis of a single standard against which every child is measured. Rather, this form of evaluation would recognize that every child has a different potential for learning to read. The degree to which children are attaining these expectations would help to determine the effectiveness of the reading program and of the classroom teacher of reading.

### B. Physical

The process through which an individual learns to read is a physical as well as a mental one. This surprises many noneducators who consider reading to be exclusively a mental activity. The erroneousness of this viewpoint is apparent when one carefully analyzes the activities inherent in learning to read.

In order to become a proficient reader, an individual must be able to see words clearly as well as discriminate auditorially among the sounds which comprise these words. Additionally, the reading act requires that a person perform both gross and fine motor skills. Just as in the case of intellectual development, each person has varying degrees of physical capability.

Although most educators would agree as to the importance of physical factors in the reading act, few reading programs actually make provision for them. Most diagnostic testing in the areas of vision, speech, hearing, and general health is haphazardly conducted and administered by individuals outside the field of education. The problem is further compounded by the manner in which the information about a student's physical condition is conveyed to teachers. Technical reports may be unintelligible to the educator and significant aspects of the test may be poorly reported.

The absence of standardized test data is not the only facet of the problem. Many teachers are reluctant to utilize informal or observational techniques to screen for subsequent referral of physical problems. Statements such as "I don't have time," "It's not my job," or "My school district doesn't allow" are frequently given as reasons for failing to do so. Diagnosis of some type must be conducted in order to insure that *each* child possesses the prerequisite physical skills necessary for the successful acquisition of reading skills.

The teacher's responsibility does not terminate with this diagnosis of each child. The reading program, through the classroom reading teacher, must instructionally make provision(s) relative to the individual differences and needs of students. For one child, this may entail occasional respites from printed matter in order to rest weary eyes. If a child has a possible hearing difficulty, the teacher may move the student's desk to a location central to instruction in the classroom. A child in poor health may need nourishment, rest during the school day, and other special assistance as warranted by the child's unique condition.

While it is not being suggested that teachers of reading become medical specialists, it is being recommended that teachers become cognizant of the physical factors which are crucial to success in reading. If a teacher suspects the existence of a physical deficiency, it is suggested that instructional and other provisions be made to accommodate the student while the suspected deficiency is being further diagnosed or treated. Chapter Three of Wilson's *Diagnostic and Remedial Reading* (*20*) presents some excellent ideas.

C. Emotional

Each child's emotional composition is unique. Each person's cultural and environmental background creates his special interests, attitudes, and motivations for learning. Family attitudes toward reading and child/parent relationships greatly influence the child's self-concept and view of school and reading.

Differences among students continue to be ignored in classroom reading instruction. Children are expected to conform to common rules of behavior; they frequently read only from a narrow range of written material; and similar modes of instruction and the same learning expectations are imposed. If each child is to realize optimal growth in reading, the teacher must recognize and accommodate the emotional differences among students.

The reading classroom should represent an environment where the individuality of a child is preserved and where a student is treated with dignity and respect. The teacher should seek to positively enhance the self-concept of each student and attempt to understand the intellectual and emotional traits of each child. Instruction as well as the classroom reward system should be adjusted appropriately.

Individuals have different interests which schools should attempt to deepen and broaden. An effective reading program will not clash with the interests of a student but should, instead, help the student find materials congruent with individual interests. These materials may serve as the catalyst for increasing a child's reading interests, for improving attitude toward reading, and for teaching or reinforcing crucial reading skills.

Research tends to reaffirm the relationship between reading achievement and one's attitudes, feelings, and self-concept and suggests that, if a teacher wants a child to attain optimal achievement in reading, then being responsive to human emotions and the teaching of reading is not an either-or proposition. The two can be quite compatible and, if each is kept in proper perspective, can result in increased reading achievement.

### D. Educational

If the phrase, "the only homogeneous group is a group of one," is true (and the author believes it is), then there are conflicts with classroom reading procedures. Usually, three to five ability groups exist within a classroom. Previous performance in reading is the customary basis upon which children are assigned to these groups. This criterion is an arbitrary and artificial one at best.

While the performance of children in reading may have been quite similar, the potentials of these students relative to reading may be quite dissimilar, their physical and emotional conditions diverse, and the proficiencies and deficiencies of each in reading markedly different. With so many discrepancies prevalent among the members, is that group really homogeneous? Will each child in the group have the same needs or the same degree of motivation relative to reading, and will each learn at the same rate and in the same manner? The answers to these questions are, of course, "No." In some classrooms, nevertheless, instruction in reading continues to be equated to three, five, or however many reading groups operate within the same basal. Each group receives similar instruction, and only an insignificant number of pages separates the top reading group from the poorest.

In an effectively organized classroom, the group does not represent an instructional panacea. Depending upon a teacher's philosophical orientation and pedagogical preference, reading groups may or may not be in existence.

The effectively organized classroom makes instructional provisions for the diverse reading capabilities and abilities of each student. The teacher is cognizant of crucial factors which can, and do, influence a child's performance in reading. Reading instruction does not occur on a hit-or-miss basis. Instead, it assumes students receive instruction in those areas necessary for increasing reading proficiency.

2. *Comprehensive, continuous diagnosis occurs in order to ascertain student reading proficiencies and deficiencies.*

Dechant (3:4) defines diagnosis as "an identification of weakness or strength from an observation of symptoms." In terms of actual classroom pedagogical procedure, however, diagnosis has taken on a far different meaning.

In a great majority of school systems, standardized tests are administered to students in the fall or spring of the year. The pupose of these survey tests is to ascertain the reading performance of students in the district. These scores, in turn, are utilized to determine the gains made by the students as a result of the past year's reading instruction.

The relative success or failure of the district's reading program is subsequently assessed. If, on the basis of the test, a high percentage of the district's students read on or above their respective grade levels, then the reading program is positively evaluated. Should the majority of students read below grade level, the reading program would likely be perceived "as not doing its job." While this type of evaluation is oversimplistic and may likely cause incorrect conclusions to be formed, the majority of school districts tend to judge their reading programs in a comparable manner.

In addition to programatic evaluation, reading scores generally are used for two other purposes: grouping and diagnosis. As was explained in the previous section of this chapter, a student's past performance in reading is the basis upon which reading groups are formed. The scores derived from these survey tests are often the criterion used to determine past performance. This can be a hit-or-miss situation, as conveyed in the previous section of this chapter.

Numerous school districts erroneously perceive these survey tests as diagnostic. Given the context in which survey tests are administered, the classroom teacher actually is provided with little valuable information about the student. Usually the teacher is given only a student's test score. Frequently, the student's subtest scores are not known by the teacher, thereby depriving the teacher of an opportunity to know a student's general proficiency in the major areas of the test. Since the actual individual test taken by the student is not given to the teacher, no opportunity is provided to analyze the pupil's answers in order to see if a pattern exists. By a pattern, it is meant that the student consistently answered correctly or incorrectly questions employing a specific reading skill.

The utilization of survey reading tests can have a place in the reading program. School districts should be aware of the constraints of these instruments, and the information derived from them must be kept in perspective. The district should encourage its teachers to carefully scrutinize the reading test of each student in order to determine whether a pattern emerges in the responses given by the child.

It should be noted that survey reading tests constitute only one small facet of available diagnostic procedures and instruments. Standardized reading instruments designated as diagnostic usually will yield much more specific information about a student's reading. In recent years, numerous informal tests and observational techniques have been designed to ascertain the reading skills, interests, instructional levels, and/or emotional needs of children within the confines of the regular classroom. These procedures may include such things as anecdotal records; exercises from professional publications; check lists; interviews; projective measures; informal reading inventories; and informal and/or systematic observation of the child during social, intellectual, and/or reading activities.

The teacher in an effectively organized classroom will pick and choose from this array of available diagnostic devices. The teacher, realizing that the reading proficiencies of children and adolescents are constantly changing, is continually diagnosing students. The type of device used will be dependent upon what the teacher perceives to be the instructional need(s) of the student. Obviously, the device and/or instrument selected will vary in each instance. This practice is congruent with the individual differences of children.

In an effectively organized classroom, diagnosis is conducted on an initial, a final, and above all, continuous basis. Heilman (8:8) correctly maintains that diagnosis should be a blueprint for instruction. Teachers of reading would do well to remember that instruction will become exemplary only when it accurately meets the reading needs of each child. Diagnosis can be the vehicle for determining these needs.

3. *Both immediate and long-range planning for reading instruction take place on a regular basis.*

It is imperative that comprehensive planning for reading instruction occur prior to the actual teaching act. This planning should deal with both immediate and long-range instructional concerns.

The major objective of immediate planning is to answer the question, "What am I going to teach tomorrow?" In attempting to answer this question, the teacher considers the reading proficiencies and deficiencies of members of her class, thus formulating the objectives for the subsequent day's instruction. The teacher may also consider such things as the amount of time to be allocated for reading, when this time will be utilized during the school day, the type(s) of instruction which will occur during this time period, and the measure(s) to be employed in order to assess the effectiveness of the day's instruction.

While immediate planning undoubtedly is essential, it is not the only important type of planning. The very nature of the teaching/learning process of reading necessitates that a teacher engage in long-range planning.

Long-range planning involves looking beyond tomorrow's lesson. In this type of activity, the teacher establishes the ultimate learning outcomes for an individual, a group of students, or the entire class. It should be noted that the existence of a lesson in a teacher's manual does not automatically insure congruence between immediate and long-range goals. It is the teacher's responsibility to continually ask whether tomorrow's lesson is congruent with the long-range goal(s) relative to reading. If the answer is "Yes," then the lesson can be taught as designed. Should the lesson not be congruent, then the planned instruction must be altered.

The process of assessing immediate versus long-range outcomes is a continual but necessary one. Thorough and consistent planning is a rather difficult, but extremely important, part of the instructional process. Although some may dismiss immediate and long-range planning as being impractical or unnecessary, it has been the author's experience that quite the opposite usually is true. Effective planning *is* the prelude to effective reading instruction.

4. *The nonteaching conditions of the educational situation are employed to their maximum usage.*

"I would be a better teacher if only my school district gave me more materials." "I can't individualize instruction. My room is too small." How often have you heard these or similar statements? Implicit in them is the contention that if financial resources were more abundant or if physical conditions were advantageous, the teacher could become effective instructionally.

During the past few years, the author has had the opportunity to visit numerous schools throughout the United States. He has seen innercity, rural, and suburban school districts ranging in fiscal resources from wealthy to financially poor. Classrooms in these districts varied greatly in terms of space, aesthetic beauty, and available instructional materials. He saw no correlation between physical conditions and effective instruction. Excellent instruction was seen both in rooms possessing an abundance or a scarcity of instructional materials. Likewise poor teaching was witnessed in these same types of classrooms. Beautiful looking classrooms have been the scene of beautiful instruction, but the author also viewed some very poor instruction in aesthetically appealing environments. Innovative and meaningful instruction has occurred in certain old school buildings, while equally decrepit settings have been the scene of ineffective teaching.

Materials and physical conditions, except in a very few instances, are peripheral to the occurrence of quality instruction, and a reading program's effectiveness should not be predicated upon these factors. One may recall that the famous one-room school *did* produce some children with excellent proficiency in reading. Yet, in some of America's most aesthetically beautiful schools, remedial reading programs exist to serve many students who are experiencing difficulty in reading.

In a well-managed classroom, the teacher of reading will realistically appraise the classroom environment. This individual will carefully assess the classroom and teaching materials available. In instances where deficiencies exist, the teacher will seek financial or other support from the school district. Should only part or none of these resources be allocated by the school district, the teacher should not "throw in the towel" instructionally for doing so would clearly be an abdication of professional responsibility.

The author recommends that the teacher seek other solutions to the dilemma. For example, if instructional materials are at a premium, can teacher-made materials serve as a substitute? Or, can the teacher use sections of materials previously utilized within the school district? If there is a scarcity of space in the classroom, can portions of the hallway (outside your classroom) be used when necessary? Clearly, these solutions are stop-gap measures to be utilized only until more positive solutions are found.

If these temporary measures prove to be failures, the teacher should alter them or cease utilization of them. The teacher should also continue to press the administration for more permanent solutions in the area of concern.

The effective teacher of reading is not the teacher who

merely has *maximum* conditions for instruction. Rather, the effective teacher of reading is one who employs the financial and physical conditions of a teaching situation to *maximum usage.*

5. *Instructional procedures are utilized which will produce optimal reading achievement for every child in the classroom.*

One year's reading growth per school year by each student is the standard upon which most teachers assess their teaching performance. If the majority of students attain one year's gain in reading, the teacher would likely consider the instruction as favorable. Conversely, if the majority of students do not attain one year's growth in a given school year, a negative viewpoint would develop. Are these assessments correct? The answer can be both "yes" and "no."

Individuals have different capacities for learning and people of high intelligence will likely find learning to read considerably easier than do individuals of limited intelligence. In addition, the *degree* of growth in reading will likely be different. Students of superior intellectual development will attain one year's growth in reading (in a single school year) with minimal effort. One year's gain in reading (in a single school year) may be an extremely difficult attainment for low intelligence students.

This situation suggests then that no single standard can be employed to assess reading achievement. If the majority of a given class are students of high intelligence, a gain of one year in reading achievement generally should not be viewed as an exemplary accomplishment. These students have the capability of accomplishing much more.

Conversely, in a room comprised primarily of students of limited intelligence and/or background of experience, one year's growth in reading per student in a single year may be an unrealistic goal. If such growth is realized within a given school year, however, the accomplishments of the students should be viewed as an extremely positive indicator of a teacher's performance. To further explore the relationship between reading achievement and intelligence, consult Bond and Tinker (*1*) and Spache (*15*).

Since the capabilities of each child in a classroom are quite different, so too are their potentials for growth in reading. Therefore, teachers should assess their effectiveness not in terms of a single standard (i.e., how many of their students gained one year in reading) but rather according to how many students achieved in reading at a level commensurate with their potentials. This standard will, of course, vary on a student-by-student basis.

Optimal achievement in reading by *every child* in the classroom can be realized only through maximum teacher effort, interest, and commitment. This implies a serious scrutiny of instructional efforts, with each teacher asking, "How can I improve the reading instruction being offered to my students?"

Reading instruction should be child-centered and designed to promote optimal and continuous achievement for each student. Students' learning styles, their unique multicultural backgrounds, and their diverse physical, intellectual, and emotional characteristics should be the basis upon which differentiated reading instruction is provided. The teacher should make provision for the learning process, paying particular attention to motivation, reinforcement, and rate and type of learning. Teaching procedures will be congruent with the principles advocated by authorities in reading. Durkin (4), Heilman (8), Spache and Spache (16), and Harris and Smith (7) provide detailed information related to reading methodology and theories of learning.

Record-keeping also plays a significant role in the instructional process for at least two reasons. First, it is imperative that a teacher know the individual differences (emotional, physical) of each child if truly effective instruction is to be given. It is virtually impossible for a teacher to rely upon memory alone to retain such varied information. By recording each child's information in a simple written format, the teacher readily refers to it in the planning and evaluation phases of the instructional process.

Record-keeping has another major purpose. By recording each day's instruction, a teacher can utilize this information as a resource in planning more meaningful, subsequent instruction for each student. The record will enable a teacher to know what specific instruction was given to each student, the success of that specific instruction, and the proficiencies and deficiencies of each child relative to the reading skill acquisition process. This practice will make possible the planning and implementing of future instruction which is congruent with the abilities and needs of each student in the classroom.

While an effective teacher of reading will undoubtedly (and correctly) teach skills to students, the human element of instruction (students) should not be neglected. Effective reading instruction will concurrently develop cognitive as well as affective growth on the part of the students. [See Quandt (*13*) for a description of this process.]

Finally, effective reading instruction does not ignore the development of lifetime readers. Lifetime readers will be produced only if reading becomes a meaningful part of an individual's life and if numerous pleasurable experiences are derived through reading. Children's literature as well as procedures such as "Sustained Silent Reading" (*12*) can make this association possible. Unfortunately, for myriad reasons, some teachers provide their students with few experiences with these materials and techniques.

6. *Evaluation of the instructional process is conducted in a continual and thorough manner.*

Most educators perceive of the instructional process as a three-phase task of planning, teaching and evaluating.

Planning focuses upon both immediate (What am I going to teach tomorrow?) and long-range instruction. Teaching, of course, pertains to the actual delivery of instruction to one's students. Evaluation is ascertaining the degree to which a teacher's immediate and long-term instructional objectives have been, or are being, attained.

While most teachers tend to place emphasis on the planning and teaching aspects of the instructional process, the evaluation facet usually suffers unfortunate neglect on the part of educators. Just as planning and teaching are integral parts of the instructional process, evaluation is an equally important facet.

Some teachers and school administrators contend that "nothing good comes from evaluation," and one can readily see the basis for this viewpoint. Evaluation, coming annually in the form of pretests and posttests, has often supplied the ammunition to critics of America's educational system. Through this medium, the public has been kept apprised of children's real or erroneously perceived reading deficiencies.

Evaluation can serve a beneficial purpose if employed in a manner suggested by Guszak (6), Karlin (10), Stieglitz (17), and others. By utilizing evaluative measures on an ongoing basis, teachers can ascertain whether their daily (immediate) instructional objectives have been attained. Evaluation can also be employed to discern the degree to which students are achieving the long-term objectives formulated by a teacher. When one considers that evaluation can be used to assess both the immediate and the long-term effectiveness of an individual's teaching, can one still legitimately contend that no good can come from evaluation?

Although evaluation can be a pretest/posttest score, it can also assume several additional forms. It should be remembered that the form evaluation takes should be congruent with what one wishes to assess. For example, teachers can probably best determine whether immediate instructional objectives are being achieved by asking (orally or in writing) students a few specific questions relative to the content. Teachers may also utilize observational signals (puzzled looks on students' faces, failure to follow subsequent phases of a lesson, etc.) in order to discern instructional effectiveness.

Specific questions and observational signals can also be used to determine the degree to which long-term instructional objectives are being met by students. The fact that these devices can be employed does not mean that they must be utilized. In some instances, evaluation can be better conducted through the use of a standardized reading test or section thereof, or some other comparable device. It should be remembered that no single measure works best in every instance. What is to be evaluated should determine the type of evaluation to be utilized.

Just as planning is the prelude to effective instruction, thorough and accurate evaluation can serve as its logical consequence. Evaluation should play a significant role in every teacher's classroom and, if properly conducted, evalua-

Mangieri

tion can provide teachers with something more than intuition to tell them whether their students are attaining optimal achievement in reading.

## Concluding Comments

In this chapter, the characteristics of an effectively organized classroom for reading instruction have been described. The degree to which these characteristics exist or are absent in a classroom will determine the effectiveness of a teacher's provision of reading instruction.

It should be noted that all of these characteristics must be present if a classroom is to function optimally and produce maximum student growth in reading.

Implementing the ideas presented in this chapter requires a considerable amount of effort on the part of teachers. Teachers should not be deterred from implementing these ideas, however, since students are the bottom line of instruction and the goal of providing exemplary reading instruction is worth optimal efforts.

**References**
1. Bond, Guy L., and Miles A. Tinker. *Reading Difficulties: Their Diagnosis and Correction*, Third Edition. New York: Appleton-Century-Crofts, 1973.
2. Cunningham, Patricia Marr, et al. *Classroom Reading Instruction K-5: Alternative Approaches*. Lexington: D.C. Heath, 1977.
3. Dechant, Emerald. *Reading Improvement in the Secondary School*. Englewood Cliffs, New Jersey: Prentice-Hall, 1973.
4. Durkin, Dolores. *Teaching Them to Read*, Second Edition. Boston: Allyn and Bacon, 1974.
5. Ekwall, Eldon E. *Locating and Correcting Reading Difficulties*, Second Edition. Columbus, Ohio: Charles E. Merrill, 1977.
6. Guszak, Frank J. *Diagnostic Reading Instruction in the Elementary School*. New York: Harper and Row, 1972.
7. Harris, Larry A., and Carl B. Smith. *Reading Instruction through Diagnostic Teaching*. New York: Holt, Rinehart and Winston, 1972.
8. Heilman, Arthur W. *Principles and Practices of Teaching Reading*, Third Edition. Columbus, Ohio: Charles E. Merrill, 1972.
9. Huck, Charlotte S., and Doris Y. Kuhn. *Children's Literature in the Elementary School*, Second Edition. New York: Holt, Rinehart and Winston, 1968.
10. Karlin, Robert. *Teaching Elementary Reading*, Second Edition. New York: Harcourt Brace Jovanovich, 1975.
11. Mangieri, John N., and Henry D. Olsen. "Five-Phase Task Force Technique: Planning Secondary School Reading Programs," *National Association of Secondary Principals*, 58 (October 1974), 66-70.

12. McCracken, Robert A. "Initiating Sustained Silent Reading," *Journal of Reading*, 14 (May 1971), 521-524, 582-583.
13. Quandt, Ivan. *Self-Concept and Reading.* Newark, Delaware: International Reading Association, 1972.
14. Sartain, Harry W., and Paul E. Stanton (Eds.). *Modular Preparation for Teaching Reading.* Newark, Delaware: International Reading Association, 1974.
15. Spache, George D. *Investigating the Issues of Reading Disabilities.* Boston: Allyn and Bacon, 1976.
16. Spache, George D., and Evelyn B. Spache. *Reading in the Elementary School*, Third Edition. Boston: Allyn and Bacon, 1973.
17. Stieglitz, Ezra L. "School and Classroom Organization for Diagnostic Teaching," in Harry Sartain and Paul Stanton (Eds.), *Modular Preparation for Teaching Reading.* Newark, Delaware: International Reading Association, 1974, 193-208.
18. Strang, Ruth, Constance M. McCullough, and Arthur E. Traxler. *The Improvement of Reading*, Fourth Edition. New York: McGraw-Hill, 1967.
19. Wilson, Richard C., and Helen J. James. *Individualized Reading: A Practical Approach*, Second Edition. Dubuque, Iowa: Kendall/Hunt, 1972.
20. Wilson, Robert M. *Diagnostic and Remedial Reading for Classroom and Clinic*, Third Edition. Columbus, Ohio: Charles E. Merrill, 1977.

The techniques for classroom organization presented by Dillner have been field tested in elementary classrooms in the Clear Lake City area and represent a cross section of rural/urban and multiethnic culturally diverse populations.

## Chapter Three   A View of an Effectively Organized Elementary Reading Program

Martha Dillner
*University of Houston at Clear Lake City*

Brown was a fourth grade teacher whose only technique for teaching reading had been the basal reader approach. Though her classes always contained students with a wide range of reading abilities, she had never used more than three different levels of basal readers because she did not believe she could adequately manage more than three groups of children during her reading class. Her most recent class consisted of children whose reading levels varied from grade one to grade six. She placed all the children reading at grade one in the first reader, all children reading at grade 2.1 to grade 3.1 in the 2.2 reader, and all children reading at the 3.2 or above in the fourth grade reader. She felt if she gave supplementary reading to the children reading material below their reading level, and carefully guided those reading above level, all could benefit from group work in the basals. She did not feel her groupings were as good as they should be but decided they were the best she could do at the time. Brown wanted to provide more individualized reading instruction for her students but simply did not know how to manage it. Thus, when the principal announced that there would be a six-week inservice program on the topic of classroom management in an individualized program, Brown determined that this would be her year to try to individualize instruction.

## Diagnostic-Prescriptive Teaching

During the first session of the inservice workshop,

Mathew, the reading consultant, told the teachers that they were going to learn how to individualize their classrooms through a diagnostic-prescriptive approach to teaching reading. In order to do this, Mathew intended to spend one week on each of six tasks which the teachers would need to complete in order to use the diagnostic-prescriptive approach. Additionally, at the completion of each session, the teachers were to go back to their classrooms and try out the step that had been focused upon during the workshop session. Six tasks are needed by a teacher in order to individualize reading instruction in a diagnostic-prescriptive manner: 1) ascertain a scope and sequence of reading skills, 2) diagnose before instruction, 3) keep records, 4) design instructional strategies, 5) diagnose after instruction, and 6) organize instruction (*3*).

## *Task One: Ascertain a Scope and Sequence of Skills*

During the remainder of the first workshop session, Mathew showed the teachers several types of scope and sequence skills charts. She explained that *scope* was the range of skills and that *sequence* was the order in which the skills should be taught. Hence, most of the sample charts used to illustrate the topic contained a scope of skills which included the categories of readiness, word recognition, comprehension, and study skills. However, some of the charts broke the skills into smaller areas, and the number of skills varied greatly from chart to chart. For example, the scope and sequence chart which accompanied one basal reader program delineated over fifty comprehension skills. However, the scope and sequence chart which accompanied a textbook used to teach reading methods in a teacher education program delineated less than thirty comprehension skills. Mathew pointed out that the skills of *making inferences, making generalizations*, and *making conclusions*, delineated in the basal reader chart, were summarized under one heading, *making inferences*, in the methods textbook. Mathew explained that neither was a right or wrong scope of skills and the list selected for use by each teacher should depend upon individual needs. A valid reason for using the basal reader chart might be that the teacher wanted each skill broken down as explicitly as possible in order to assure that no dimension of the reading skills would be overlooked. An equally valid reason for using the methods textbook might be that the teacher felt a smaller number of skills would be more manageable. Additionally, the same teacher might argue that when students were asked to complete one of the more general skills, they would also learn the skills inherent within that more general skill. Thus, one teacher might prefer that his students specifically practice the skills of making inferences, making generalizations, and making conclusions while another teacher might believe that when she asked her students to practice making inference skills, they would also be practicing making generalizations and making conclusions. This situation would be particularly true if the children were asked to make the type of inferences which did require making a generalization and/or drawing a conclusion. While the former teacher might argue that the children would not learn all three unless the skills were presented separately. The latter teacher might argue that if she had to teach three times as many different skills, she would not be able to develop enough lessons for the children to adequately learn each. Hence, Mathew summarized that there would be a trade off between a few lessons on each of an explicitly stated list of skills or many lessons on each of a more generally stated list of skills.

Mathew asked the teachers to note the order in which the reading skills were presented on both charts. Each chart had the skills arranged in general levels at which the skills would probably be best taught. The skills for each instructional level varied somewhat from the others. For example, a child who was just beginning to read would need skills from a readiness level chart and might be presented a skill such as *using left to right progression*. However, a child who was reading at the fourth grade level would use an intermediate level chart which would not contain the skill of using left to right progression. Rather, the intermediate level chart would probably contain a skill such as *notetaking*, not likely to be found at the readiness level.

The reading skills within each level appear to be in a general order of progression from simple to more difficult. On the intermediate level chart, the skill of *locating detail* is placed before the skill of *locating main idea* because the reader probably has to be able to use the skill of locating detail before he can locate a main idea.

Mathew emphasized to the teachers that placement of a child on any scope and sequence of skills chart should be determined by reading level and not by grade level. If a child reads at the fourth grade level and is in the first grade, he should be taught the skills listed on the intermediate level chart and not the readiness level chart. Likewise, a fourth grade student who is a nonreader should be presented skills from the readiness level chart and not the intermediate level chart.

*Brown ascertains a scope and sequence of skills.* After the meeting, Brown went home and carefully examined the scope and sequence of skills of the three basal reader texts which she had been using with her three groups. Then she perused the scope and sequence of skills chart given to her by the reading consultant and decided to use the chart from the methods textbook as her master list of skills; it seemed less cumbersome to her than did the more expansive basal reader charts. However, Brown did extend the scope of the chart she selected by delineating more explicitly a few of the reading skills which she felt particularly important for her pupils to know. Hence, she added *scanning* to the master list as a specifically stated subskill of *adjusting rate to purpose.*

Since the reading levels of Brown's students ranged from grade one to grade six and she felt she could only manage three groups, she determined that she needed to use scope and sequence charts on three general reading levels. She would omit the level containing the readiness skills as she had no nonreaders in her classroom. Her first list would be geared for intermediate level readers (those fourth graders who read at the fourth grade level or above). Her second list would be for primary level readers (those fourth graders who read at the second or third grade level). Her third list would be for beginning readers (those fourth graders who read at the first grade level). In comparing the three charts, she noted the skill of using the table of contents was not on the beginning level chart and that the skill was first presented on the primary level chart. Since Brown felt the emphasis on content area reading in grade four made the skill needed even by the weakest reader, she added that skill to the beginning reader chart.

Dillner

## Task Two: Diagnose before Instruction

At the second workshop session, all teachers shared their personalized Scope and Sequence of Skills charts and then listened as the consultant discussed the need to diagnose before beginning reading instruction. During the brainstorming session which followed, several teachers stated that the facts acquired from the school's cumulative record about each child's aptitude and achievement would be helpful for determining each child's reading needs. One teacher commented on the need for determining the interests of each child in order to assign reading materials that would be motivating. The consultant agreed with the teachers that these things were important and then focused upon two types of reading diagnoses which teachers should make within their own classrooms: 1) locating each child's instructional reading level, and 2) locating specific reading skills needed by each child at that level.

*Locating instructional reading level.* After some discussion on the use of standardized reading tests and various other less formal measures for locating reading levels, Mathew demonstrated techniques for developing, administering, and interpreting an informal reading inventory (IRI is more fully discussed in Chapter Five). She gave each teacher a copy of an IRI and demonstrated its use. Each teacher practiced administration of that particular IRI.

*Locating specific skill needs.* Finally, Mathew showed the teachers how to assess the skills needed by each child. She stressed that each child *must* be assessed on materials written on his or her instructional level. Hence, if John reads at the third grade level, and Sue reads at the first grade level, they would be assessed on their uses of context clues on third and first grade materials, respectively. Regardless of whether John and Sue were in first or third grade, their preassessments on each reading skill should be written on their instructional reading levels.

*Sources for preassessment materials.* Mathew explained that preassessments could be obtained from a variety of sources. She demonstrated how a portion of a basal reader worksheet could be used to preassess specific reading skills. She discussed how sections of commercially available diagnostic tests could be correlated with each teacher's diagnostic-prescriptive program. She then asked the teachers to share with one another ideas they had developed which could easily be used as preassessments.

*Format of a preassessment.* Regardless of the source used to locate material suitable for use as a preassessment, at least three items should always be used to validly assess a skill. For example, if teachers want to measure competence with context clues, they would have to construct a preassessment which contains a minimum of three questions about context clues. The criterion level for passing each skill would have to be set by each teacher. That is, one teacher might feel that John knows context clues if he can answer two out of three correctly, while a second teacher might expect John to respond correctly to all three.

Mathew told the teachers that preassessments could be formal or informal—not formal as in a standardized test but as designed by the teacher to diagnose a specific skill. For example, a teacher might plan to teach context clues, develop a written test to determine which children need instruction on the skills, and then plan instruction based on the results of the assessment. This would be a *formal* assessment. On the other hand, the same teacher might notice that Phil is unable to complete any of his science assignments which require that he use the index of his science textbook. This would be an *informal* assessment.

Mathew demonstrated to the teachers how preassessments could be administered individually, in small groups, or in large groups. She explained that the size of the group would depend upon the number of students for whom the skill was relevant as well as the nature of the skill to be taught. If only one child was on the readiness level, it would be foolish for the teacher to assess the entire class on the readiness skill of *left-to-right progress.* Likewise, if the teacher wished to measure *oral interpretation,* it would be necessary to listen to each child individually. Because the large group mode is the most economical with the teacher's time, Mathew spent some time demonstrating how teachers could use it to obtain individual assessments. For example, a teacher might read aloud a mystery story and then ask her students to make three inferences about the main character. All children, regardless of reading level, would be able to make a response. Additionally, the teacher might ask the children to read a mimeo and then answer questions concerning main idea. Though all children would be performing the task simultaneously, each child would be given a passage on his or her reading level.

*Brown diagnoses her class.* Since Brown had previously given an IRI to all her children during the first week of school, she already had a list of the instructional reading levels for each child. Hence, she took out the three basal readers she had been using with her three groups and noted which reading skills were to be taught in each basal for the coming lesson. Her first grade basal was focusing on *naming short and long vowels* and *following directions.* Her second grade basal (2.2 level) was focusing on *naming vowel diphthongs* and *locating details.* Her fourth grade basal was focusing on *identifying the schwa sound* and *discriminating fact from opinion.* Hence she made up a preassessment on each of these six skills. For four of the skills, she simply adapted worksheets from a basal reader series not used by her children. Additionally, she used a portion of a commercially published diagnostic test to measure the children's competence with the two remaining skills.

Furthermore, when she had asked the children to use their table of contents during their social studies assignment, she noticed that few of the children seemed to be able to do so. Therefore, in addition to the six skills she had selected from the basal reader lessons, she made up formal preassessments for the skill of *using a table of contents,* which she administered to every child in class regardless of basal reader grouping. An example of the small group, formal assessment which she gave to the children using the 2.2 reader is shown in Figure 1.


**Figure 1**

*Directions.* This is a story about a shell collection. First read it to yourself and then answer the questions about it.

Every day, when the sand was hot from the morning sun, the boy ran down to the water to play. He loved the mornings. Very few people were on the beach, and he could swim and play by himself.*

*Locating Details*
1. How often did the boy go to the beach? _____
2. Why was the sand hot? _____
3. When did the boy like to play in the water? _____

*Naming Vowel Diphthongs*   All the words below are from the story you read. Put a "yes" by the ones which contain a vowel diphthong.

1. boy _____
2. down _____
3. beach _____
4. few _____
5. swim _____

*Using a Table of Contents*   Use your reading book to answer these questions:

1. On what page does the story "The Shell Collection" begin? _____
2. How many stories are there in your book? _____
3. What story was written by George McCue? _____

---

Selection from "The Shell Collection" by Dina Anastasio, from the Holt, Rinehart and Winston Readers, *The Way of The World* (Grade 2.2), edited by Lyman C. Hunt and others. New York: Holt, Rinehart and Winston, 1973. Reprinted by permission.

Close examination of Brown's preassessment for the children in the 2.2 reader reveals these characteristics: 1) Since the children read at the 2.2 grade level, the preassessment is taken from second grade material. 2) Brown has included at least three items on each of the three skills she is assessing. 3) Since this material has been carefully prepared and will be given only to the children in the 2.2 reader, a small group, formal assessment was the appropriate format for her to use. 4) In order to preassess using a table of contents, she has to watch the children while they are taking their preassessment to ascertain whether they turn to the table of contents to find the answers or simply locate the correct response by flipping through the pages of their 2.2 reader.

After developing the preassessments for all the skills she had selected, Brown then administered the appropriate set of preassessments to each child. A portion of her notes about each child's performance on preassessment is reproduced in Figure 2.

### Figure 2*

Eric   Reads at fourth grade level. Assessed on intermediate level skills chart. Missed three out of five questions on the schwa sound; missed none on fact from opinion and none on using a table of contents.

Jack   Reads at the 2.2 grade level. Assessed on the primary level skills chart. Missed two out of three questions on details; missed two out of five on vowel diphthongs; and missed none on using the table of contents.

Paula   Reads at the grade one level. Assessed on the beginning level skills chart. Missed four out of five on naming short and long vowels; missed none on following directions; missed all three questions on the table of contents.

| Ervin | Reads at the fourth grade level. Assessed on the intermediate skills chart. Missed five out of five questions on the schwa sound. Missed one out of five in distinguishing fact from opinion; missed none in using table of contents. |
|---|---|
| Jane | Reads at the fourth grade level. Assessed on intermediate level skills chart. Missed two out of five questions on the schwa sound; missed none on distinguishing fact from opinion; missed none on using the table of contents. |
| Bobby | Reads at the sixth grade level. Assessed on intermediate level skills chart. Missed no questions on the schwa sound; missed no questions on distinguishing fact from opinion; missed no questions on using a table of contents. |

*Reproduced teacher notes.

## Task Three: Keep Records

At the third inservice session all teachers discussed their progress with the diagnoses of students during the previous week. They expressed concern about how to keep track of each child's performance on each reading skill. It was apparent to all the teachers that they needed at least two types of records: one to help the teacher keep track of each child's progress and one to help the child know when to move from task to task.

*Teacher records.* Though Mathew knew there were many useful ways to keep teacher records, she offered a record keeping form which she herself had found particularly useful. Mathew demonstrated the form by using the performance records of Brown's students. She then described to the rest of the teachers how they should interpret the filled in chart.

By looking at the chart of Brown's students, it can be seen that each child's name is placed across the top, and that the reading skill being assessed is placed down the lefthand side. A key is used to indicate whether a skill has been assessed. Additionally, the key provides an indication of whether the child mastered the skill or not on the preassessment as well as whether the child mastered the skill upon completion of instruction.

*Pupil records.* Mathew showed the teachers that their management tasks would be decreased if they would teach their students to be responsible for some of their own record keeping. There were many ways to manage the children's progress through a series of recommended tasks. Among the simplest was that of the "contract system." In this system, each child is given a folder with the youngster's name on it.

## Figure 3*

Portion of Beginning Reader Chart (Reading Levels preprimer through first reader)

| Objective Name | Paula | | | | |
|---|---|---|---|---|---|
| Naming Short & Long Vowels | 0 | | | | |
| Following Directions | ✓ | | | | |
| Using a Table of Contents | 0 | | | | |

Portion of Primary Reader Chart (Reading Levels grade 2 and grade 3)

| Objective Name | Jack | | | | |
|---|---|---|---|---|---|
| Naming Vowel Diphthongs | 0 | | | | |
| Locating Details | 0 | | | | |
| Using a Table of Contents | ✓ | | | | |

Portion of Intermediate Level Chart (Reading Levels grade 4 and above)

| Objective Name | Eric | Ervin | Jane | Bobby | |
|---|---|---|---|---|---|
| Identifying the Schwa Sound | 0 | 0 | 0 | ✓ | |
| Discriminating Fact From Opinion | ✓ | ✓ | ✓ | ✓ | |
| Using a Table of Contents | ✓ | ✓ | ✓ | ✓ | |

Suggested Key: Blank Space - Not Assessed
  ✓ - Passed Assessment
  0 - Did Not Pass Preassessment; Needs Instruction
  ∅ - Did Not Pass Preassessment; Has Received Instruction and Passed Postassessment

---

*Adapted from *Learning to Teach Reading in the Elementary School* by Joanne P. Olson and Martha H. Dillner. Copyright ©1976 by Macmillan Publishing Company, Inc. Reprinted with permission.

Inside the folder is a list of activities to be completed in order to learn a needed reading skill.

Since Poindexter had been using a contract system successfully for several years, he showed the other teachers the folders used by several of his sixth grade pupils. In developing his contract system, he and his pupils had worked out a mutually acceptable amount of work for the student to do in order to meet each objective. These agreements between each pupil and Poindexter stated 1) the learning objectives, 2) the choice of activities by which the objectives could be accomplished, 3) the criteria that had to be met for a particular grade, and 4) the method for evaluating successful completion of objectives (3).

Dillner

The student had some freedom of choice among activities, but Poindexter retained the power of approval and based grades upon the work. Students who wanted to get an "A" would contract for more work than those who wanted to get a "B" and so forth. Since there were always more activities and materials available in the contract than one would have to complete in order to receive a particular grade, the use of contracts helped develop the student's decision-making powers as well as provided for completion of activities which were the most motivating to the students. Poindexter then showed the teachers how Fred Phillips had progressed through his contract (3:194-196).

### Figure 4

Name: Fred Phillips                                    Date ended October 7
  Began: September 30
  Objectives:
  After completion of this contract, the student will be able to
  1. Identify all words with their meanings given by context clues in chapter four of *Blue Pony*
  2. Follow a given set of directions
Contract for "C"
  Requirement:
  1. Complete 2 out of the 6 activities listed on context clues and 1 out of 4 of the activities listed on following directions and successfully complete the posttest given by Poindexter.
Contract for "B"
  1. Complete at least 4 out of the 6 activities listed on context clues and 2 out of 4 activities listed on following directions and successfully complete the posttest given by Poindexter.
Contract for "A"
  1. Complete at least 5 out of the 6 activities listed on context clues and 3 out of 4 of the activities listed on following directions and successfully complete the posttest given by Poindexter.

---

| Activity Name | Date Assigned | Date Completed | Date Verified | Person Verifying |
|---|---|---|---|---|
| "Making a Dart Board" | 9/30 | 10/5 | 10/7 | JP* |
| "Worksheet #1 - Context" | 9/30 | 10/7 | 10/7 | JP |
| "Context Bingo" | 9/30 | 10/7 | 10/6 | KR** |
| "Filmstrip on Context" | 9/30 | 10/5 | 10/5 | PR*** |

---

\* Poindexter's initials. He verified completion of the dart board and worksheet when checking Fred's folder on October 7.

\*\* A peer's initials. This student had passed the preassessment on context clues and was the "caller" for the "Bingo" game.

\*\*\* Another peer's initials. This person helped set up the filmstrip projector for Fred.

**Figure 5***

Name of Skill

Name of Children

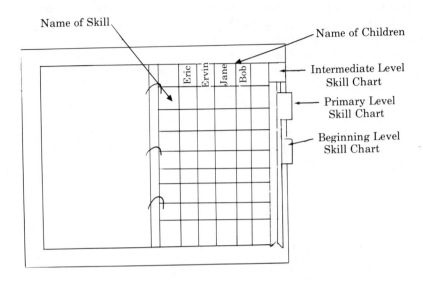

Intermediate Level
Skill Chart

Primary Level
Skill Chart

Beginning Level
Skill Chart

Eric
Ervin
Jane
Bob

Brown's Notebook

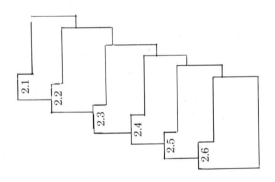

2.1
2.2
2.3
2.4
2.5
2.6

Key:  2.1 = Game using schwa sound
      2.2 = Basal worksheet on schwa sound
      2.3 = Crossword puzzle using schwa sound
      2.4 = Basal worksheet on schwa sound
      2.5 = Newspaper activity using the schwa sound
      2.6 = Worksheet on the schwa sound

*Adapted from Lapp (1).

Dillner

*Brown plans her record keeping system.* During the week following the inservice session on record keeping, Brown spent time making a notebook for class records and a filing system for activities she had located to teach each skill. For example, since Eric was reading at the fourth grade level and needed the skill of *identifying the schwa sound,* she located fourth grade level materials which provided practice with this skill. Each time she located an exercise concerning the schwa sound, she placed it in a manila folder and put a number "2" on the tab of the folder. She had labeled each of the reading skills which she was going to teach by number and "identifying the schwa sound" was the second skill listed on her intermediate level scope and sequence of skills chart. She eventually located five more exercises on the intermediate level on identifying the schwa sound. She decided to use a decimal point to differentiate each activity from the others and marked her six folders concerning the schwa sound "2.1", "2.2", "2.3", "2.4", "2.5", and "2.6", respectively.

Then Brown spent a few minutes writing a note to Eric about his choice of activities. She decided not to use as formal a contract system as Poindexter had but rather to write notes to individual children telling them the tasks to be completed during the week. Her system gave each child a choice of activities, but did not include a choice of grades. She determined that she would grade each child by the quality of the material in his or her folder at the completion of each grading period. Additionally, since she had thirty pupils in her classroom, and she did not wish to spend an inordinate amount of time writing notes to children, she decided to check each child's folder once a week. That way if she examined six folders a day she could assess each child's progress every five days. An example of her note to Eric is shown in Figure 6.

In a like manner she wrote notes to all the children on the intermediate reading level who needed improvement on identifying the schwa sound. Since note writing consumed much time, she did not make activity folders for all the skills she had preassessed. Rather, she decided to develop instructional activities for only one skill per group for the present. She would use the material which accompanied the basal reader series for each group to teach the children the skills on which she did not have time to develop activity folders. During her

## Figure 6

Hi Eric,

    I really liked the way you presented your book report yesterday. The collage idea was super! Please complete the activities below before next Wednesday. If you need someone to play the game in folder 2.1, check with Ervin, Jane, or Bobby as they need to practice this same activity.

DURING READING PERIOD:

    Whenever you finish your basal reader activities work in folders 2.1, 2.2, 2.3, 2.4, 2.5, or 2.6.

    Choose another book for fun reading and drop me a note in this folder telling me the title. I will ask you more about your book later.

DURING REST OF DAY:

    If you have spare time or finish any content area assignments early, work on the activities above.

Note: Eric had passed the preassessment on fact from opinion and the table of contents. However, if he had needed more help on these skills, Brown would have taught these two skills during the basal lesson. At this point in time, she was just beginning to coordinate all her materials and was easing into the contract system one skill at a time.

Adapted from Lapp (1:65).

week of planning, she located and developed activity folders for identifying the schwa sound for the intermediate level readers, naming long and short vowels for the beginning readers, and locating details for the primary level readers.

## Task Four: Designing Instructional Activities

    At the fourth workshop session, the teachers discussed their progress in keeping records. Then Mathew brought up the topic of designing efficient instructional strategies. She explained that each teacher needed to develop initial teaching lessons as well as reinforcement lessons on each needed skill. In an initial teaching lesson the child is *taught* the reading skill. In this type lesson the teacher herself usually explains or demonstrates the skill. Often the teaching is done in conjunction with the preparation or skill building step of a basal reader lesson. Sometimes the teaching is done during small group sessions which the teacher has organized in order to specifically teach a few children the same skill. The teacher,

Dillner

however, does not always have to be present during the initial teaching lesson if she can provide direct instruction in another manner. Alternatives to the actual presence of the teacher include teacher aides, peer tutors, and self-checking instructional packets which are often composed primarily of audiovisual components.

During reinforcement lessons children should be asked to *practice* what they have been taught during the initial teaching lesson. Reinforcement activities often include worksheets, games, and discussions. Mathew emphasized that direct teaching (during the initial teaching lesson) and practice (during the reinforcement lesson) are two entirely different aspects of learning a reading skill. Though some games are constructed in such a manner that they do teach the skills, most games are reinforcement activities. Usually, children cannot be expected to play a game in which they score a point for each correctly identified schwa sound (reinforcement lesson) unless they have first been taught what a schwa sound is (initial teaching lesson).

Mathew spent the remainder of the workshop session demonstrating how to locate activities for both initial teaching and reinforcement lessons. Representative sources of initial teaching activities included teaching suggestions in the teacher's edition of various basal reader series, self-contained instructional packets published commercially such as the "Listen and Think" series put out by the Educational Development Laboratories, and teaching suggestions obtained from methods textbooks used in college level reading courses.

Possible resource materials for reinforcement lessons can be found in the same sources as those used for gathering ideas concerning initial teaching lessons. Professional journals for both teaching and reinforcing ideas can be consulted. Teachers were urged to share ideas which they developed themselves and which they had used successfully with their students.

*Brown locates and organizes instructional materials.* Having scores of ideas gathered throughout the years from previous workshops and professional conferences, Brown decided to develop a series of lessons on each skill by first looking through materials which she already possessed.

The first step in converting all the resources into a manageable format had already been done for her. She decided that the manila folder system which she had tried out the previous week should be expanded to include four: 1) folders used by each student to receive reading assignments, 2) folders to hold activities ready to be completed by the children, 3) folders for filing teaching ideas useful for the initial teaching lesson, and 4) folders for reinforcement activities needing construction before the children could use them.

The first activity Brown located focused upon the schwa sound at the intermediate level. Several copies of a worksheet from a fourth grade basal reader workbook were inserted into a folder marked "2.7" and the folder was placed in the box of activities already being used by the children.

Next, Brown located an idea for a game in which the children played detective and had to use the schwa sound correctly to succeed. Since the game required her to make a game board, she placed the description of the game into a folder marked with a red "2" (meaning the activity needed further development).

One idea for teaching the schwa sound included the suggestion that a teacher ask a child to demonstrate the schwa sound. If the child did not know the schwa sound, the teacher was to ask the child to make the sound a person would make if he were hit in the stomach. The teacher would then tell the class that the schwa sound is similar to the "uhh!" sound a person might make upon being struck in the stomach. Finally, the teacher was to show the class several examples of words containing this sound. Since this activity was appropriate for an initial teaching lesson, Brown placed it in a folder marked with a blue "2" (meaning an initial teaching lesson to be presented by a teacher).

Finally Brown located an audiotape and worksheet on the schwa sound which had been developed by another fourth grade teacher. Since this material was self-instructional, Brown placed it in a folder marked with a green "2" (meaning an initial teaching activity which could be used by a child without the help of a teacher. Brown then placed that teaching activity in the same box as the reinforcement activities on the schwa sound.

The four types of folders and the box containing the student activities can be seen in Figure 7.

# Figure 7

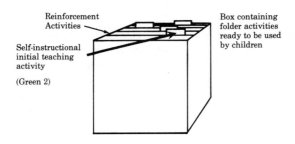

Reinforcement Activities

Self-instructional initial teaching activity

(Green 2)

Box containing folder activities ready to be used by children

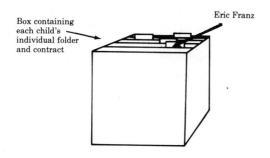

Box containing each child's individual folder and contract

Eric Franz

(Red 2)                                      (Blue 2)

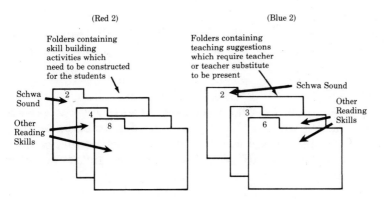

Folders containing skill building activities which need to be constructed for the students

Schwa Sound

Other Reading Skills

Folders containing teaching suggestions which require teacher or teacher substitute to be present

Schwa Sound

Other Reading Skills

## Task Five: Diagnosing after Instruction

At the fifth workshop, the consultant stressed the need to diagnose after instruction. The format of a postassessment is similar to that of a preassessment and can be developed from the same sources used to develop preassessment items, the obvious difference between the two being time of administration.

*Continuous assessment.* Mathew pointed out to the teachers that one of the most important concepts presented during the workshop sessions is that of *continuous assessment.* Teachers had been shown how to construct and administer a preassessment on each reading skill before they taught a lesson on that skill. This time they were to postassess after instruction to determine whether the skill had been mastered by each child. Continuous assessment meant to frequently evaluate a child's need for a skill as well as mastery of a skill after instruction.

*Brown postassesses her students.* During the week following the fifth workshop session, Brown located, developed, and administered postassessments on each of the skills she had selected to teach her pupils. The task was simple as most of her postassessments were constructed from ideas she had located earlier when developing her preassessments.

Upon postassessment, she discovered that most of the children seemed to have learned the skills she had been teaching. However, she wondered whether Eric really knew the skill of identifying the schwa sound as her postassessment on that skill was given to Eric immediately after he had completed two worksheets on the skill. She felt that if she gave him the postassessment again, he might not know the skill. She decided to ask the consultant what sort of timing would be best between lessons as well as between lessons and postassessment.

## Task Six: Organizing Instruction

The final workshop focused on precisely the type of questions Brown had about the timing of instruction. Mathew told the teachers that in order to best organize instruction, they needed to 1) carefully plan their lessons and 2) schedule instruction for optimum learning.

*Lesson planning.* Mathew did not spend much time on techniques for planning lessons. She emphasized that the teachers' lesson plans submitted to their principal at the beginning of the week were adequate. Each lesson plan required by the principal contained a set of behaviorally stated objectives which the children were to complete each day. In addition, the lesson plans contained a list of materials which the teachers would need in order to teach the objectives and a description of the procedures to be used by the teacher in order to teach the desired objectives. Finally, the principal required teachers to postassess the children on the successful completion of the objectives. Since this format fit nicely into the diagnostic-prescriptive technique presented by Mathew, she saw no reason to ask the teachers to plan their lessons differently.

*Scheduling instruction.* Timing of the presentation of each initial teaching lesson, reinforcement lesson, and post-assessment was important for maximizing each child's learning of a reading skill. The teachers were shown a variety of ways in which they could schedule instruction for optimum learning. Mathew stressed the flexibility of scheduling in terms of each teacher's individual teaching situation. For example, those in a self-contained classroom could schedule according to their own perceptions about when each lesson ought to be presented. Teachers in a team teaching situation would have to schedule their instruction based upon when they would see each child and when each child was scheduled for reading instruction. Though there were many ways to schedule instruction, Mathew felt that leaving a day or two between each lesson was probably best. She felt that presenting an initial teaching lesson, two reinforcement lessons, and a postassessment on the same day would be less effective than the technique of spacing out the activities. To her, distributive practice was more helpful in placing the reading skills into each child's long term learning than was immediate recitation of a skill just presented.

Mathew then helped Brown outline a feasible schedule for instruction and suggested that each skill she wanted to teach be preassessed a few days before that skill was needed in the basal lesson. That way, if Brown needed to make up activities on needed skills, she would have time to do so. Then the consultant suggested that Brown present an initial teaching lesson followed by an immediate reinforcement lesson to give the child a chance to practice the new skill. Next, Mathew suggested that Brown schedule two more reinforcement activities on the two following days. Finally, the consultant suggested that a postassessment be given two or three days after the last reinforcement. A schedule of the instructional plan is shown in Figure 8.

**Figure 8**

|        | Monday | Tuesday | Wednesday | Thursday | Friday |
|--------|--------|---------|-----------|----------|--------|
| Week 1 |        |         | Preassess on 7 skills |   |        |
| Week 2 | Initial teach 7 skills** 1st reinforcement*** | 2nd reinforcement**** | 3rd reinforcement**** |   |        |
| Week 3 | Postassessment* |   |   |   |        |

    \* small group, formal during basal lesson
       4th grade basal: schwa sound, fact from opinion, table of contents
       2.2 basal: vowel diphthongs, details, table of contents
       1 basal: short and long vowels, following directions, table of contents

   \** small groups during basal lesson; those who passed skill work independently on extension activity

 \*** immediately after lesson children practice skill in either basal materials or folder activities

\**** folder activity done anytime during day or during a portion of basal lesson

Mathew spent similar sessions with individual teachers to help each one determine what type of scheduling was best. Additionally, the consultant stressed that the schedules developed were only examples and that teachers should feel free to adjust them in any way they saw fit.

*Brown schedules her instruction.* During the next week, Brown followed the planned schedule and was pleased with the progress of the children. Since Ervin did not pass his postassessment after his first three reinforcement activities, Brown located a few more reinforcement activities on the skill of identifying the schwa sound and put a note in Ervin's folder telling him to complete the activities before the following Tuesday, at which time he took a second postassessment and was able to complete the activity successfully.

On the other hand, Jane completed her three reinforcement activities early and then was assigned extension activities on the skill. One of these activities suggested that Jane make up several games using newspaper words containing the schwa sound. Jane successfully constructed two games, using words from the sports section of the newspaper. The activity was so creative that Brown placed it in a folder marked 2.8 and placed it in the box for other children to use. Other members of the class thought it was fun to play the game and asked for an opportunity to make up games of their own. Eventually all were given an opportunity to make up games which the teacher evaluated and then, usually with only minor adjustments, placed in folders for other children to enjoy.

References
1. Lapp, Diane. "Individualized Reading Made Easy for Teacher," *Early Years*, February 1977, 63-67, 73.
2. *Listen and Think.* Huntington, New York: Educational Development Laboratories, 1962.
3. Olson, Joanne, and Martha Dillner. *Learning to Teach Reading in the Elementary School.* New York: Macmillan, 1976.

Flood describes well-managed classrooms and provides a sequence of procedures for developing and managing effective secondary programs.


**Chapter Four  A View of an Effectively Organized Secondary Reading Program**

James Flood
*Boston University*

"Today we decided Steinbeck is a better writer than Shakespeare, Austin, our school librarian, and John Lennon," Bob announced to his mother one evening. "What?" inquired his mother.

Bob:  "Yeah, Robin, Frank, Maggie, and I filled out these charts and we decided."

Mom:  "When did you do this incredible task?"

Bob:  "In English class. We set up categories like we were judges. Jonesie [Bob's teacher] gave us five passages to read, but he didn't tell us who wrote each one. We judged them and Steinbeck came out first."

Mom:  "But how did you decide?"

Bob:  "We set up categories."

Mom:  "Oh, like whether you liked the passage."

Bob:  "Yeah, and characterization and setting and theme and all that stuff."

Mom:  "Oh, what a nice idea."

Bob:  "Yeah, it was fun. Tomorrow we're rating newspapers, and next week we're doing poems."

Bob's mother, Mrs. Kurmis, knew something was awry. Bob never said anything about school was fun; and he never, never said the word "poem." He hated, loathed, despised, and abhorred the word. What was happening? Mrs. Kurmis decided to visit the class to see this miracle worker in action and to discover for herself if the rumors which she had heard about Mr. Jones were true. Did he really individualize his instruction?

Jones had been an English teacher in an innercity school for ten years—years of whole group instruction, years of prepared lectures for half groups. Since he had abandoned all hope of ever having 100 percent attendance, he knew he had to try a different approach to his teaching. He also knew that every class he had taught in the past ten years had been heterogeneously grouped despite all the labeling to the contrary. Each class had some good readers, some poor writers, some adequate spellers, some dictionary users, some orators, a few mustaches, and a few bouffants. He sat down one day and decided to do something about homogeneous groups of students.

When Kurmis arrived early the next day, Jones explained that he was trying to individualize his teaching so that *every* student could learn something; so that *every* student's needs could begin to be met. He realized that this was a rather comprehensive and ambitious goal, but he also knew that his whole group presentation approach was a failure; it had frustrated him and his students.

Before he began his new program, he decided to reread Piaget, Dewey, and Bruner. He knew they didn't always agree with one another, but there was a repeated refrain in their writings: "Base your instruction on involvement." Jones thought about his most successful teaching experiences and realized his students actually *liked* solving murder mysteries and writing TV advertisements and listening to popular lyrics and reading novels when *they* selected them. They liked his classes when *they* were involved, when *they* were directing their own learning. Jones explained to Kurmis that his program was intended to interest students by keeping them involved at the fullest level he could manage.

Kurmis was intrigued; she decided to stay for the first period class. The door opened. "Egad, the Sweathogs in person: Horshak, Barbarino, Washington, and Epstein," she thought, watching the banter. They seemed to be checking some sort of chart near the door. Magically, and almost calmly, they grouped themselves and started working on projects. The Sweathogs were transformed before her eyes into industrious, interested students.

She asked Jones to explain the whole procedure: "What

have you done?" He said this was his individualized program. "Eureka, and it only took three years to organize it," he laughed and started to explain his system.

## Definition

First, Jones decided to establish a working, useful definition of individualization (3). He knew he had individualized his instruction on occasion, but he had not done it systematically. He realized he was individualizing by interests when he permitted students their choices in reading materials and choices of topics for writing assignments. He also knew there must be more to an individualized system than just allowing choices. He knew that he did not want to totally discard whole group presentations, and he also knew he could not work with every student on a one-to-one basis every day. He had done some group work in the past with his class, and he found that it worked fairly well. He concluded that individualized instruction for him could encompass all three of these teaching formats: *whole class presentations, small groups,* and *individual work.*

Considering grouping practices, Jones realized that there were several ways in which he could group students by interests, knowledge, and/or skills. The groups could work on the same materials (multiple copies) or they could work on different tasks. These teaching formats are illustrated on the chart shown.

**Teaching Formats**

| BASIS FOR GROUPING | MATERIALS | TYPES OF GROUPS | | |
|---|---|---|---|---|
| | | SMALL GROUPS | WHOLE GROUPS | ONE PERSON |
| Interest or Knowledge or Skills | Same Material | X | X | X |
| | Different Material | X | | X |

Flood

# Framework

Now that Jones had some idea of the possibilities for instructional grouping, he decided to construct a framework for his program.

## Step One:  Establish Goals

Since he had had several years of teaching experience, Jones felt comfortable stating his goals for this particular class. He listed three general goals.

*Skills.* To improve students' language skills in reading, writing, speaking, listening, and viewing.

*Knowledge.* To enable students to acquire basic information (knowledge) about forms of literature, film, and modes of writing.

*Interest.* To encourage students to broaden their interests in the communication processes.

After forcing himself to state his goals, Jones realized that each goal was totally dependent upon the experience of each student. He fully realized that improving Sharon's skills in reading was quite a different task from improving Pat's skills in reading. The second step, then, was to assess individual student needs, abilities, and interests in order to plan personalized programs for each.

## Step Two:  Assess Student Abilities and Needs

Assessment can be conducted in many different ways. Standardized pencil and paper tests were only one way to gain information about students. When Jones used norm-referenced, standardized tests, he chose diagnostic tests which provided him with information about the components of a skill as well as an overall measure of the skill itself; for example, in reading he chose a test that gave information about word analysis skills and different components of comprehension. Jones also found that he could gather valuable information from his own observations and from informal teacher-made criterion referenced tests. When he used his own tests, he found he could tailor the test to the particular student or class.

In addition to skills and knowledge information, Jones also gathered data about student interests within and outside the English curricula. He found that he needed to record this information in order to store it and to use it to plan appropriate programs for each student.

After he had gathered all of this diagnostic information, Jones felt that he was prepared to make assignments from various texts. A new problem arose. Which texts should be used?

## Step Three: Assess the Materials

Now that Jones had a great deal of hard data telling him that his students were unique—that all of them did not have the same reading and writing skills—he felt he had to locate suitable materials for each of them that would challenge without frustrating. He set about his task by determining the readability of the materials he was going to use. He used standard readability formulas (Dale-Chall and Fry) as well as his own measures (his intuitive formula that assessed literary devices, concept complexity, and idiomatic language).

Jones also used his information about student interests and preferences as a compelling and sound directive for choosing materials and for matching these materials with individual students.

## Step Four: Establish Grouping Patterns

Jones realized that he was able to assess student abilities and interests, as well as the difficulty of materials. He knew what he wanted his students to learn, but suddenly he came to the "How do I do it?" question. Since no two students had the same needs or abilities, it was useless to pursue whole group presentation. He knew he wanted to group his students so they could start at their own appropriate points and progress at their most comfortable (but productive) rates. However, he remembered the experience of a friend who had decided to individualize and who had written contracts for each of his 120 students. It had taken the friend two full months to write a two week contract for each student. After five days in his program, he was ready for a vacation. The experiment was a patent disaster and was abandoned.

Jones decided to start his program on a limited basis. In fact, he started with a single class, using only two groups. Although he changed group composition to accommodate interests, he never used more than two groups for the first six months.

After becoming comfortable with the idea of groups, Jones used the following format.

1. Jones set up a bulletin board on which he hung a sign explaining the group pattern for the day—one of three arrays:

A
| Whole Group |
| --- |
| Assignment: Speeches |

B
| Individual Work |
| --- |
| Assignment: Edit Your Writing |

C
| Groups |
| --- |
| |

If the "C" array (Groups) appeared, he would include group composition and task assignments coded by Learning Packet Number. Sample arrays are shown.

| GROUPS | | | | |
| --- | --- | --- | --- | --- |
| Learning Packets (*Skills*) | | | | |
| L.P. #1 | L.P. #2 | L.P. #2 | L.P. #2 | L.P. #2 |
| Jim | Rena | Joe | Cleo | Judy |
| John | Roy | Jill | Clem | Joy |
| | Rita | Jack | Claph | Justin |
| | Rob | Jane | Chip | Jenny |
| | Ron | Jessa | Clark | Jeremy |

| GROUPS | | |
|---|---|---|
| Learning Packets (*Interest*) | | |
| L.P. #3 | L.P. #4 | L.P. #5 |
| Jim | John | Clem |
| Rena | Roy | Joy |
| Judy | Jessa | Jeremy |
| Cleo | | Jack |
| | | Jill |
| | | Rita |

| GROUPS | |
|---|---|
| Learning Packets (*Knowledge*) | |
| L.P. #1 | L.P. #2 |
| Judy | Rita |
| Jim | Rob |
| Jack | Jeremy |
| Rena | Jane |
| Joe | Jill |
| Cleo | Chip |
| Clem | Clark |
| Jessa | Ron |
| Justin | Roy |

2. The learning packets were kept in a file cabinet. Students were expected to borrow and return these packets. Each year his learning packet file increased. By starting slowly (just two groups), Jones allowed himself time to create ample interesting and useful materials.

3. Groups were established to improve *skills* (e.g., punctuation, reading for explicitly stated information) or to have students increase their knowledge about a particular topic (e.g., History of Old Globe Theater), or to have students work on *interest* tasks (e.g., astrological signs).

4. Although he might have five groups operating simultaneously, Jones realized that each group did not need a different learning packet. Since all or some of the five groups could be working on the same material, he provided multiple copies of one specific learning packet.

## Step Five: Prescribe

Jones realized he had to prescribe an instructional program that would be appropriate for each student. The prescription was based directly on assessment of each student's needs and interests and on Jones' beliefs about what was important to teach within the content of the English curriculum. The learning packets were designed to meet these individual needs.

## Step Six: Evaluate

Realizing his program still had a major problem (paper work had increased) Jones used the following procedures:

1. All *skills* learning packets were self-correcting. Students had to show their completed work before they were given the answer key.
2. *Interest* learning packets were designed to include oral reports so that students were receiving immediate feedback, and Jones was provided with an inclass opportunity to evaluate progress.
3. *Knowledge* learning packets were followed by traditional unit tests.
4. Some writing assignments were corrected by students, but Jones tended to correct the assignments himself. The system, nevertheless, freed him from correcting 120 compositions every other Sunday night because he staggered the assignments, so that only a few students were writing each day. Some time became available to correct writings with students during the class period.

## Managing the Program

It became crucial to have three checklists for each student: 1) an Interest Checklist, 2) a Skills Checklist, and 3) a Knowledge Checklist. Jones composed these lists for each class and compiled them in a bound notebook, which provided him with a concise profile of each student. As soon as he discovered an interest the student had, he jotted it down on the interest checklist. He believed strongly in this practice because of an incident that happened to him two years before. One morning, as he was driving to school, he spotted three of his former students on the streets. He remembered their names, even their grades, but he couldn't remember any interests they had. It occurred to Jones that knowing student interests might be a good way to start his program. He decided to create an interest checklist that would serve as a record of student interests in several categories: books, TV, movies, and content interests (botany, astrology, automobiles, medicine). He showed his Interest Checklist to Bob's mother. A sample checklist is shown below.

| Interest Checklist | | | | | | |
|---|---|---|---|---|---|---|
| Books | TV | Movies | | | Materials Loaned | |
| | | | Title | | Out | In |
| | | | 1. | | | |
| | | | 2. | | | |
| | | | 3. | | | |
| Academic (Content) Interests | | | 4. | | Interest Activities | |
| 1. | | | 1. | | | |
| 2. | | | 2. | | | |
| 3. | | | 3. | | | |
| 4. | | | 4. | | | |
| 5. | | | 5. | | | |

Remembering that morning when he spotted former students, Jones realized that he knew their grades, but he didn't know anything about their skills. Delores didn't write well, but he couldn't remember the precise difficulty. Dan's reading score was below grade level, but Jones didn't fully understand what that meant and had no idea what skills Dan needed to develop. With the help of other teachers in the department, Jones created a skills checklist that was manageable and efficient. It did not include so many skills that it became useless nor did it include a list of unaccessible skills. The skills checklist looked like the sample shown.

The third checklist, a Knowledge Checklist, was designed to take the place of Jones' traditional grade book. In addition to recording unit test scores, he used the checklist to help record the names of students who already knew certain parts of the knowledge content of his course. (He vividly remembered an exchange he had with an eighth grade teacher who insisted on "teaching" a Globe Theater unit to all students despite the fact that several students in the class had taken a minicourse on Play Production which included a unit on the

**Skills Checklist**

| | YES | NO | MOSTLY | COMMENTS |
|---|---|---|---|---|

I. Reading/Thinking

A. Word Analysis
Structural Analysis
   tense markers
   morphemes
   affixes
      prefix
      suffix
   roots

B. Vocabulary

C. Comprehension
Explicit Information
   details
   supporting evidence
   cause and effect
   main idea

Implicit Relationships
   synthesis
   inference
   main idea
   transfer
   application
   judgment

D. Study Skills
Library
   reference books
   organization
Dictionary

II. Writing
A. Structure
   Sentence structure
   Paragraphing
   Organization in passage
   Spelling
   Vocabulary

B. Creative Expression

C. Journalism
Newspaper
Magazine

D. Language Usage
   Grammatical structures
   Mechanics
      agreement of verbs
      agreement of subject and verb
      consistency
      diction

|  | YES | NO | MOSTLY | COMMENTS |
|---|---|---|---|---|
| III. Listening | | | | |
|   A. Follow Directions | | | | |
|   B. Comprehension<br>    Details<br>    Evidence<br>    Cause and effect<br>    Main idea | | | | |
| IV. Speaking<br>  A. Organization<br>  B. Expression<br>  C. Persuasion<br>  D. Creative Dramatics | | | | |
| V. Viewing<br>  A. Comprehension<br>    Details<br>    Main idea<br>    Cause and effect<br>    Evidence | | | | |
|   B. Film Production<br>    Writing<br>    Filming<br>    Editing | | | | |

Old Globe Theater.) Jones found that the Knowledge Checklist presented below helped him to remember these scattered bits of information.

## Cautions

Overwhelming management problems occur in implementing a totally individualized program. Individualization does not necessarily mean that each student works on a separate task. Rather, it means that each student has a program that meets his/her own needs. The format of instruction can be whole group, small group, or individual. Groups are extremely efficient because students can learn from one another, and the teacher can manage (diagnose, prescribe, and evaluate) the total program effectively. Teachers wishing to begin an individualized program should

1. Start slowly, with a program of individualization within one class in which they are most comfortable (level is

# Knowledge Checklist

| | Test 1 | Test 2 | Test 3 | Test 4 | Test 5 | Test 6 |
|---|---|---|---|---|---|---|
| **I. Literature** | | | | | | |
| 1 Short Story/Novel | | | | | | |
| 2 Poetry <br> narrative <br> ballad | | | | | | |
| 3 Drama <br> comedy <br> tragedy | | | | | | |
| 4 Nonfiction <br> biography <br> diary | | | | | | |
| **II. Film** | | | | | | |
| 1 Short Selection | | | | | | |
| 2 Narrative | | | | | | |
| 3 Full Length | | | | | | |
| 4 Documentary | | | | | | |
| **III. Written Composition** | | | | | | |
| 1 Prose Writing <br> narrative <br> expository | | | | | | |
| 2 Expressive Writing <br> poetry <br> short story | | | | | | |
| 3 Journalism <br> news <br> editorial | | | | | | |
| 4 Biography <br> diary <br> journal | | | | | | |
| **IV: Oral Communication** | | | | | | |
| 1 Discussion | | | | | | |
| 2 Folktales, Storytelling | | | | | | |
| 3 Formal Presentations | | | | | | |
| 4 Conversation | | | | | | |

unimportant). In the beginning, work should be with just two groups in order to provide enough materials, create enough learning packets, and give students sufficient feedback.

2. Try to involve the entire department. The greater the number of teachers involved, the greater the number of learning packets that can be created. A department chairperson or a lead teacher should serve as a coordinator for assigning needed learning packets based on teacher interests.
3. Share ideas and materials in order to make individualization a successful experience for every teacher and every student, for the whole task of individualization is so overwhelming that no single teacher can do it alone.

**References**
1. Dillner, M., and J. Olson. *Personalizing Reading Instruction in the Middle, Junior, and Senior High Schools.* New York: Macmillan, 1977.
2. Lapp, D., and J. Flood. *Teaching Reading to Every Child.* New York: Macmillan, 1978.
3. Lapp, D. "Individualizing Made Easy for Teachers," *Early Years,* 7 (February 1977), 63-73.
4. Lapp, D. "Beyond the Redbirds, Bluebirds, and Yellowbirds," *Reporting on Reading,* 5 (March 1979).

Intili and Conrad introduce a design for planning a managed, individualized classroom and suggest implementation, management, and learning procedures.

## Chapter Five   Planning the Well Managed Classroom

Jo-Ann K. Intili
*Stanford Univeristy*

Helen Conrad
*Columbiana County Board of Education*
*Lisbon, Ohio*

## A Look at Management (1)

The classroom is noisy. Many students rove around the room: one or two sharpen their pencils; others search for interviewees to discuss their favorite character in this week's book; some schedule a conference with the teacher or seek answers to questions. This third grade class is real. To the eye of an unpracticed observer, it seems to be controlled bedlam. Every once in a while one child punctuates the din with a loud, "Keep it quiet, I can't think." Some students actually stand on their heads while others sit watching faces turn first pink, then red, then purple. A few even take notes on the experience. The teacher moves about the room or meets with students in scheduled conferences. Sometimes she answers questions. She seems more or less oblivious to the general scene.

What is a well managed class? Is this one? Teachers are frequently evaluated on the order in their classrooms, especially beginning teachers (2). We all have our definitions, and sometimes they seem directly related to the amount of noise and activity in the class. Yet, a quiet class can be as poorly managed as a noisy one or vice versa.

Ms. Shamus' class barely appeared to be managed at all. Yet, spending time there revealed it to be a finely balanced system which was running extremely smoothly. Students seemed to know what to do. If you asked the third graders

"What are you working on?" "Why?" "How will you find out what to do next?" "What will you do if the teacher is unavailable?" most of them could answer constructively (20 out of the 27 in the class) and most of them were performing adequately. Only one or two were relatively uninvolved in the instructional process at any particular ten minute period, and rarely were they the same students.

Every class is managed to some extent: just by there being a schedule when students pick up reading books or worksheets. The heart of the management issue is getting and keeping the students meaningfully engaged in the learning activities. Management concerns can be divided into four parts: 1) task design and allocation; 2) selection of an authority of supervision strategy; 3) design of a feedback system which keeps in touch with all students; and 4) student cooperation and requirements for commitment. The parts are interrelated so that each affects all others. A teacher has to invest time in system maintenance or the system will not stay in tune.

## Task Design and Allocation

This concern refers to the system used for deciding the task(s) on which students are going to work. Both character of the task and the number of tasks students work at simultaneously have implications for the nature of the management process implemented.

Some tasks are more or less routine. Learning the spelling or pronunciation of ten particular words which are often missed is an example of a task that can be considered routine. Learning how to read a table of contents is another. Such information must be mastered by everyone. These types of tasks may be more appropriate for large group instruction than certain other tasks, such as the practicing of reporting techniques. The character of tasks has to be analyzed to determine the way the tasks are to be carried out and what demands will be placed on the teacher's time. The absolute clarity of procedures, the availability of resources, and the student-student interaction opportunities must be considered.

One teacher who tried to have students individually work on the same worksheet on pronunciation, silently at their desks, discovered first hand that silence quickly eroded as everyone mouthed the same words and created one giant whisper. Nobody could hear themselves. The teacher tried to maintain silence and help as needed. Some students, especially those in the back, quickly tuned out and turned to giggling when they decided the teacher could not give them any form of immediate feedback on what they were doing.

This example illustrates the type of demands for management skills which are inherent in a teacher's conception of a task—even those tasks which appear to be simple. These skills require the teacher to think about 1) the number of students who can work on a task and still have it appropriate to their needs; 2) whether the format of the task is going to allow students the needed concentration to accomplish it; 3) the amount and character of teacher intervention required to keep the students productively engaged; 4) the availability of needed resources such as extra paper, scissors, tape recorders; 5) the clarity of various procedures such as for the use of scarce resources or for solving a sticky problem, i.e., the clarity of teacher expectations for student behavior and student expectations for teacher behavior; and 6) the extent to which students perceive teacher expectations as reasonable and proper. Teachers sometimes think their expectations are quite clear. Yet, students often cannot express what those expectations are and sometimes do not agree and may not comply with them. Thus points 5 and 6 are not trivial; neither are they necessarily a function of the hardheadedness of certain students. Principals, for example, who feel the criteria for evaluation of teachers are quite clear are often surprised to find out that teachers have a totally different though equally clear conception of what the criteria are (2). The problem is communication; and this problem becomes increasingly important when the task structure becomes more individualized—that is, when there are a number of different tasks simultaneously occurring.

Analyzing the character of the tasks can highlight the problems and prospects of an intended experience. Consider the worksheet pronunciation incident. First, some students worked who did not need to, and others could not do the task. Evidently the teacher had not diagnosed the needs of the students, and it turned out the task was inappropriate for quite a few of them. Furthermore, there were too many students

*Planning*                                                           63

involved for the task to fit their diverse strengths and weaknesses. There was too much noise; students could not hear because the spatial arrangements did not fit the task requirements. Too much teacher intervention was required. Procedures were not made clear; few students profited and most were not greatly interested in the task.

What could have been done? Treating the task orally, as a whole group, where the teacher directly oversees what is happening would have been one way of attacking the task. This method would limit individual performance to a point where the teacher could have contributed the required timely feedback and could directly assess when some students needed a modified task. In this structure, the teacher's personal charisma and authority would have had to suffice to ensure student commitment to the task. Doing a small group or peer tutor setup with students who were already competent in the task distributed among the groups may also have worked. However, if teachers and students were not clear on the nature of the expectations for performance, and the procedures to be used when a group was stuck, it still would not have worked. Some tasks can be productively and enjoyably handled in a whole group instructional framework; other tasks may not be suitable to this format. Individualization does not mean that *every* task has to be performed individually. It neither precludes small group work nor whole class instruction; rather, it focuses on student needs and varies task structure to meet them.

Shamus evidently had thought out the task design and allocation procedures before she embarked upon the observed periods. Students were working on tasks designed to fit their particular skill needs or, in some cases, interests. Students who were working on tasks requiring quiet were in a special section of the room while those who were noisier or required more space were in another section. Students as well as the teacher could intervene in the scene to request greater quiet or answer particular questions. Thus, teacher time was not so scarce as it was in the other class situation. The expectations for how a task was performed were both clear and were thought to be reasonable by the students and teachers and were directly related to the needs and interests of the students. It took a lot of time to build such a system. Sometimes it worked better than others. How it was going and its problems or prospects were discussed among the class as a whole.

## Selection of a Supervision Strategy

How can I try to ensure high quality outcomes? and How can I keep track of what is going on? The first impulse is for the teacher to want to see and monitor everything, including how a task is performed and the outcomes. For direct supervision to succeed, the teacher has to be able to see at a glance exactly what is going on—who is working and who is not; why an individual is not working; and, if there is a dispute in progress, who started it. The consequences of acting on inadequate information, when the teacher cannot see, are only too apparent (3). Yet, the occasions when a teacher can see at a glance are confined to whole class or large group instruction. Although these situations present their own management problems, at least the teacher can more or less see what is happening.

In individualized classes, or with small group work, the problem is more difficult. Supervising alone, a teacher either has to be in five to thirty places at once or has to delegate responsibility for supervision to others, at least in some areas. The teacher need not give up all hope for quality control; but does need to decide which tasks require closest surveillance. One teacher, for example, gave students great latitude in selecting tasks and procedures for working on them. The teacher composed and taught skill groups on the basis of the needs assessment from the written products of selected tasks. The skill groups were under much tighter surveillance than other tasks. They were a means for this teacher to keep in close touch with the learning process (4).

Each supervision strategy has its pluses and minuses, and certain questions must be considered: Do I want to deal with the ramifications from this one? What happens if I ignore this or that element? Do I want to deal with this alone—without another adult for at least moral support? Why engage in a complex, time-consuming management system so students can learn ten particular words? These are reasonable questions. If there is a simple task, it may be more efficient and enjoyable all around—it may be a nice change to some students—to accomplish it in a simple and direct manner. A combination of methods can be used (5).

The direct supervision strategy requires teacher ability to see what is happening. Thus, it is more suitable in situations where most of the class is treated as a group. Grouping the class together has its own problems, however, increasing the potential for problems. Since all students depend upon the teacher to tell them what to do next, any dropped pencil interferes with a student's ability to hear; any student movement or stray work distracts from the act in the center ring; any giggle can spread like wild fire. If the task is not clear, if a student or the teacher is itchy, or if someone has butter-fingers, the whole process begins to drag and undermine student commitment to the task.

Another method available is to make students as a group responsible for supervision of themselves on certain tasks. This approach makes sense especially when the teacher cannot see what is going on at a glance. In her class, Shamus laid out clear procedures to follow in the tasks themselves. A general set of rules does not apply here because the require-ments of simultaneous tasks may differ in a number of respects, such as the amount of student-student interaction. Too complex a set of rules to follow is required to cover every wrinkle involved in instruction using multiple tasks. Shamus had procedures specified with the tasks. Then she had conferences with students over the outcomes of the tasks and how the process was working. Students, themselves, monitored how they worked on the tasks; Shamus gave them feedback about how the work was fitting into the whole picture. Students gave her feedback as well. During the period, if students had questions, they tried to answer for themselves as a group; if they could not, they put up some special signal indicating they needed teacher attention. In the interim, students worked on something else, thus cutting down on the traffic problem. Occasionally, when a question or problem was urgent (there were criteria they had all discussed pertaining to this decision) a student went to Shamus directly.

One student managed to almost slip through this system. He rarely seemed to signal for help when the teacher was near him, and he seemed engaged in the tasks. Students regularly kept logs of what they were doing, using schedules made out themselves at the beginning of the week telling what they were going to work on and when. Shamus examined this student's log and schedule; both seemed adequate but the student did not seem to be making progress. Intermittent mastery tests connected to the tasks showed no progress. Shamus could not figure it out and for a few days tried to keep herself particularly informed about what this student was doing. It turned out that every time the teacher was in the student's vicinity, he turned off the signal (took down the feather) indicating he needed teacher help. When the teacher was out of his vicinity, he restored the sign. The up signal legalized working on various puzzles and games not directly connected with the task until the teacher came around. Shamus soon discovered the student's system.

The method of making the group responsible reduces pressure on teachers for immediate decisions, but much preparation time is required. The teacher has to make sure the tasks are interesting and motivating for students. Success depends upon maintaining student cooperation and interest in what is happening. The teacher also has to make sure tasks are appropriate to specific student needs. Otherwise the system may end in frustration for everybody with bottlenecks of too many unanswered questions. If the students are selecting the tasks themselves, the teacher has to make sure they have adequate skills in task selection so that tasks which are too easy or too hard are not selected. Quintessentially, this strategy depends upon feedback given just at the point a student needs it. Yet, some students will request help more often than others; so there is a tendency for certain students to get lost. One teacher discovered a student who was not participating and who was doing poorly—she seemed to be slow. The teacher tried to find out from the student what the matter was. A change in tactics brought no change. Then, for a few consecutive periods, the teacher jotted down notes about whom she talked to, for how long, and on what topic. The nonachieving student was receiving much less time than other students. Most students were asking for help, but this pupil was not seeking assistance. Consequently, she was almost lost.

When the teacher increased (equalized) her time with the student, student skills improved. Teacher time, then, must be distributed equitably among all students in the class. Adequate means of sharing must be made available; otherwise, bottlenecks will disrupt the flow.

Giving some of the power to the group to evaluate how things are going is one means of decentralizing the supervision structure. Obviously, it is less appropriate when students work in a large group and more effective when students work at different paces or on different tasks.

Individuals can become responsible for their own task performances. Contracts, of course, are one means. In this case, the demands for task clarity are most stringent for no two people are working on the same thing. Thus, the teacher is the only person a student can ask for help. Since there are more tasks, the teacher must be in more places and has greater difficulty in making sure there are adequate resources to complete each task.

## Design of a Feedback System

The nature of the feedback system becomes more important as the classroom structure becomes more individualized. The teacher becomes dependent upon the student to furnish relevant and accurate information about individual interests and help needed. The teacher must get this information but is too busy to gather it accurately alone. Students, however, are not trained to pinpoint educational problems, especially their own. Students need assistance in focusing on and remembering information about a task process that can help teachers facilitate their learning process. Student logs, journals, or post task questionnaires are tools which can focus student attention on specific aspects of their own performances.

Relying on students for information does not completely relieve teachers of the burden. Teachers still must maintain easily accessible records, easily used, indicating what students have been doing and their particular areas of strength, weakness, and enthusiasm. Teacher notes made during the class period, charts of skills and interests indicating particular areas of mastery and characteristics of task performance, are good ways of keeping on top of the situation, in terms of how individuals are working. Occasional focus on the operation of class process as a whole is also necessary to keep the management system in tune.

Attention is needed to avoid certain trouble spots in the management system: traffic patterns in the class (student-student interaction and interference patterns); teacher-student interaction patterns (which students are talked to about what, how often, and the relative amounts of praise and criticism); which tasks seem to work better than others; and needed extra resources which may be unavailable. Observations in these areas can indicate patterns of social interaction among students which restrict classroom experience; the unwritten rules which seem to guide student-student interaction and may disrupt teacher expectations of (and task requirements for) cooperation among students; and uneven teacher-student interaction patterns. These observations can point to the underlying causes of bottlenecks where the potential for disruption is great.

Both content and frequency of feedback to students are important. Aside from student progress on skills, class process is an important element of teacher feedback to students that is broader than, "Jimmy, I don't like the way you work with Victor." It is meant to include comments relating to broadening friendship patterns, competition versus cooperation, student interests and boredoms, and student judgments concerning the amount of help they need compared to the attention they are receiving.

Unless there is some systematic approach to the feedback process, however, teachers will only be getting information from some students on some areas, and will only be reviewing some of the information. Here, in particular, there is need for aides or extra teachers in the class. It is helpful to have other sources of information besides yourself and to distribute the labor to handle the complex feedback system. One group—a teacher and an aide—did it this way:

- Conferences were scheduled with students once every two weeks; each conference took about twenty minutes and covered a variety of areas.
- In between times the teacher informally responded to student requests and needs and initiated tasks.

- Everyday both teacher and aide wrote down brief observations of individual children in a small notebook. At the end of each day the teacher and aide spent twenty minutes together using the class list to go over whom they had seen, whom they had missed, what they had observed, and what this all meant for the next day. "Steven is not finishing his tasks; we should make sure he does. We missed Jaime today; let's make sure we see her tomorrow. Everybody is having problems with the directions for this task...."
- Students posted schedules each week of what they were going to do and when. These were visible to all. A schedule could be changed by a student or by a student in consultation with a teacher, but it could not be taken down until the end of the week. Both teacher and student consulted it to see how things were going. A set amount of reading, spelling, and math had to be done each week.
- Students kept logs of what they were doing, what they were feeling about it, and why. This took twenty minutes to be done at their discretion during the day. Logs were made in a small book, and their content was directed by the student's wishes and student-teacher negotiations. Logs were handed in to the teacher the day before the scheduled student-teacher conference.
- Weekly class meetings were held to discuss events to be planned, how things were going, and any problems that came up.
- About once a month, the teacher and aide tried to focus on the management and instructional process to check out the interaction patterns on a systematic basis.

## Student Commitment

Student commitment to the ongoing class process is essential, especially as the class structure becomes more complex and the teacher is less able to supervise directly what is happening. To a great extent, success depends upon the ability to deliver feedback to students at just the right time. When there is a long lag time before needed feedback and students are stuck with nothing to do, the opportunities for distraction and disruption increase exponentially.

Student commitment and cooperation also are affected by the extent to which instruction is relevant to their interests. Providing humorous and exciting activities is one way of attracting student cooperation. Another way, which creates many more management problems, is giving students discretion over how they spend their time and what they work on. When students themselves choose what they will work on, and the tasks are interesting, their investment in the system increases. Some teachers have given students discretion for selecting what they work on, when, how long, in what location (within or outside the classroom), with whom, and what deadlines and restraints are set in their work process. Student discretion over more than one of the above dramatically increases management difficulties; therefore, the teacher's philosophy, the amount of student commitment that will be gained, and the management problems engendered has to be carefully balanced early in the experience. Initially, the amount of student discretion should be low, until students become used to and skilled at making the decisions involved and teachers have worked out the management bugs.

## Basic Concerns of a Management System

First, *devise a task structure appropriate to the needs and interests of individual students.* Sometimes this may involve large group instruction; sometimes, a smaller group format; and sometimes, tasks constructed for individuals.

Depending upon the characteristics of the tasks selected, *a strategy for supervising the task performance has to be implemented.* This is the second crucial element of a management system. The supervising strategy has to take into account the availability of resources required by the tasks; the amount of teacher time which will be needed to assist students in accomplishing tasks and how that time will be distributed to reduce wait time and bottlenecks; and what sort of products will give the teacher a good idea of whether the student has mastered the concept adequately.

Third, develop *a systematic approach to delivering timely feedback to students.* This pertains to getting around to all students, having a record keeping system which is easy to use and accessible, with information on student performance and management process in a number of different ways; and pumping students for additional information about task performance.

Fourth, focus on *student commitment toward the instructional process*. This involves centering instruction as much as possible on student interests and granting students some degree of discretion over how they spend their time during class.

Now, how does one go about setting up such a process? Obviously, running a successful individualized learning program is not a snap. Outcomes from individualized programs are mixed. When the teacher gives *all* responsibility for instruction to the students, many classes become chaotic. Research findings show that in situations where students are left to proceed by themselves, without supervision of any sort, the outcomes are often not good. Also, to the extent the tasks are unclear and the management system is not working, the teacher will be swamped with requests for help. The teacher working alone in the class, therefore, must recruit parent volunteers, acquire an aide, team up with another teacher, or rethink the implementation of such a complex individualized program.

## How to Begin an Individualized Program

Shamus first spent time observing other classes that were individualizing instruction, talked to other teachers, and looked at materials. One must see how it works and see what reaction one gets from the administrator(s) in the school, what help can be mustered, and what resources can be used.

Shamus, obviously, decided she wanted to go ahead with the challenge; and she liked the assumptions that she understood were behind it:

- To learn, a student has to be actively involved in an instructional process appropriate to where he/she is at the time.
- Tasks tailored to student needs improve specific skills.
- Student responsibility for their own instruction builds

active learning time and increases task engagement, both necessary precursors to learning.

• Tasks built on student interests also actively involved the student in the instructional process.

Shamus, however, was unsure what individualization meant in practice. She questioned what individualization meant for her classroom. What spatial arrangements? Previously, she had worked with two or three reading groups. How many did she have to have to be individualized? How many different tasks were actually involved when seven groups, of four students each, worked on reading? How many different materials did this imply? Was individualization going to be students working at different paces in the same materials, or were there going to be substantially different tasks and objectives? What type of discretion should she first give the students? She had yet to decide upon a program to enlist parent support—she wanted to wait on this a little, until she had her act together a bit more. She had to get the record keeping system and the management tools organized so the process would be more or less routine. She still would have to train an aide and determine their respective roles and activities during the instructional period. It would have been ideal if the aide or another teacher could have worked with her setting up the system, but she seemed able to get only consultation from a teacher friend occasionally and an aide to help her later.

## The Content of Instruction

Shamus first made a list of major objectives for the year. She included monthly themes she wanted to cover and the types of activities these themes could involve. She even made a stab at analyzing what the ramifications would be for the management system by focusing on the special supplies required; the amount of space a task would take; the number of students who could work on such a task in a group without having it get out of hand (large group, small group, individual); the amount of noise the task would probably generate (high, medium, or low); the amount of student-student cooperation the task involved; and the amount of teacher help required.

Space was allowed for comments on any special characteristics of the system. She called it her Grande Instructional Plan (preliminary version).

The setting up of the plan and its (partial) completion took about a week or a week and a half. All the goals were listed. Some of the activities, however, were more or less blank. Shamus tried some of her ideas out on her friend. She decided at first to design activities for larger groups—perhaps four of them. Three or four learning centers would also be set up, representing different themes. Students would work there during a scheduled portion of the day. The learning centers during this initial phase would be primarily for supplementary materials relating to the major activities. She had to find out what the pupils knew, what they liked to do, and what their weaknesses were. Scores on subscales of the standard tests of basic skills test results could be useful, but a more accurate perception would have to develop from observations of task performance and conferences. She would have to work out some diagnostic procedures. She was going to start out with a small model of individualization and expand it as she began to know the students better and when both were used to what individualization involved.

Of course she knew that she would undoubtedly modify the Grande Plan: themes would be switched to accommodate particular interests or events; activities would be adjusted to particular skill needs or styles. One big problem in starting such a program is that of amassing enough tasks and required supplies. Teachers report that they spend much time the first year amassing tasks and building a repertoire. Shamus had been gathering tasks for a year; therefore, her first two weeks could be organized.

*Space.* Spatial arrangements are important. Some tasks are noisy, some quiet; some require a number of special resources and need to be near a supply shelf; some tasks require cooperative group work; others require solitary work. Clearly, room arrangements have to be flexible. When students, in groups of three, sit on the floor and figure out what trail the two troopers followed, space must be available. Space is needed as well for the students who perform quiet and lonely tasks. Instead of continually changing the rules, certain areas should be kept for quiet tasks. The characteristics of the tasks also have to be taken into account so that supplies are handy.

Individualized classes are noisy and rugs help to absorb noise and cushion footsteps. Rugs are also comfortable to sit upon. Attractive, comfortable surroundings with cozy corners for pleasure reading help create the desired mood. Children love cubbyholes and often do better work when they can be off by themselves. A loft provides cozy space; perhaps parents and students can be drawn upon to build one for the class. In Shamus' class someone donated lumber and pieces of carpeting and, just before school, parents, pupils, and the teacher build a loft. Large packing crates, set on their sides with their bottoms cushioned, also provide neat holes for reading.

One should not forget to earmark space for class meetings and skill group work sessions. Also, students need storage spaces—places to get messages from the teacher, places to store things not currently in use, and places to post schedules. Mail drawers (small boxes with cork fronts to pin schedules on) work well for this.

*A Floor Plan*

Special arrangements are easier to manipulate in the newer, more flexible buildings. In older buildings, however, it is still possible to create an exciting environment. Several resources which might be helpful are listed at the end of this chapter. Shamus' floor plan reserved the left side of the classroom for quiet—the right, for noisier activities. The loft was about 5'6" high; underneath, there was space on one side for a magic carpet reading area; and on the other was space for desks. On top of the loft, children read or did their work; there were games, puzzles, and books available both on top of and underneath the loft. The mail boxes were embedded in the sides of the loft. Shelves held mail boxes with names. Learning center areas allowed work spaces and supply shelves in close proximity. Desks were arranged in single and multiple student formations. Dividers to separate students who needed privacy for concentration were made from large pieces of cardboard and attached to desks.

## Developing Tasks and Ordering Supplies

Well before the class begins, one has to decide what texts are going to be used, what type of products and how many are going to be required for the tasks. The testing and evaluation program also has to be worked out so that there are task mastery evaluations along with an evaluation of whether students are pulling together the skills being taught and are beginning to grasp underlying concepts. Materials for supplementary activities for students during wait time should not be forgotten.

## Record Keeping System

In addition to worksheets and tests, there are other forms that need to be developed for the management of the program. These include forms for 1) observations of individual student performance; 2) observations of class process, 3) schedules for student use, 4) logs for student comments, 5) student contracts or work inventories, and 6) progress charts.

A small loose leaf notebook, listing the names of the students in the class alphabetically, can be used for jotting down observations of student performance.

A number of references which can be used for looking at class process are listed at the end of this chapter. One could also prepare sheets with space for comments on student-student interaction, teacher-student interaction, traffic flow, bottlenecks, and other management or learning approach considerations. Examples of appropriate forms appear in Chapter Ten.

Many of these forms will be needed. Schedules should provide enough space to separate morning and afternoon activities and allow students to write exactly what they will be doing during the day.

Students can make their own logs the first week of school. So, there is nothing to prepare; however, one will have to determine the first facets of performance that students should report—their likes or dislikes about the tasks might be a good starter.

Student contracts or work-study agreements have to be prepared, indicating to students what they are supposed to do, and what they have done. For learning centers, however, if one doesn't use contracts, there can be sign-in/sign-out sheets where students inscribe their names and state when they attend and for how long. This record will show when most of the students have been through a learning center and when it has to be changed. It will also provide feedback on how long students take to complete the tasks. Charts indicating the skills students are to cover and their mastery of them might also be useful.

Each teacher must determine which records are needed to keep track of whether instruction is meeting student needs. Some teachers keep these records in their heads. Shamus tried to, but found always there were some things forgotten. At first, she tried a complicated computer-based record keeping system which earmarked student strengths and weaknesses, provided charts, and finally gave her so much data that she didn't have time to analyze it properly. She seemed to spend more time in management than in teaching; obviously the system was wrong for her. She devised her own system—the one mentioned here. At first, she was overwhelmed with the number of forms to be prepared. Then she realized that the students would be keeping most of the records themselves; and, all told, the system would not take too much time.

## Parents

The time came for showing parents what their children would be getting into and explaining how parents could help. A session in the classroom would be a good way to start. The goals and underlying rationale should be explained, along with how student progress would be evaluated. Parents should be made to feel that their children will make progress. A session in which parents actually participate in some of the activities often sparks enthusiasm.

## The First Day

By the middle of the first day, Shamus relaxed and decided to admire the three ring circus that was her class. Only one or two students had had previous experience in individualized classes. The room was filled with interesting materials and provocative space. Every student wanted to try out everything at once. Early in the day, after some activities to help students get acquainted, a tour of the room was arranged, accompanied by a demonstration of how some of the special tasks worked. Use of the mailboxes, the contracts (the task allocation system), and the way in which the room was designed to work in general also had to be explained. The children were full of enthusiasm to begin their work. The pupils worked industriously. By the middle of the day, Shamus took the time to see what would need to be reinforced with students at the end. She had a meeting, just before clean-up, to review any problems with the system.

## Summary

Shamus spent many hours preparing for this class. Once in progress, she still had to spend a fairly substantial portion of time looking over individual accomplishments, making sure tasks were appropriate, and in finding new tasks. Shamus' method of individualizing instruction was only one way of approaching the concept of designing an instructional program to meet the specific needs and interests of a given group of students. Programs for other teachers and other classes will be different, but the essential features will still be there: the need to determine individual tasks for individual students and then find a way to make sure students learn without becoming frustrated.

**Notes**

1. Based on a chapter by E.G. Cohen, J.K. Intili, and S.H. Robbins, "Task and Authority: A Sociological View of Classroom Management," in D. Duke (Ed.) *78th Yearbook of the National Society for the Study of Education*, Part II. Chicago: NSSE, 1979.
2. For more on how teachers are evaluated, see S.M. Dornbusch and W.R. Scott, *Evaluation and the Exercise of Authority*. San Francisco: Jossey Bass, 1975.
3. In *Discipline and Group Management in Classrooms*, J. Kounin writes more about the implications of not being "with it," as he calls it. New York: Holt, Rinehart and Winston, 1970.
4. A description of this class is presented in more depth in the paper by Cohen, Intili, and Robbins.
5. The use of large group instruction has been assumed by many to be a hallmark of an authoritarian teacher and, therefore, has no place in an individualized program. This is too bad. In some instances, the results

Intili and Conrad

may be better than for individualized situations—i.e., when the individualization is not well managed and when the large group instruction is accompanied by a reasonable task. W. Gordon and L. Adler show these results in their report on "Dimensions of Teacher Leadership in Classroom Social Systems," Project No. 1084, December 1973, UCLA. F. McNeil and P. Elias also suggest this in "The Effects of Teaching Performance on Pupil Learning," *Beginning Teacher Evaluation Studies*, Phase 2, Vol. 1. Princeton, New Jersey: ETS, 1976.

**Bibliography**
*70 Activities for Classroom Learning Centers.* Dorothy M. Lloyd. Instruction Handbook Series.
*The Learning Center Book: An Integrated Approach.* Tom Davidson and others. Santa Monica, California: Goodyear Publishing.
*Innovation without Renovation.* Richard Morton and Jane Morton. New York: Citation Press.
*Individualized Teaching in Elementary Schools.* Dona Kofod Stuhl and Patricia Angalone. West Nyack, New York: Parker.
*Room to Learn.* Joan Dean. New York: Citation Press.
*Classroom Learning Centers.* John E. Morlan. Belmont, California: Fearon.
*The Workshop Approach to Classroom Interest Centers.* Barbara Kilroy Ingram, Nancy Riggs Jones, and Marlene LeButt. West Nyack, New York: Parker.
*Personalized Reading Instruction.* W. Barbe and J.L. Abbott. West Nyack, New York: Parker.
"Reading: Managing the Classroom Reading Program." Roselmina Indrisano. *Instructor*, January 1978, 117-120.
*Educator's Self-Teaching Guide to Individualized Instruction.* Rita Dunn and Kenneth Dunn. West Nyack, New York: Parker, 1975, 50-73, 112-156.
*Looking in Classrooms.* T.L. Good and J.E. Brophy. New York: Harper and Row, 1973.

Stieglitz provides a workable plan for implementing an effective reading program based on initial assessment and describes various formal and informal instruments and procedures for effective diagnosis.

## Chapter Six   Initial Assessment for Individualization

Ezra L. Stieglitz
*Rhode Island College*

Many teachers remember their first meeting of a group of students at the beginning of the school year: the excitement, the enthusiasm, the anticipation, the knot in the stomach. Beyond such feelings, teachers contemplating the start of a school year usually have many questions related to the educational program:

- What are the major goals of instruction for the school year?
- What minimum skills are needed in order to meet these goals?
- How prepared are the students to meet these goals?
- What materials are available to meet the needs of every student in the class?
- Which approaches to instruction will the students respond to best?
- What should be done to determine whether the goals of instruction have been met?

Each of the above questions is related, in one way or another, to the need to individualize instruction in the classroom. When selecting materials, for example, the needs of the pupil must be considered in order to choose proper materials. Similarly, when choosing an approach to teach a word identification or comprehension skill, the method that will be most suitable for the learner must be selected.

Assessment plays a central role in the establishment of

an individualized program. According to Harris and Smith (*12*:101), "...it enables a teacher to identify a reading level where the child can work effectively on a daily basis, and each child's pattern of strengths and weaknesses."

The emphasis of this chapter is on diagnostic procedures that can be used to assess pupils' reading performances at the beginning of the school year. The topic of continuous or ongoing assessment is addressed in Chapter Seven.

This chapter begins with a discussion of the role of the teacher in a diagnostic program and the two levels of diagnosis in the classroom. Next, the various types of standardized and informal devices available for collecting diagnostic information are described, followed by the presentation of a systematic plan for assessing students' reading needs at the start of a new semester. Finally, the reader is introduced to sources of information on diagnostic tools in reading.

## Diagnosis in the Classroom
### *What Is Diagnosis ?*

Diagnosis is a term that is used interchangeably with *assessment* and *diagnostic teaching* in the literature. According to Kennedy (*18*:19), "Diagnosis...is the process of finding exactly what kinds of reading behavior a pupil exhibits, determining whether they are good or bad, and deciding what to do about them." Sartain (*25*:45) states that "...diagnostic teaching is highly differentiated instruction based upon careful assessments of individual backgrounds, personal adjustments, aptitudes, and achievements." No matter how one defines it, diagnosis should always lead directly to the improvement of reading through the reinforcement of strengths and correction of difficulties.

Diagnosis is often viewed as a procedure that reading specialists should assume responsibility for when working with disabled readers in a special reading center or clinic. Diagnosis of reading performance should also be seen as an essential part of classroom instruction. Sartain supports this view in stating, "Diagnostic assessment must be practiced with every child in order to guide his maximum progress rather than with only those children who are in major difficulty."

## Levels of Classroom Diagnosis

Diagnosis in the classroom occurs at two levels. At the first level, it is used by classroom teachers to provide them with information on general achievement of a class in reading. At the second level, diagnosis is used to identify specific student strengths and weaknesses in reading.

### Level I: Diagnosis of General Achievement

The main purpose of this stage in the diagnostic process is to discover the level at which reading instruction should take place for every child in the class; in other words, to determine each pupil's functional or instructional reading level. This is defined as the level at which the student will profit most from instruction. All instruction should, therefore, be geared to this level.

It is essential that functional reading levels be established early in the school year since teachers must have this information in order to place their students in the proper reading groups. Also, teachers need this information to select appropriate reading and subject matter materials. When pupils receive instruction from materials that are too simple, they are not challenged enough to attain maximum growth. However, if the books are too difficult, they may become discouraged and lose interest in reading.

An appraisal of students' general reading performance usually uncovers areas of weakness that require further assessment and necessitates a more specific form of diagnosis.

### Level II: Diagnosis of Specific Skills

The major purpose of this stage in a diagnostic program is to secure enough specific information about a pupil to guide teachers in planning for direct and appropriate instruction. Assessment devices are used at this level by classroom teachers to reveal specific student strengths and weaknesses in the major skill areas of reading. These are word identification, comprehension, and study skills.

Diagnosis at this level depends upon continuous individual assessment throughout the school year. As stated by

Stieglitz

Sartain, this is essential "... in order to determine each pupil's level and pattern of progress to guide planning for continued instruction" (25:45).

Diagnosis in the classroom is distinguished from diagnosis in the clinic mainly in terms of the level of comprehensiveness. In the classroom, teachers use diagnostic procedures to 1) assess the reading levels of their pupils, 2) study their reading strengths and weaknesses, 3) correct as many of their reading difficulties as possible, and 4) identify individuals who appear to have special instructional needs requiring the services of a specialist.

In a clinical setting, diagnosis is more intensive and comprehensive. At this level, reading specialists usually have to conduct detailed studies of pupils' reading problems. Also, it may be necessary to obtain additional information from other specialists such as guidance counselors, social workers, physicians, and psychologists. A complete case study may have to be done in order to get an overall picture of a child and his needs.

## The Role of the Teacher in Classroom Diagnosis

The classroom teacher is a key figure in any plan to implement a program of diagnostic assessment. The entire effectiveness of the program depends largely on the expertise of the teacher. Because diagnostic assessment must be practiced with all children, it is essential that every classroom teacher be able to 1) demonstrate a good knowledge of diagnostic tools and techniques, 2) determine the general level appropriate for group or individual reading instruction, 3) assess reading achievement periodically in order to determine each child's general status, and 4) analyze in some detail each child's difficulties in any of the major areas of reading. Given a teacher who possesses these skills, along with adequate materials and good facilities, the goal of establishing a diagnostic classroom is readily attainable.

## Sources of Information for Classroom Diagnosis

In order to determine the learning needs of every student in the classroom, teachers should refer to as many sources of information as are available. To accomplish this task, teachers need to have a thorough understanding of the standardized and informal devices necessary for collecting diagnostic information. Examples of such devices are included in the discussion that follows. More detailed information on how some of these instruments can be used by teachers to implement a program of classroom diagnosis will be introduced in the next section of this chapter.


## Standardized Tests

Standardized tests are often used in the elementary classroom to provide teachers with some measure of each student's performance in reading and other related areas. Generally, a test is said to be standardized if it is based upon norms, can be used with large segments of the school population, yields objective data, and includes data which establish its reliability and validity. Standardized tests differ from informal devices mainly by the nature of their construction and design. During the standardization process, these tests are administered to a representative sample of the population which is supposed to comprise a cross section of the total school population. As a result of this process, the appropriateness of the test items is determined and the scores of the standardization sample are reported in the form of norms. Norms are usually presented as grade equivalent scores, percentile rankings, or stanine scores. Assessment instruments developed in this manner are known as norm referenced tests whose purpose is to show how individuals and groups compare with the students on whom the test was standardized.

Test score results are reported for each student as he progresses through the grades in the cumulative record folder. The cumulative folder provides teachers with a record of each student's performance on different kinds of standardized tests. These include reading readiness tests, survey reading tests, achievement batteries, diagnostic or analytic tests, and tests of mental abilities.

*Reading readiness tests* are intended for use in kindergarten and first grade and, according to the publishers, are designed to determine which pupils are or are not likely to make progress in beginning reading instruction. The tests are composed of a series of subtests on those skills that are believed prerequisite for success in beginning reading.

While no two tests sample the same skills in identical fashion, readiness tests, generally speaking, include items for measuring skills in auditory discrimination, visual discrimination, knowledge of letter names, and listening comprehension.

Whereas reading readiness tests are used to predict success in reading, *reading survey tests* are used to provide a measure of the level of proficiency a student has attained in reading. Survey tests are usually administered to groups of pupils by classroom teachers near the end of the school year. The areas of reading assessed by these tests are broad. Typically, most survey tests consist of two subtests (vocabulary and comprehension) and yield three scores: a vocabulary score, a comprehension score, and a total reading score. Care should be exercised when interpreting the results of survey tests since these instruments are intended to only provide general information about reading level.

Reading survey tests are sometimes included in a battery of tests designed to measure achievement in several basic areas such as arithmetic, social studies, and science. The reading portion of this test can often be purchased separately if desired.

*Diagnostic tests* (also known as analytical tests) should be administered to pinpoint deficiencies in reading when more specific information is needed. Diagnostic tests are more specialized than survey tests since they concentrate on specific areas of the reading act. The Gates-McKillop Reading Diagnostic Tests (Teachers College Press) for example, sample reading behavior in each of the areas of word recognition: oral reading, words; flash presentation, words; untimed presentation, phrases; flash presentation; knowledge of word parts; recognizing the visual form of sounds; and auditory blending. Diagnostic instruments are available as group or individual tests. Since group tests are easier to administer and score than individual tests, they are usually selected by classroom teachers. Individual diagnostic tests are usually reserved for use by reading specialists.

The final example of a standardized instrument is the group test of *scholastic aptitude* or *mental abilities*. The main purpose of this test is to provide information regarding the approximate level on which pupils are expected to achieve. Although such tests have some limitations, when used with discretion, the results of mental abilities tests can give valuable information to teachers.

## Informal Devices

Informal or nonstandardized tests do not have norms. Nevertheless, they can be equally or even more valuable than standardized tests to the classroom teacher in need of diagnostic information regarding each student's performance in reading. Examples of informal devices include: informal reading inventories, word lists, criterion referenced tests, basal reading programs with an assessment component, the cloze procedure, miscue analysis, teacher observation, trail teaching, and teacher made tests.

*The informal reading inventory* (IRI) is administered individually to provide useful information about a student's general and specific levels of achievement in reading. The test usually consists of a series of graded passages from preprimer through grades six or eight. Accompanying each paragraph is a set of questions to test comprehension. During the administration of an IRI, the student reads the selections orally to the teacher until the material becomes frustrating either in terms of accuracy of pronunciation or comprehension of ideas in the passages. The results are used to determine a student's independent, instructional, hearing comprehension, and frustration levels in reading. Besides furnishing teachers with an estimation of these levels, the data from an IRI also provide diagnostic information on specific strengths and weaknesses with word identification and comprehension skills. While an IRI is usually administered as an oral test, it can be given as a silent test when only a comprehension score is needed.

*Word lists* are useful tools when an informal device is needed to quickly evaluate a student's ability to recognize words. Typically, a word list test consists of columns of graded words drawn from basal reader glossaries and established lists such as the Dolch and the Thorndike. Beginning with the list with which the student is most likely to be successful (one year below actual grade level is the usual rule of thumb), the student pronounces the words at each succeeding level until he fails to pronounce a certain number of the words correctly. By observing a student's performance with the words, the teacher can use the results as an initial step in determining whether the pupil can read materials written at a specific level. This procedure is usually part of an informal reading inventory where it is used to estimate the approximate starting level for the reading of the graded passages.

Another type of word list that should be used to test word recognition is one that attempts to identify the high frequency words that pupils do or do not have in their recognition vocabularies. Hillerich's "Starter Words" is an example of such a list and is presented in Chapter Seven.

*Criterion referenced tests* have gained increased attention in recent years. They are being used more and more for program planning and classroom diagnosis. A criterion referenced test is designed to assess mastery of specific objectives. A typical objective might read: "Given ten letters from the alphabet, the student will identify the letters as either consonants or vowels, with no more than two errors." Whereas norm referenced tests can be used to compare performances, criterion referenced measures do a better job of describing performance of individuals and groups.

Criterion referenced tests are used basically as part of a skills management system. According to Johnson and Pearson (*14*:757-758), the commercially developed systems and the locally available systems share these components:

1. A sequentially ordered set of behavioral objectives for the various reading skills monitored by the system.
2. A set of subtests (or a set of test items) with one or more items designed to measure each objective.
3. A rule or set of rules for deciding what level of achievement constitutes mastery of each objective.
4. A resource file listing specific workbook pages, ditto masters, games or kits, and teaching strategies which teachers can use to provide instruction and practice for children who fail to attain specific objectives.
5. A method of reporting to teachers which students have or have not mastered which skills.

More and more publishers are producing *basal reading programs with an assessment component* which may include silent group mastery or achievement tests at the end of each unit and criterion referenced or level masters tests to check pupil performance in decoding, vocabulary, comprehension and study skills. Because these devices are usually keyed to the objectives of the reading program itself, the teacher can use the results of these tools to monitor a student's progress through a series of readers.

The *cloze procedure* can be a useful device for measuring general understanding of written material. The technique "is based on the gestalt idea of closure—the impulse to complete a structured whole by supplying a missing element" (*28*:249-250). In the cloze procedure, the reader is presented with a series of passages from which certain words have been omitted. Words are deleted in a consistent pattern, e.g., every fifth or every eighth word substituted with a blank of standard length. The individual taking the test reads the passage and writes in the missing words. The percentage of correct responses is then calculated and from these percentages, independent, instructional, and frustration reading levels are determined.

Special expertise in test development is not required in order to construct a cloze test. The classroom teacher should find this procedure easy to use with either individual pupils or groups of students.

In recent years, much attention has been given to *miscue analysis* as a procedure for diagnosis and evaluation. A miscue is an oral response made by the reader which deviates from the expected response. Goodman and Burke (*9*:5) state that miscues "... are not random errors but, in fact, are cued by the thought and language of the reader in his encounter with the material." What distinguishes this procedure from other diagnostic methods is the stress placed on a qualitative as well as a quantitative analysis of reading proficiency. For example, in the administration of the *Reading Miscue Inventory* (*9*:49) the teacher is required to answer the following questions about every miscue:

1. Is a dialect variation involved in the miscue?
2. Is a shift in intonation involved in the miscue?
3. How much does the miscue look like what was expected?
4. How much does the miscue sound like what was expected?

5. Is the grammatical function of the miscue the same as the grammatical function of the word in context?
6. Is the miscue corrected?
7. Does the miscue occur in a structure which is grammatically acceptable?
8. Does the miscue occur in a structure which is semantically acceptable?
9. Does the miscue result in a change of meaning?

These questions illustrate that an analysis of oral reading can reveal much about a child's reading strategy—more than could be obtained from simply counting errors without regard to their nature.

The use of *teacher observation, trial teaching*, and *teacher made tests* are diagnostic tools available to all teachers.

Observation should be viewed as an acceptable and basic technique for appraising the child's reading growth. The careful observation of student reactions to teacher's questions, responses to the items on a worksheet, or oral paragraph reading from a book may provide the teacher with information not readily obtainable from other sources.

Trial teaching can furnish the teacher with additional insights into the nature of a reading problem. Using this technique, the teacher first identifies a problem with a skill or concept that previous diagnosis has indicated a child needs to learn. The teacher then designs a lesson for this child. During the lesson the teacher notes how well the student is able to accomplish the learning task. Finally, the teacher uses the insights gained from observing the student perform to adjust subsequent instruction.

An effective program of classroom diagnosis need not rely upon the availability of standardized tests and/or commercially prepared informal tests. Teacher made devices such as informal tests or skill exercises may be just as or more useful in permitting the teacher to focus on the reading behavior that he feels is relevant to a given situation.

## Planning for Initial Classroom Diagnosis

There are numerous ways to organize a classroom for diagnostic teaching. However, whatever approach is taken, a plan for classroom diagnosis at the beginning of a school year can only be effective if it is systematic, flexible, and functional. A plan for diagnosis is systematic if it contains a definite set of procedures. These procedures serve as a guide to teachers in their implementation of a program based on continuing assessment. In referring to this plan, teachers should know how to initiate the program, make use of the diagnostic tools available, and monitor the progress of students during the school year.

Besides being systematic, a good design for classroom diagnosis must also be flexible. A plan that is too rigid could lead to pointless testing situations for children. According to Wilson (*31*:37), "An efficient diagnosis . . . is one which includes those measures needed by the educator to properly arrive at a solution to the problem; it eliminates those which have questionable value in relation to the final objective of diagnosis." A flexible diagnostic program allows classroom teachers to use alternative strategies for assessing the reading strengths and weaknesses of every pupil. Since a student's performance may be affected by the type of instrument used, it is essential that teachers have access to a variety of devices. For example, when a student responds negatively to the format or contents of a particular test and, as a result, does not perform as anticipated, the teacher must be able to refer to an alternative source that is a measure of the same behavior.

Finally, an effective scheme has to be functional. A plan is only of limited value if it is too cumbersome for the average classroom teacher to implement or if it requires skills in diagnosis that teachers may have never acquired.

The remainder of this chapter is devoted to the presentation of a design for initial classroom assessment. This plan consists of the following steps:

1. Establish instructional goals for the reading program.
2. Construct or select a ready-made pupil record sheet for summarizing the diagnostic findings.
3. Review the contents of the cumulative record folders.
4. Determine the general achievement levels in reading for every child in the class.
   (Level I: Diagnosis of General Achievement)
5. Perform a specific diagnosis of each student's reading strengths and weaknesses.
   (Level II: Diagnosis of Specific Skills)

Steps 1-4 are usually implemented at the beginning of the school year. Step 5 is ongoing throughout the school year.

## Step 1. *Establish Instructional Goals for the Reading Program*

It is important to understand that before assessment can take place in the classroom, the teacher must first determine what it is that needs to be assessed. A test is worthwhile only when it provides the teacher with information about how students are achieving in relation to the goals established for instruction. As a first step in implementing a diagnostic plan, therefore, it is essential that the instructional goals of the reading program be identified. It is up to the teacher, at this point, to distinguish the high priority reading skills from the low priority skills. In other words, the teacher has to determine which aspects of reading should be emphasized and which should not. Although goal setting at this time can be difficult, some decisions must be made early to give the program coherence and structure (12:103).

With the goals for the reading program clearly established, the teacher is now able to select diagnostic tools that will measure their attainment. As time passes, these goals of reading instruction are eventually translated into learning tasks or specific objectives, and the assessment devices used to measure these objectives are more precise.

## Step 2. *Construct or Select a Ready-Made Pupil Record Sheet*

In order to arrive at judgments about the degree to which the objectives of the reading program are being achieved, the teacher should maintain a careful record of each student's performance during the school year. The classroom teacher may find it useful to record essential information on a device that will be referred to as a *pupil record sheet*. An example of a pupil record sheet is provided in Figure 1.

## Figure 1. Sample Pupil Record Sheet
INTERMEDIATE GRADE CHECKLIST OF TEACHER OBSERVATION
ON PUPIL'S READING*

Name _____ Grade _____ Teacher _____

I. Word Recognition Techniques

    A. Sight Recognition
        1. Is able to recognize most of the general vocabulary words at sight which are found in general reading and content reading _____

    B. Phonetic Analysis
        1. Is able to use phonetic analysis to determine the pronunciation and meaning of an unknown general vocabulary term _____
        2. Is able to use phonetic analysis to determine the pronunciation and meaning of specialized vocabulary terms from content area textbooks or reference books _____

    C. Structural Analysis
        1. Can recognize a base or root word
           Examples—invents, invented, and inventing _____
        2. Knows the meaning of the following prefixes and can use them in determining the pronunciation and meaning of unknown general vocabulary terms found in readers and tradebooks and specialized vocabulary terms found in content textbooks _____
        3. Can understand the function of the following suffixes
           Examples—ly, ful, les, ness, er, and en _____
        4. Can correctly divide polysyllabic words into syllables _____
        5. Is able to understand and apply the principles of accent
           a. In a word of two syllables, the first syllable usually is accented _____
           b. Words of three syllables usually are accented on the first or second syllable _____
        6. Is able to understand the function of primary and secondary accent _____

    D. Picture Clue Usage
        1. Is able to use a picture in a reader, a tradebook, or a content textbook to determine the meaning of an unknown word on the same or nearby page _____

    E. Context Clue Usage
        1. Can apply context clue usage effectively in determining the meaning of an unknown word in a reader, tradebook, or a content textbook _____

    F. Dictionary and Glossary Usage
        1. Can use the dictionary or the glossary in a textbook effectively in locating the pronunciation and meaning of unknown words which are met in a reader, tradebook, or content textbook _____
        2. Is able to understand alphabetical sequence _____
        3. Is able to use guide words _____
        4. Is able to use the pronunciation key _____
        5. Can choose the correct dictionary definition for use in the context of the unknown word _____

Stieglitz

II. Comprehension Skills

  A. Literal Comprehension
    1. Is able to answer literal and factual questions which have been
      posed from reading done in readers, tradebooks, or content
      textbooks
      Example—What was the first word which Helen Keller learned
      to say? _____

  B. Interpretive Comprehension
    1. Is able to answer interpretive questions (inferring, drawing
      conclusions, drawing generalizations, summarizing, and read-
      ing between the lines) which are posed from reading in readers,
      tradebooks, and content textbooks
      Example—Why does Helen Keller believe that her mother
      helped her so very much when she was young? _____

  C. Critical Reading
    1. Is able to answer questions which call for critical or evaluative
      responses done from readers, tradebooks, or content textbooks
      Example—Do you believe that Helen Keller's mother should have
      allowed her to be independent? Why or why not? _____
    2. Is able to evaluate propaganda techniques _____

  D. Creative Reading
    1. Is able to follow up his reading from readers, tradebooks, or
      content textbooks in a problem-solving situation such as by
      creative writing, an oral book report, a written book report, role
      playing, or creative dramatics _____


III. Study Skills

  A. Finding the Main Idea
    1. Can locate a main topic sentence in a paragraph _____
    2. Can state a directly stated main idea in a paragraph in his own
      words _____
    3. Can state the implied main idea in a paragraph in his own
      words _____
    4. Can give another title for a story or a book which was read _____

  B. Locating Details
    1. Is able to locate the significant details in a paragraph _____
    2. Is able to locate the irrelevant details in a paragraph _____

  C. Following Directions
    1. Is able to follow a one-step direction _____
    2. Is able to follow a two- or three-step direction in proper
      sequence _____

  D. Organizational Skills
    1. Can outline a chapter using main headings and subordinate
      headings _____
    2. Can take acceptable notes from a content textbook _____
    3. Can summarize a paragraph in his own words _____
    4. Can summarize an entire selection in his own words _____

E. Location of Information
    1. Can use textbook aids such as table of contents, index, and glossary    _____
    2. Can locate information in content textbooks and reference books    _____

F. Graphic Aids
    1. Can interpret maps, charts, tables, and diagrams    _____

IV. Silent Reading

  A. Enjoys silent reading as determined from reactions during silent reading    _____

  B. Is interested in reading readers stories, tradebooks, and content textbooks silently    _____

  C. Has proper posture and book position while reading silently    _____

  D. Does not use lip movement or whispering while reading silently    _____

  E. Does not use head movement while reading silently    _____

  F. Is able to read silently in thought units    _____

V. Oral Reading

  A. Enjoys oral reading before an audience    _____

  B. Has good expression in oral reading    _____

  C. Observes punctuation marks while reading orally    _____

  D. Can read orally in phrases or thought units    _____

*From *Reading Diagnosis Kit* by Wilma H. Miller. ©1974 by The Center for Applied Research in Education, Inc., New York, New York. Published by The Center for Applied Research in Education, West Nyack, New York.


Devices of this type usually come in the form of checklists or rating scales. Teachers can construct their own record sheets or select a ready-made one. Either way, the contents of the pupil record sheet should relate directly to the instructional goals of the reading program.

The pupil record sheet has many uses in evaluating reading instruction. It provides the teacher with basic information about a student's reading performance at a glance. It can be used by the instructor to determine whether progress is being made with a pupil. It can be used as a guide for observing student performance in the classroom. It can help the teacher to bring together isolated bits of information in order to discover patterns of growth (or lack of growth) in reading. The teacher can then use this information for grouping students into various skill and interest groups.

## Step 3. *Review the Contents of the Cumulative Record Folders*

As a pupil progresses from grade to grade, a record of the student's work in school is usually kept in a cumulative record folder. This folder is a valuable diagnostic tool because it provides teachers with an overview of a student's past performance. The data found in this folder furnishes teachers with information needed to conduct a preliminary assessment of each student's achievement in reading and other areas. Teachers can use the cumulative record folder as an initial source of information for recording data on the pupil record sheet. As a result of reviewing the cumulative records, teachers can become acquainted with their students prior to the start of classes and can draw some tentative conclusions as to what degree the goals established in the first step can be met. Based on the results of this preliminary assessment, teachers might find it necessary to modify their instructional goals.

Teachers who review the contents of the cumulative record folders early in the school year will find it a valuable tool for planning a program of diagnostic teaching in the classroom. The folder usually includes a history of each pupil's performance on standardized reading tests and other tests of achievement and aptitude. The folder may also contain report card ratings, teacher comments, a list of materials used for reading instruction and useful data about a student's health. In addition, the folder may include space for recording significant incidents that could have some bearing upon a pupil's success in school (e.g., interviews with guidance counselors, data from a core evaluation team). Finally, the cumulative record folder may provide teachers with the names or roles of personnel who can provide additional information on a child's performance in school (e.g., reading resource teacher, school psychologist, special education director).

There are numerous ways in which teachers can use the information in the cumulative record folder. The results of standardized reading tests, report card ratings, and comments from previous teachers can be used to classify students for purposes of grouping in reading. It is assumed, however, that the assignment of children to reading groups at the beginning of the school year is done on a tentative basis. As more information on each pupil becomes available, the composition and number of groups will most likely have to be revised. In addition to data from reading tests, scores from the subtests of achievement batteries along with report card ratings can alert classroom teachers to possible pupil weaknesses in subject areas such as science, social studies, and mathematics.

Many school systems report the results of group tests of mental ability on the cumulative record card. Information from mental tests can be compared with reading test results in order to determine if a student is achieving up to potential. Generally, the brighter a pupil is the higher are expectations for the student to read at or above grade level. However, since proficiency in reading is required for the completion of many group tests of mental ability, the pupil who has a reading problem to begin with will be at a definite disadvantage. It is, therefore, recommended that the results of group mental ability tests be used with discretion when predicting reading achievement for poor readers.

The teacher should examine the data on the cumulative record card to determine if there are any significant patterns in achievement. The writer remembers one fourth grader who, based upon information in the record folder, was reading above grade level at the completion of first and second grades. However, the student's test scores at the end of third grade showed a dramatic decline in reading achievement and performance in most other academic areas. As a result of discussions with the third grade teacher and the school's guidance counselor, it was learned that a disruption in this student's home life occurred during the previous school year and this may have had an adverse effect on overall performance in school.

Sources of additional information are usually found in the cumulative record folder. If, for example, it is noted on the folder that a pupil has been receiving instruction from the school's reading specialist, contact with this member of the faculty could provide classroom teachers with valuable insights into a student's problems in reading. With the passage of the new federal law for the handicapped (PL 94-142), a greater number of children with handicaps who have not had the benefit of an educational program, or who have received instruction but only in the environs of special classes, will be mainstreamed into regular classrooms. The cumulative record folder should alert the teacher as to who these children are and which specialist(s) in the school system should be contacted for additional information and assistance.

Although the cumulative record folder is an invaluable source of information, cautions in the use of the folder should be noted. Teachers should remember that not all of the information included in the folder may be completely free from bias. A previous teacher's negative perceptions of a child may prejudice a future teacher's appraisal of this same child. It is for this reason that some educators advocate not looking at the cumulative folders until after initial impressions of pupils have been formed. It is the opinion of this writer that the reasons for using the cumulative record as a diagnostic tool at the beginning of the semester far outweigh those reasons for not using it. With the proper precautions, a competent teacher should be able to use the data in the folders without unfairly prejudging students.

*Step 4. Determine General Achievement Levels in Reading*

The purpose of diagnosis at this level is to survey the class for general strengths and weaknesses in reading and determine each student's functional reading level. Diagnosis of general achievement serves as the foundation upon which all subsequent diagnosis is based.

Teachers can use a number of assessment devices to examine the reading performance of a class. These include standardized reading survey tests, informal reading inventories, the cloze procedure, the maze technique, and word lists. Each of these instruments can be used separately or in combination to determine reading achievement levels, but only those tests which are likely to help the teacher arrive at pertinent results should be used.

The results of most standardized reading survey tests

show how well students are reading when compared to the general population of children tested. It was indicated earlier that standardized test scores are usually recorded on the pupil's cumulative record card. Teachers can use this information to survey class performance in reading by referring to the most recently reported scores in the folder. Since many school systems administer standardized survey tests in the spring, these test results are probably recent enough so that they can be used by classroom teachers in September. Older test scores will be of limited value only.

Survey tests yield total grade placement scores as well as separate scores for each of two or more subtests. For example, a student entering fifth grade who earns a total grade equivalent score of 4.1 (fourth grade, first month) is, according to the test results, achieving in reading about one year below his actual grade level.

Teachers can use the results of a survey test to determine the average and range of reading achievement levels in a class. A knowledge of the range in reading levels helps teachers to establish realistic goals for reading instruction. For example, the teacher assigned to Class L when given the information listed in Table 1 would need to organize the reading program differently from the teacher assigned to Class M.

**Table 1**
Range of Reading Survey Scores for Two Hypothetical Fifth Grade Classes

| Class L | | Class M | |
|---|---|---|---|
| Grade Equivalent Scores (Total) | No. of Pupils | Grade Equivalent Scores (Total) | No. of Pupils |
| 8.0 - 8.9 | 2 | 8.0 - 8.9 | 0 |
| 7.0 - 7.9 | 4 | 7.0 - 7.9 | 0 |
| 6.0 - 6.9 | 5 | 6.0 - 6.9 | 11 |
| 5.0 - 5.9 | 5 | 5.0 - 5.9 | 12 |
| 4.0 - 4.9 | 3 | 4.0 - 4.9 | 4 |
| 3.0 - 3.9 | 4 | 3.0 - 3.9 | 0 |
| 2.0 - 2.9 | 3 | 2.0 - 2.9 | 0 |

Knowledge of grade equivalent scores can help teachers to divide the class into smaller groups for instructional purposes. The teacher of Class M will, in all likelihood, find this a much easier task to accomplish than the teacher in Class L.

In either case, it is important for both teachers to realize that since the scores obtained provide only approximations of reading level, groups formed in September will have to be restructured periodically as more diagnostic information becomes available.

The teacher should also use the results to assess the general and individual instructional needs of the pupils. This task can be accomplished by studying the subscores of the total test. A class's scores in the comprehension subtest may, for example, reveal a general weakness in this area, for which further diagnosis is necessary. Review of the total reading score can be misleading as the data in Table 2 show.

**Table 2**
Reading Subscores for Two Students with the Same Total Scores

|  | William | Joan |
|---|---|---|
| Word Knowledge | 4.3 | 4.0 |
| Word Discrimination | 5.7 | 3.7 |
| Comprehension | 3.2 | 5.5 |
| Total | 4.4 | 4.4 |

Teachers should study the data from each child's subtest scores in order to pinpoint areas of weakness in reading. Once a problem area is identified, teachers can then use additional diagnostic tools to arrive at a more specific assessment of the student's reading problem.

As a result of reviewing the cumulative record folders and summarizing the scores from standardized reading survey tests, the teacher should have developed an overall impression of the class. By now, the teacher should have some idea of where to begin instruction. Since the above sources only provide a rough estimate of a pupil's functional level in reading, additional confirming evidence is needed in order to support hunches. Informal assessment procedures can be used by teachers to determine both where to begin instruction with a pupil and how to identify the level of reading materials the student can handle.

The informal reading inventory is an often used method of informal assessment in the classroom. The IRI is based on the premise that achievement in reading occurs at four levels: the independent level, the instructional level, the frustration level, and the hearing comprehension level. At the independent level, a child is supposed to read a book on his own without any outside help and with a high degree of fluency, accuracy, and comprehension. Material written at a student's instructional level can be read by a pupil but only with the guidance of a teacher. The instructional level of reading is regarded as the teaching level.

Teachers should avoid presenting students with material written on their frustration levels for this is the level at which reading becomes a laborious task. The hearing or listening comprehension level is the highest level at which students can understand the ideas and concepts in material that is read to them. An assumption made here is that, given the appropriate skills in word recognition, the student will be able to read and comprehend this passage without help.

These levels on an IRI are based on certain criteria that should be applied when evaluating a student's performance. It was pointed out earlier that during the administration of an IRI the pupil is asked to read to the teacher passages of increasing difficulty. After each selection is read, questions are asked by the teacher to test comprehension. When the inventory is scored, the following criteria are applied to each of the paragraphs to determine the different reading levels designated (15:12):

| Level | Word Recognition | Comprehension |
| --- | --- | --- |
| Independent | 99% | 90% |
| Instructional | 95% | 75% |
| Frustration | Below 90% | Below 50% |
| Listening Comprehension | ———— | 75% |

The instructional level is of greatest importance to classroom teachers. This is the level to which all instruction should be geared. Teachers can use this knowledge to accurately place students in reading material. It is important to note that in comparing a student's performance on an IRI to performance on a standardized survey test, there is a tendency for the grade equivalent scores on the survey test to be higher than the instructional level determined by an IRI. Since survey test scores tend to place a student's reading achievement level somewhat above the student's actual level in reading, one could conclude, therefore, that the IRI results provide the teacher with a better estimation of actual reading level.

The cloze procedure is another tool that can be used by teachers to estimate reading levels. A distinct advantage of the cloze technique is that it can be adapted for individual or whole group use.

A cloze test can be constructed from a set of leveled materials such as a basal reading series. In constructing a cloze exercise, the developer should first assemble a series of passages, each one about 250 words in length, that represent material written at different grade levels. Except for the first and last sentences, words from each selection should be deleted in a consistent pattern—usually every fifth word (5:287). An example of a cloze exercise is provided below (30:4):

### Make an Escape Plan

Don't wait for fire. Figure out now where (1) _____ get out if your (2) _____ and halls are full (3) _____ smoke and fire. In (4) _____ apartment house, take your (5) _____ to the fire stairs (6) _____ practice going down together. (7) _____ you have an outside (8) _____ escape learn how to (9) _____ it. If you live (10) _____ a house find a (11) _____ way to get outside (12) _____ your usual halls and (13) _____, maybe through a window (14) _____ a roof, or by (15) _____ ladder to the ground. (16) _____ sure that escape windows (17) _____ be opened easily and (18) _____ large enough to climb (19) _____. Maybe, get a rope or chain ladder for your house.

| | |
|---|---|
| 1. to | 11. different |
| 2. stairs | 12. besides |
| 3. of | 13. stairs |
| 4. an | 14. onto |
| 5. family | 15. a |
| 6. and | 16. Be |
| 7. If | 17. can |
| 8. fire | 18. are |
| 9. use | 19. through |
| 10. in | |

The cloze test should not be timed. When scoring the test, credit should be given for exact words only. Synonyms are not counted as being correct. This procedure is recommended in order to make it easier to score the test. The following percentages of correct responses indicate whether the material used in the test is at the student's independent, instructional, or frustration level (5):

| Cloze Test Percentage Score | Reading Level |
| --- | --- |
| 58% to 100% | Independent |
| 44% to 57% | Instructional |
| 43% or below | Frustration (p. 287) |

Upon applying these criteria, the teacher will end up with reading level approximations for each student as the following example illustrates:

| | Grade Level of Passage | Student's % Score on Cloze | Level |
| --- | --- | --- | --- |
| Passage 1 | 3.0 | 75% | Independent |
| Passage 2 | 4.0 | 60% | Independent |
| Passage 3 | 5.0 | 48% | Instructional |
| Passage 4 | 6.0 | 20% | Frustration |

A variation of the cloze procedure is the maze technique (10). The maze technique consists of a series of graded passages which may be selected from any story or book. Passages should be about 120 words in length. The text is modified by substituting approximately every fifth word with three alternative words. The alternatives should include: 1) the correct word, 2) an incorrect word that is the same part of speech (noun, verb, adjective, etc.) as the correct word, and 3) an incorrect word that is a different part of speech. The placement of the words should vary. An example follows:

below
It took the mechanic three hours to repair the stove.
goats

paid
The mechanic wanted to be lost with a check.
thing

A score of 60 to 70 percent correct indicates optimal teaching level (instructional level). If the child performs at 50 percent accuracy or below, the material at that level is probably too difficult. When a pupil reaches 85 to 100 percent accuracy, then the material is probably too easy (10).

A fourth instrument that can be used to provide

information on general reading level is the graded word list. Lists are readily available and can be easily administered by classroom teachers. It should be kept in mind though that word lists, although handy to use, provide only a rough estimate of reading level at best. The San Diego Quick Assessment is an example of this type of device (20). The test consists of thirteen graded lists of words. The lists are derived from words randomly drawn from basal reader glossaries and the Thorndike List. During the administration of this test, the student pronounces words aloud from increasingly difficult lists until three or more words are missed at a particular level. This, according to the authors, indicates the level at which the material will be too difficult for a student to read. When a student misreads no more than one of the ten words incorrectly, this is considered to be a student's base or independent level. Two errors on a list indicate instructional level.

The words used in the San Diego Quick Assessment are listed below (20):

| Preprimer Level | Primer | First | Second | Third | Fourth |
|---|---|---|---|---|---|
| see | you | road | our | city | decided |
| play | come | live | please | middle | served |
| me | not | thank | myself | moment | amazed |
| at | with | when | town | frightened | silent |
| run | jump | bigger | early | exclaimed | wrecked |
| go | help | how | send | several | improved |
| and | is | always | wide | lonely | certainly |
| look | work | night | believe | drew | entered |
| can | are | spring | quietly | since | realized |
| here | this | today | carefully | straight | interrupted |

| Fifth | Sixth | Seventh | Eighth | Ninth |
|---|---|---|---|---|
| scanty | bridge | amber | capacious | conscientious |
| certainly | commercial | dominion | limitation | isolation |
| develop | abolish | sundry | pretext | molecule |
| considered | trucker | capillary | intrigue | ritual |
| discussed | apparatus | impetuous | delusion | momentous |
| behaved | elementary | blight | immaculate | vulnerable |
| splendid | comment | wrest | ascent | kinship |
| acquainted | necessity | enumerate | acrid | conservatism |
| escaped | gallery | daunted | binocular | jaunty |
| grim | relativity | condescend | embankment | inventive |

| Tenth | Eleventh |
|-------|----------|
| zany | galore |
| jerkin | rotunda |
| nausea | capitalism |
| gratuitous | prevaricate |
| linear | risible |
| inept | exonerate |
| legality | superannuate |
| aspen | luxuriate |
| amnesty | piebald |
| barometer | crunch |

Although word list tests are primarily used to arrive at a quick estimate of reading level, the results can also be used to reveal basic weaknesses in word attack skills.

## Step 5. Perform a Specific Diagnosis of Reading Skills

The main function of diagnosis at this level is to provide teachers with specific information on every pupil's reading behavior. Diagnosis at the specific level uncovers weaknesses in word identification, comprehension, and study skills. However, while a pupil's reading weaknesses naturally might be the concern of the classroom teacher, diagnosing for strengths is equally important. Wilson (*31*:37-38) states: "Since instructional adjustment should start with areas of strengths, deliberate diagnosis to determine those strengths is necessary."

There are numerous diagnostic tools available to assess pupil progress in each of the major skill areas of reading. Two of these devices, standardized survey tests and informal reading inventories, while providing information on general achievement levels in reading, can also be used as tools for determining specific skill strengths and weaknesses. Other techniques to be discussed include reading miscue analysis, classroom observation, criterion referenced tests, workbook and worksheet pages, and teacher made devices.

The standardized reading test can also serve as a diagnostic instrument when the results are used in certain ways. One way to accomplish this is to orally review the test items with a student in order to obtain additional insights into the student's reading problem. The student is encouraged, during the meeting, to describe his process for selecting appropriate synonyms for words or for answering questions related to selected articles. Using this procedure, the teacher is able to determine whether the student has a good, logical reason for answers or is only making a wild guess. The teacher can also discover whether the student is misreading the item or does not understand the intent of the question.

The teacher can also analyze the test items in order to discern patterns in errors. An analysis of this type could reveal problems in answering comprehension test items related to finding the main idea or anticipating outcomes.

Besides its usefulness in determining students' reading levels, the IRI can also be used to identify specific skill needs. An analysis of the errors or miscues made during the oral reading of the paragraphs and a student's responses to the comprehension questions asked by the examiner provide the teacher with important information about a student's reading behavior.

In reviewing the literature, one finds disagreement regarding what constitutes an oral reading error which becomes apparent when different oral reading tests are compared. In the Gilmore Oral Reading Test (Harcourt Brace Jovanovich), for example, hesitations and disregard for punctuation are scored as accountable errors while in the Classroom Reading Inventory (William C. Brown), they are not.

The procedure suggested by Harris and Sipay (11) is a good example of a system for scoring oral reading miscues and is used in this discussion. The authors make a distinction between major and minor miscues. Their system focuses attention on the quality rather than the quantity of errors made by the pupil. Harris and Sipay (11:173) recommend that the following scoring system be used in scoring reading miscues.

1. Count as one miscue each: a) any response that deviates from the printed text and disrupts the intended meaning and b) any word pronounced for the child after a five-second hesitation.
2. Count as one-half miscue each: any response that deviates from the printed text but does not disrupt the intended meaning.
3. Count as a total of one miscue, regardless of the number of times the behavior occurs: a) repeated substitution such as *a* for *the* and b) repetitions.
4. Do not count as miscues: a) miscues that conform to cultural or regional dialects, b) self-corrections made within five seconds, c) hesitation, or d) ignoring or misinterpreting punctuation marks.

**Table 3**
Marking System for Oral Reading Miscues

| Type of Miscue | Score | Description | Rule for Marking with Example |
|---|---|---|---|
| Mispronunciations | 1 Miscue | When a word is pronounced incorrectly and does not make sense in the sentence. | plon<br>The new pillow was filled with goose feathers. |
| Substitutions | 1 Miscue | When the printed word is substituted by a word that disrupts the intended meaning. | sat<br>She woke up early in the morning to watch the sun come up. |
| | ½ Miscue | When the printed word is substituted by a word that does not disrupt the intended meaning. | home<br>Ben lives in a very big house. |
| Words Pronounced by the Examiner | 1 Miscue | When the examiner must pronounce the word after five seconds. | Nancy was given a calculator as a birthday present. |
| Omissions | 1 Miscue | When a whole word, word parts or group of words is omitted and it disrupts the intended meaning. | The dog hid under the sofa. |
| | ½ Miscue | Same as above but does not disrupt intended meaning. | The man bought a very big car. |
| Additions (Insertions) | ½ Miscue | When an extra word is added. | green<br>He cut the grass in the morning. |

| | | | |
|---|---|---|---|
| Reversals | 1 Miscue | The confusion of single letters, reversal of words or the reversal of the order of words in a sentence. | big<br>The pirate liked to dig for buried treasure.<br>saw<br>The sky was blue.<br>The cat saw a mouse.<br>for<br>The mouse saw a cat. |
| Repetitions | 1 Miscue | When two or more words are repeated. | She rode to the park on her bicycle. |
| | Not counted as Miscue | When one word or less is repeated. | She rode to the park on her bicycle. |
| Hesitations | Not counted as Miscue | When hesitation occurs but the proper pronunciation is given before five seconds. | The baby took a nap in the afternoon. |
| Dialect Variations | Not counted as Miscue | When a pupil reads orally in accordance with his dialect. | Many New Englanders do not pronounce the /r/ in words such as hard and car. |

5. Count repeated errors on the same word as only one miscue, regardless of the type of error made.

The information in Table 3 is based on the Harris and Sipay procedure and provides the teacher with guidelines on how to score the word recognition miscues made during the oral reading of passages from an informal reading inventory. The teacher can use this system to analyze the types of errors made by students and then implement strategies that match remediation to miscues. Suggestions for these types of activities are included in an article by Maring (21).

## Reading Miscue Analysis

Tortelli (29) has developed a technique for gathering information concerning a student's reading behavior that is based upon principles established for the *Reading Miscue Inventory Manual* (9). The procedure is described below:

1. The student reads aloud a copy of an unfamiliar story.
2. The teacher writes down on another copy of the story all the student readings that are not contained in the original text. For example, if the student reads aloud "the dog" instead of "old dog," the teacher would write the word "the" above the word "old."
3. When the student has finished reading orally, the teacher folds a sheet of paper into four columns, labeling the first "unexpected readings"; the second, "intended readings"; the third, "language"; and the fourth, "meaning"; and then numbers the paper from one to ten under these headings.
4. The teacher lists on this sheet of paper, in the first column, ten of the student's unexpected readings, that is, readings that are different from the text. In the second column, the intended readings, the words that occur in the text.
5. The teacher considers whether the unexpected readings sound like language. In other words, is each reading "grammatically correct?" If it is, the teacher writes "yes" in the third ("language") column; if not, "no." For example, the student who connects two sentences by either omitting words in the text or adding others is altering the grammar of the text. If it is like the child's speech, it is considered gramatically correct, for that child; otherwise, it is not grammatically correct. Upon reading the following,

An old farmer and his son were taking their donkey to town to sell. They had not gone far when they saw some girls at a well.

one student read:

An old farmer and his son were taking their donkey to town to sell *while* had not gone far when they saw some girls at a well.

By omitting the period and subject of the second sentence, the reader produced a reading that does not sound like language. It is "grammatically incorrect." Therefore, a "no" is recorded in the "language" column.

6. The teacher examines each unexpected reading from the perspective of meaning, asking if each of the student's unexpected readings means the same as the printed textual item, the intended reading. If the meaning is different, "no" is entered.

7. The teacher then totals the number of unexpected readings in the "language" column that "sound like language" and the number of readings in the "meaning" column that have the same meaning as the textual items. The number of yesses is recorded at the bottom of each column.

When reviewing the data, if the majority of a student's unexpected readings sound like language, it is apparent, according to Tortelli, that the reader should focus more on the meaning of the words read. It is up to the teacher, then, to prepare lessons that stress the comprehension of written language.

*Classroom observation* is a natural and logical way for the teacher to gather diagnostic information. In fact, informal daily observation is probably one of the most efficient and informative appraisal procedures that can be used by classroom teachers.

Informal observations should be conducted by teachers to determine whether pupil placement in instructional groups at the beginning of the school year is appropriate. Since the results of standardized tests and informal inventories provide the teacher with only an estimate of actual reading level, additional evidence is needed to either support or refute these results. Through careful observation on a daily basis, the teacher can determine whether a student has or has not been correctly assigned to an instructional group. A student's group assignment should be revised as soon as improper placement is discovered.

Observations made during the school day help teachers to assess pupil strengths and weaknesses in reading. A teacher, for example, might observe that one pupil who is poor in comprehension is overanalyzing words; another child who is good in using phonic skills is ineffective in using context clues as an aid to word identification; a third child may have a limited sight vocabulary; and a fourth child, though able to understand material at a literal level, has difficulty comprehending at the higher levels.

Observations made during study periods and/or free reading periods may reveal student attitudes toward reading and toward themselves as readers. It should be apparent from such observations whether a child reads with enjoyment or indifference, with poise or anxiety, cooperatively or with resistance.

Finally, informal observations may disclose physical problems that could affect performance in reading. For example, tearing of the eyes, squinting, and complaining about headaches may be manifestations of visual problems. Inattentiveness and inability to follow directions may be indications of problems with hearing.

The insights acquired from the children's reading behavior during classroom observations should be recorded on the pupil record form used to monitor the progress of each student. Information gathered from the careful observation of pupils in various reading situations should be used to verify and complement the data from other sources.

It was pointed out earlier that diagnosis at the specific level should uncover both a student's strengths and weaknesses in reading. Criterion referenced tests are useful because they help classroom teachers determine which skills the student has and has not acquired. Given this information, teachers can build upon a pupil's reading strengths in order to correct his weaknesses.

Teachers can construct their own criterion referenced test items when there is a need to find out what a pupil can or cannot do. In order to accomplish this, test items should be written to assess mastery of specific objectives in reading. The item below is typical of one that could be used to assess a student's attainment of the following objective: "After reading a short selection, the student will be able to select the main idea of this passage."

Sample Item from a Criterion Referenced Test*

Summer had been great fun, but it was now time to return to school. All the children in the neighborhood were getting ready. Mark had bought a bright, new plaid shirt and some jeans. Gretchen had purchased a new knit dress. Connie was going to wear her new pleated skirt. How attractive they would all look on the first day of school!!

The best title for this story would be _____.
a. Going to School        c. Shopping for Clothes
b. New School Clothes      d. Mark's Jeans
e. I don't know.

*From William C. Blanton et al., Reading Survey Test to accompany *Power Reading 2.*

If the performance standard is set at 80 percent and there are five such items devoted to the main idea, then the student would have to answer at least four correctly in order to master the objective.

Criterion referenced tests can be designed by teachers or extracted from workbook exercises and commercially prepared worksheets. Teachers who prepare their own items should be knowledgeable in the areas of reading and test design.

Teachers who wish to base their entire program on a criterion referenced approach can adopt one of a number of skills management systems available commercially. Included among these are *Power Reading* (BFA Educational Media), *Fountain Valley Teachers' Support System* (R.L. Zweig), and *Wisconsin Design for Reading Skill Development* (National Computer Systems). Stallard (27) compared fifteen objective based reading programs. Her analysis should help educators who are trying to choose a program to meet the needs of students in a particular school.

Exercises from workbooks and worksheets can be used to quickly check pupil mastery of reading skills. These exercises serve as initial tests of reading skills. If behavioral objectives relative to specific skills are stated, the pupil attainment of these skills can be monitored through the use of these materials. However they are used, exercises from workbooks and worksheets can enable teachers to conduct an on-the-spot diagnosis of reading problems.

Teachers can collect exercises from a variety of sources and file each one according to the type of skill and the difficulty level of the skill. Then, whenever it becomes necessary to assess the attainment of a certain skill, the appropriate exercise can be easily retrieved. Teachers should consider placing a plastic film or laminate over the papers in order to render the materials reusable.

Teacher made tests may be more useful than standardized tests or commercially prepared informal tests when teachers need important data about children's reading performance. Heilman (*13*:335-336) discusses the advantages that such tests have for classroom use:

> First, they are simple to construct since the teacher has available graded reading materials from the preprimer level through the upper grades. Second, the child can be tested over longer passages of sustained reading than are characteristically found on standardized tests. Third, the use of teacher made tests avoids the formality of the usual test situation...Finally, the teacher made test is inexpensive and demands no more teacher time for administration and analysis than do other tests.

Teachers can devise their own evaluative instruments to assess student growth in areas such as word attack, comprehension, and study skills. Many fine examples for accomplishing this are presented in Chapter Seven.

## Collections of Diagnostic Measures

An excellent collection of suggestions for informal assessment in reading is found in *Informal Reading Diagnosis: A Practical Guide for the Classroom Teacher* (*24*). The devices in this book may be utilized in an initial diagnosis of groups or individual children or for an ongoing evaluation of a reading program. The authors have identified devices for assessing perceptual discrimination skills, word analysis skills, oral and silent reading, study skills, and attitudes and appreciation in reading.

Another fine source of assessment tools is the *Reading Diagnostic Kit* (*22*). Included in this book are examples of informal reading inventories, observation checklists, inventories in the word recognition techniques, content area reading inventories, cloze exercises, interest inventories, and incomplete sentences tests. The authors also present descriptions of standardized oral reading tests, survey tests, diagnostic tests, and listening comprehension tests.

## Summary

In order to make reading possible through effective classroom organization, it is essential that a plan for initial and ongoing assessment of student needs be carried out. A plan

Stieglitz

for diagnosis must relate to the classroom teacher's instructional goals for the reading program. Diagnostic tools such as standardized tests, informal reading inventories, the cloze and maze procedures, workbooks and worksheets, classroom observations, criterion referenced measures, and teacher made tests can be utilized to determine general achievement levels in reading and individual patterns of strengths and weaknesses. The cumulative record folder is also a valuable diagnostic tool because it provides teachers with an overview of a student's past performance.

However, any plan for classroom diagnosis is as good as the teacher who is responsible for implementing it. Cleland (3) sums up the feelings of many educators regarding the role of teachers in implementing an effective program of classroom diagnosis:

> Appraising a child's strengths and weaknesses in reading should be approached with humility. While patterns of test scores are of great value in assessing a child's progress toward desirable goals, the considered judgment of the tester as he observes the child's reactions to the testing situation is of inestimable value in interpreting these patterns of scores. The tester must always be cognizant of the limitations of standardized instruments. Many behavioral manifestations cannot be measured by paper and pencil tests; they, therefore, must be observed, studied, collated, and interpreted in the light of the patterns of scores obtained from standardized instruments. There is NO substitute for the considered judgment of the teacher in classroom evaluation.

References
1. Bond, Guy L. "Diagnostic Teaching in the Classroom," in Dorothy L. DeBoer (Ed.), *Reading Diagnosis and Evaluation*. Newark, Delaware: International Reading Association, 1970.
2. Breedlove, Wanda Gale. "The Diagnostic Teaching of Reading," in Robert E. Leibert (Ed.), *Diagnostic Viewpoints in Reading*. Newark, Delaware: International Reading Association, 1971, 19-29.
3. Cleland, Donald L. "Classroom Evaluation: Can It Be Effective?" (Mimeographed)
4. Dallmann, Martha, et al. *The Teaching of Reading*, Fourth Edition. New York: Holt, Rinehart and Winston, 1974.
5. Ekwall, Eldon E. *Diagnosis and Remediation of the Disabled Reader*. Boston: Allyn and Bacon, 1976.
6. Gates, Arthur I., and Anne S. McKillop. *Gates-McKillop Reading Diagnostic Tests*. New York: Teachers College Press, 1962.
7. Gilliland, Hap. *A Practical Guide to Remedial Reading*. Columbus, Ohio: Charles E. Merrill, 1974.

8. Gilmore, John V., and Eunice C. Gilmore. *Gilmore Oral Reading Test.* New York: Harcourt Brace Jovanovich, 1965.
9. Goodman, Yetta, and Carolyn Burke. *Reading Miscue Inventory Manual: Procedure for Diagnosis and Evaluation.* New York: Macmillan, 1972.
10. Guthrie, John T., et al. "The Maze Technique to Assess Monitor Reading Comprehension," *Reading Teacher,* 28 (November 1974), 161-168.
11. Harris, Albert J., and Edward R. Sipay. *How to Increase Reading Ability,* Sixth Edition. New York: David McKay Company, 1975, 173, 201-204, 412-419.
12. Harris, Larry A., and Carl B. Smith. *Reading Instruction: Diagnostic Teaching in the Classroom,* Second Edition. New York: Holt, Rinehart and Winston, 1976.
13. Heilman, Arthur W. *Principles and Practices of Teaching Reading,* Fourth Edition. Columbus, Ohio: Charles E. Merrill, 1977.
14. Johnson, Dale D., and P. David Pearson. "Skills Management Systems: A Critique," *Reading Teacher,* 28 (May 1975), 757-764.
15. Johnson, Marjorie S., and Roy A. Kress. *Informal Reading Inventories.* Newark, Delaware: International Reading Association, 1965.
16. Karlin, Robert. *Teaching Elementary Reading: Principles and Strategies,* Second Edition. New York: Harcourt Brace Jovanovich, 1975.
17. Karlin, Robert. *Teaching Reading in High School: Improving Reading in Content Areas,* Third Edition. Indianapolis, Indiana: Bobbs-Merrill, 1977.
18. Kennedy, Eddie C. *Classroom Approaches to Remedial Reading.* Itasca, Illinois: F.E. Peacock Publishers, 1977.
19. Lapp, Diane, and James Flood. *Teaching Reading to Every Child.* New York: Macmillan, 1978.
20. LaPray, Margaret, and Ramon Ross. "The Graded Word List: Quick Gauge of Reading Ability," *Journal of Reading,* 12 (January 1969), 305-307.
21. Maring, Gerald H. "Matching Remediation to Miscues," *Reading Teacher,* 31 (May 1978), 887-891.
22. Miller, Wilma H. *Reading Diagnostic Kit.* New York: Center for Applied Research in Education, 1974.
23. Otto, Wayne, Richard A. McMenemy, and Richard Smith. *Corrective and Remedial Teaching,* Second Edition. Boston: Houghton Mifflin, 1973.
24. Potter, Thomas C., and Gwenneth Rae. *Informal Reading Diagnosis: A Practical Guide for the Classroom Teacher.* Englewood Cliffs, New Jersey: Prentice-Hall, 1973.
25. Sartain, Harry W. "The Modular Content of the Professional Program," in H.W. Sartain and P.E. Stanton (Eds.), *Modular Preparation for Teaching Reading: A Professional Program for Preservice and Continuing Education.* Newark, Delaware: International Reading Association, 1974, 45-46.
26. Silvaroli, Nicholas J. *Classroom Reading Inventory,* Third Edition. Dubuque, Iowa: William C. Brown, 1976.
27. Stallard, Cathy. "Comparing Objective Based Reading Programs," *Journal of Reading,* 21 (October 1977), 36-44.
28. Strang, Ruth, et al. *The Improvement of Reading,* Fourth Edition. New York: McGraw-Hill, 1967.
29. Tortelli, James P. "Simplified Psycholinguistic Diagnosis," *Reading Teacher,* 29 (April 1976), 637-639.

30. U.S. Department of Health, Education, and Welfare, Social and Rehabilitation Service. *Look Out! It Burns!* Washington: Government Printing Office, 1969.
31. Wilson, Robert M. *Diagnostic and Remedial Reading for Classroom and Clinic*, Second Edition. Columbus, Ohio: Charles E. Merrill, 1972.
32. Zintz, Miles. *The Reading Process: The Teacher and the Learner*, Second Edition. Dubuque, Iowa: William C. Brown, 1975.
33. Zintz, Miles. *Corrective Reading*, Third Edition. Dubuque, Iowa: William C. Brown, 1977.

Hillerich explores several approaches for assessing continuous growth and need in word recognition and comprehension, discusses interest as an essential variable, and offers suggestions for integrating the cognitive and affective dimensions of the learner.

## Chapter Seven   Continuous Assessment of Instructional Needs in Reading

Robert L. Hillerich
*Bowling Green State University*

The previous chapter deals with the essentials of initial diagnosis of status in reading. This chapter presents specific techniques for continuous assessment

1. of reading level, which will enable proper pacing and placing of children in whatever type of program is being used;
2. of language and phonic skills, which will include basic language development and consonant and vowel letter/sound associations;
3. of the ability to use context and of the recognition vocabulary necessary so that some of the print can be used as context;
4. of structural analysis skills, including prefixes, suffixes, base forms, and compound words; and
5. for the many comprehension and study skills.

The chapter concludes with a discussion of the affective area of reading—an area that does not call for specific diagnosis in the sense of identifying skill needs, but one that the effective teacher must certainly be aware of and provide for.

First, the role and kind of testing one would use in a diagnostic/prescriptive approach to the teaching of reading must be clarified.

## A Different Kind of Testing

Traditionally the procedure in many classrooms has been one of teaching and then testing to determine whether children have learned what was taught. Currently, this teach-test approach has been revised by adding another element: test-teach-test. The teacher tests (diagnoses) students to find out where they are (their reading level) and what they need (their skill deficits). Then the teaching takes place to supply whatever deficits are identified from the pretesting. Finally, posttesting determines whether the deficits identified in pretesting have been provided for.

Of course, the test-teach-test cycle is not new in remedial situations. Special reading teachers have followed such a procedure all along. The value of such an approach is that it does save time in the long run. It avoids attempts to teach children what they already know, and it enables identification of what they do not know.

Another important facet of the pretesting-teaching-post-testing lies in the use of criterion referenced tests as opposed to the traditional norm referenced tests. This difference was discussed in Chapter Six.

The concern throughout this chapter will be with criterion referenced testing, including a concern for testing only with items that are important to reading success. Topics for assessment are taken in an approximate order for instruction. Certainly no research has proved a definite continuum of reading skills, but the following order is a sequence that can be followed in any classroom.


## At What Level is this Student Reading?

While the identification of reading level is discussed in the chapter on diagnosis, in this chapter on continuous assessment it is also one of the most important items a teacher must consider. First of all, one assesses level to accomplish one purpose only—to assure that the pupil is placed in the appropriate level of reading material. The determination of a child's reading level gives little if any information about that child's skill needs, but it does indicate the level of reading difficulty of the material that can be used as a vehicle for the development of whatever skills are needed.

If this author were asked to specify the one improvement in reading instruction in this country that would contribute most to increased achievement in reading, the answer would be the proper placement of children in materials. In fact, in many schools, 20 percent or more of the pupils are attempting to read in materials that are too difficult for them. For example, when a new reading program was adopted in one school system, the staff tested each child with the placement test to assure that each one would begin that program at the proper level. Within just one year, 20 percent of the children were already above their instructional level in those materials! Other examples of proper diagnosis without proper pacing or continuous assessment abound in schools.

Several kinds of materials have been used in efforts at continuous assessment of reading level. These include group tests and individual tests such as commercial placement tests accompanying reading programs, informal tests, and commercial oral reading tests.

*Group tests.* There is no way that scores from a group, norm referenced reading test can be used to determine an individual child's reading level. Group tests tend to overestimate the reading level of individuals, but there is no rule of thumb to determine the extent of overestimation. In some cases, group tests underestimate reading level.

With poor readers, group tests tend to give no information at all, since such poor readers fall near or below the "guessing score" on a group test (3).

*Individual tests.* Yes, a test to determine reading level of an individual with any assurance of accuracy must be administered individually. Before teachers proceed with giving individual tests to twenty-five to thirty children in their class, a point must be made: There is no need to administer an individual test for reading level to all children. Any child known to be at or above grade level does not need to be given such a test, since children at that level can read the material designed for use in their grade. It is academic how much above level students can read, since the grade level materials can be used as a vehicle for whatever skills are needed. Children can learn skills from materials below their reading level; they usually cannot learn from materials too difficult for them to read. In other words, the concern in assessing reading level is to provide appropriate instructional materials for those children who cannot read the material designed for their grade level. Hence, in most instances, the classroom teacher will be giving an individual test to 50 percent or less of the class. ("Enrichment" and reading materials beyond grade level should be amply provided for more capable pupils in the other 50 percent of the reading program. See "The Affective Domain" section of this chapter.)

A number of options are available in terms of the kind of individual oral reading test to be used. Many modern basal reading programs have accompanying placement tests and/or informal reading inventories (IRI) for obtaining a proper fit between the reading level of the child and that of the material. Using such tests in September, however, offers no assurance of proper placement in January; assessment must be continuous.

Another option, instead of the test accompanying the basal program, would be to use the reading materials in the manner of an IRI in order to determine at what level the child can read in that program. The characteristics of an IRI and the procedures for administering one are discussed in Chapter Six.

In the classroom, on a day to day basis, an IRI can be used even more informally as a quick check on the student's match with whatever material is at hand. At any time in the school year—or with any material a student might be reading—the teacher may want to recheck by merely marking off a hundred words just ahead of where the student is reading in a given book and having the student then read that portion aloud and answer four questions about it. The teacher should use this informal technique every two months or so, or when a child seems to be having difficulty with material.

Commercial tests are also available and range from the formalized "informal reading inventory" of Silvaroli or Spache to individual oral reading tests such as the Gray or Gilmore. However, an IRI made from materials being used by the child is much preferred since the purpose is to match the child to the material. If the teacher uses a commercial test, that teacher will get a norm referenced reading level and then will have to determine the reading level of the book in which the child is to be placed. Such double measures, each having its own error of measurement, double the possibility of error.

## Assessing Skill Needs

Just as placement tests usually accompany modern basal programs for determination of reading levels, so too management systems are available for the assessment of skill needs. In addition, separate management systems, such as the Wisconsin Design, Fountain Valley, or Criterion, may be purchased for use with any reading program.

If a commercial management system is used, it behooves the staff to do a careful evaluation of the content in order to eliminate some of the items to be tested since many of these skills are doubtful contributors to success in reading. To use the entire package is likely to turn teachers into testers and bookkeepers who have little time for teaching.

There are two basic criteria for evaluating assessment or practice exercises. The first and most obvious criterion for such an evaluation is to ask: Does this skill contribute to better reading? Commercial programs abound with examples of purported skill activities that do little more than waste precious instructional time and, worse, that frustrate pupils and teachers. This chapter discusses examples of such items, including overemphasis on learning words, as well as the fallible vowel rules and syllable rules, all of which ought to be carefully evaluated before teachers allow such skill activities to intrude on class time and to detract from time spent in actual reading.

The second criterion to be applied to any assessment or practice activity is the question: Do these items actually deal with the skill they claim to be assessing or providing practice in? Application of this criterion requires that the teacher work and think through the process involved in solving whatever problem is presented to the child in the activity or assessment.

While this chapter deals with assessment, not organization, it is important at this point to recognize that assessments of skill needs usually should not lead to one-to-one instruction. Such a procedure is impractical and inefficient in a class-size group. Assessments should lead to determination of skill needs that for instructional purposes will result in flexible grouping. Children will be grouped by common skill needs for instruction in those skills, as discussed in Chapter Three.

The following discussion of skill needs begins at the nonreading level. Teachers will enter the skill sections at various points, depending upon the level of development of their pupils.

## What Language Skills Does this Student Need?

It is axiomatic among teachers of reading that no one can be taught to read in a language that that person does not speak and understand. Obviously then, at one extreme is the child who does not speak or understand English because of a different language background. That child must begin at the oral English level and learn to speak and understand a moderate amount of English before being given instruction in reading in English. However, this factor does not preclude instruction in reading in the child's native language, if that is practical, during the interim in which the child is learning oral English. Evidence suggests that instruction in reading in the native language while learning to speak and understand the second language makes a contribution to learning to read in the second language once the student has developed oral skill in that second language.

*Dialect.* Principles developed from research in teaching children from different language backgrounds, however, cannot be carried over and applied to children who speak a different dialect of English, whether that dialect be "substandard," Bostonian, Black, Midwestern, or some other type. All of these are English and any one may be treated as substandard in some communities where, by implication, standard English is defined as the English spoken by the majority group to which the teacher belongs.

In working with children who speak a dialect that varies from the norm of the community, it is clear that one must accept and encourage the student's own language. Dialects should not be "corrected" nor speech altered in the elementary years. Children from different dialects can learn to read successfully in standard printed English, as do any other youngsters, providing the child's spoken language is accepted and encouraged.

Dialects may be at variance with standard English in terms of pronunciation, syntax, or vocabulary. Nevertheless, standard forms of English can be presented in print: The Bostonian learns that /pak/ is spelled *park*, just as the Black dialect speaker learns that /bof/ is spelled *both*, and the Midwestern youngster learns that /krik/ is spelled *creek*.

Regardless of dialect, everyone needs language development skills to be successful in the beginning stages of reading. Hillerich (6:36-50) offers a more complete treatment of this area.

*Auditory discrimination.* Obviously the individual cannot function at all in the language if that person cannot hear differences in sounds—an ability reading teachers label "auditory discrimination." It is doubtful that any person who speaks and understands English (and who does not have a physical impairment) has a serious problem in auditory discrimination. However, to check on this, the teacher may take pairs of pictures or objects whose names differ by only one sound, name the two in a pair, and ask the child to point to one. For example, given a lock and a rock on the table, the teacher can name the two and ask the child to point to "lock." Pairing *hat/bat, yarn/barn, wing/ring*, and so on, the teacher can check through the various consonant sounds in initial position and can also use the same procedure for final consonant sounds and for vowel sounds, right down to the fine distinction of *pen/pin* (*1*).

Such a procedure avoids the auditory memory problems and the understanding of "same" and "different" that complicate interpretations of some commercial tests such as the Wepman (6:47).

*Vocabulary.* Another aspect of language development is vocabulary: words to name objects, people, or activities that the child has been exposed to, as well as understanding the basic function words of the language so often used for instructional purposes (*in, on, same, different*). Admittedly, no one has been able to state the precise words or the number of vocabulary words an individual must have in order to be successful in reading. Therefore, such an assessment is a kind of dipstick to determine whether the individual has a reasonable store of words for listening/speaking.

To perform the assessment, the teacher can ask the child to identify pictures of common objects and activities. The teacher can also use pictures to ask the child to perform certain functions, such as "put the hat *in* the box," "*on* the box," and so on, in order to determine if the child's deficit in vocabulary must be remediated before instruction in reading can be successful.

Finally, along these same lines, competencies such as the ability to follow oral directions should be assessed by giving simple one, two, and three step directions for the child to follow.

*Listening comprehension.* The ability to function in a language includes the ability to think in that language. A simple test of listening comprehension is important to determine whether the individual can understand that which is spoken or read. A one-paragraph story can be read to the child, and the child then can be asked to tell what the story is about. In the process, the teacher can also identify whether the youngster is able to recall events in the proper sequence. In the retelling, young children sometimes tell a story in jumbled fashion. Then the teacher can recheck on sequence by asking what happened first, what happened next.

*Oral language development.* The extent of oral language development should also be assessed in the case of an individual who is not reading at all. There are formal methods, such as number of words per T-unit, that can be used (*9*); but the teacher can make a fair judgment of oral language development by listening to the child talk about a picture, a series of pictures, or an experience. In other words, from a sample of the individual's oral language the teacher should be able to judge adequacy. Inadequacy is indicated if the individual speaks in three- or four-word utterances (whether simple noun-verb sentences or fragments), tends to omit adjectives and adverbs (including at times even the articles), and uses no prepositional phrases. Such an individual certainly needs further development of oral language before being expected to read successfully.

*Letter form discrimination.* Finally, as one approaches the actual reading skills, one of the basic steps is to determine whether the individual has had adequate experience in order to distinguish letter forms (often called visual discrimination).

Assessment of this type should not be concerned with the gross kinds of visual discrimination often dealt with, since one does not need to note the difference between a triangle and a square—or between a dog with a tail and one without—in order to learn to read. In fact, practice in distinguishing the triangle on its base from one sitting on a point can actually be misleading preparation for the reading act: A triangle is a triangle no matter how it is turned, but a *b* is a *d* if it is turned around.

Nor should the assessment be concerned with the individual's ability to name the letters: Such knowledge is a good predictor of future success and fits in well with other *non*diagnostic measures, but knowledge of letter names is not necessary for success in reading. Students need to establish the letter/sound association; they do not need to know the letter name: What does "double you" have to do with *wagon, water*, or *wind?*

Assessment for letter form discrimination must deal with the letter forms and must focus on discovering whether the individual has had enough experience with printed letters to be aware of some of the fine differences that distinguish one letter from another. The teacher may make up sets of three or four letters in which the first letter is repeated among the others. These sets should be graduated from those letters easily distinguished (*m, c, l, v*) to more difficult ones (*c, o, e, a* or *b, d, p, q*). The child is to find the one that is the same as the first letter. (Of course, the teacher must be certain beforehand that the child understands the instructional language "the same.") Sets may take the following form.

| | | | | |
|---|---|---|---|---|
| n: | c | l | d | n |
| k: | a | k | m | l |
| b: | d | b | p | q |

Having identified that the individual is functioning adequately in these areas, the next step in the continuum with the person at a nonreading or beginning level of reading is assessment of phonic skills.

## What Phonic Skills Does this Student Need?

Philosophies of reading vary in the area of phonics from extreme synthetic approaches to analytic approaches, i.e., from an early and heavy emphasis on letter-sounds to a more moderate progression with an early emphasis on meaning. Few reading teachers, however, would deny the importance of some kind of phonics in the early stages of learning to read.

Phonics involves developing an understanding of the symbol/sound or letter/sound relationships in terms of consonants and vowels, whether these relationships are developed by a rules oriented method, by a stimulus-response method of learning to pronounce each letter sound in isolation, or by an inductive approach such as analysis of known words or through linguistic patterns.

In the following section, the author offers suggestions for assessing a student's reading from a middle of the road view.

*Consonant sound associations.* At the lowest level of reading skill, one might assess the consonant letter/sound associations first since these tend to be the most basic. They are the most frequently used letters in English, have the most consistent symbol/sound relationship, and are the beginning point in phonics in most reading programs. These consonant sound associations may be assessed informally in the process of listening to children read orally or even in the process of administering an informal reading inventory.

For those seeking a more organized kind of assessment, commercial phonics tests are available or are easily constructed by the teacher. The point to remember with any phonics test is, if such tests are administered as group tests (as they direct), they are not measuring reading skill in phonics at all; they are measuring spelling skill in a multiple choice fashion. To demonstrate, following are two example items from such a phonics test (6):

|    |     |     |     |
|----|-----|-----|-----|
| 1. gam | fam | tam | nam |
| 2. rem | lem | sem | bem |

Usually such tests direct the teacher to give the child an answer sheet, have the child look at the first row, and mark the one that begins like "fish" and "funny." If the youngster draws a circle around *fam*, that youngster is *not* demonstrating any reading phonics but rather the ability to make a multiple choice guess for spelling. In the reading act, one is faced with print first and must determine—out of the whole world of sound—the sound a given letter represents. As this test is administered, the child is given the sound (fish) and must determine which of four words begins with the proper letter that represents that beginning sound. This latter is a much easier task than is the reading task.

Such tests can be converted to reading tests, but they must then be administered *individually*. Such a test will be administered only to those children about whom the teacher is doubtful.

To administer such a test as a reading test, the teacher must first circle the answers on a sheet, sit down with the child, point to the first row, and tell the child, "I'm going to say all of these except the one with a circle around it. Then I want you to say that one." The teacher then reads, "gam...tam...nam" and expects the child to read "fam." If the child succeeds, that child obviously has established the sound association for the consonant *f*.

Following this pattern, the teacher may develop a nonsense syllable test for all of the consonants in initial position and may also want to check for use of these sound associations in final position if students have mastered them in initial position. For slightly more advanced students, the teacher may even want to develop this kind of test for the variant consonant spellings, such as the *kn* and *pn* spelling of /n/, *ph* for /f/, and so on.

It seems wise to use nonsense syllables instead of real words in this kind of testing, especially with older disabled readers. If real words are used, the child may be able to call some of them as a result of recognizing the words rather than through use of the skill being tested.

*Vowel sound associations.* Early in this chapter a point was made that children ought to be assessed for those items considered important for reading success. While most reading

Hillerich

programs attempt to teach some generalizations about vowels—and some even base their beginning approach on the vowels—evidence suggests that the vowel generalizations do not make a significant contribution to increased reading skill. This is true, first of all, from analyses of the nature of the language itself, where studies ranging from Clymer (*1*) to Hanna (*4*) demonstrate the fallibility of vowel generalizations.

The former revealed that, out of twenty-four vowel rules agreed upon in four basal reading programs, only six were true 75 percent of the time, and two of the six did not give any help to children. The latter reported that a computer, programmed with 203 rules, was able to spell the 17,000 words in the study with only 49 percent accuracy.

Probably more important are the results of several studies of the effectiveness of teaching vowel generalizations to children (*6*:121-123) which indicate that such teaching does not contribute to increased reading skill.

Nevertheless, teachers who want to assess letter/sound relationships for vowels can develop the same kind of phonics test as was used for consonants (holding the initial and final letters constant and changing the medial vowel letter) as indicated in the following two sets (*5*):

1. voy    vay    vuy    voay
2. koat   keut   koit   keat

Care must be taken in the construction of such a test so two likely possibilities are not presented for the same sound. After all, the same vowel sound is spelled in a number of ways, and the same letter or letters can represent a variety of vowel sounds. For example, in a pilot study, this author included *zub* and *zube* in the same group to test the vowel sound heard in *tube*. Half the first graders marked each of them. Actually, the *u*-consonant-*e* spelling of that sound is used only about one-third as often as the *u* spelling. Hillerich offers a detailed frequency check of the vowel letter/sound combinations (*6*:Chapter Six).

## What Context and Word Recognition Skills Does this Student Need?

Assessment should include only those items deemed

important to success in reading, and testing results ought to lead to instruction. Otherwise, precious time is wasted. Hence, teachers who believe in an extreme synthetic approach to reading—whether sounding out the letters in isolation or using linguistic patterns—might want to skip this section. Such programs do not emphasize a semantic context nor do they see word recognition in the same light as presented here.

In contrast, however, many programs do recognize that context should be used along with phonics in order to identify a strange word in print.

*Assessing use of context.* Informally, in the process of listening to oral reading or while administering an informal reading inventory, the teacher should be aware of the kinds of word errors a child makes: When a child miscalls words, is there a pattern to the substitutions or mispronunciations? If the words the child says consistently tend to be words that make sense but bear little resemblance to the word in print, that child is obviously using context; the problem may be in having limited phonic skill or in the inability to apply that skill. In contrast, if a child tends to substitute or mispronounce words so that what is said resembles the printed form but makes no sense, then that child is using phonics but is not reading for meaning and is not paying attention to context.

To assess the use of context more formally, the teacher may want to develop an instrument made up of sentences, either discrete or in a running selection. Delete a word from each sentence and ask the child to read the sentence and supply a word that would make sense.

In developing such a test, care should be taken that the words in the rest of the sentence do supply adequate contextual hints that will lead to a limited number of appropriate words, if not to a single word.

Secondly, it is important that the position of the missing word vary. If the missing word always comes at the end of a sentence, children may get in the habit of stopping when they come to an unknown word rather than continuing on with the balance of the sentence—or even with the next sentence—in order to get the additional contextual clues that would help them identify the word.

Third, in developing assessments for the use of context,

Hillerich

use a variety of kinds of context so that children are able to use different kinds of context and do not become skilled in only one. Following is a brief listing of some of the kinds of context that youngsters can be exposed to.

Types of Context for Children to Experience

| | |
|---|---|
| Synonym: | Not many animals lived in *arid* or dry lands. |
| Apposition/Restatement: | *Arid* lands, those with little water, support less life than other kinds of land. |
| Definition/Description: | An *arid* land is a very dry land. |
| Example: | A desert is an *arid* land. |
| Contrast: | We find less life on *arid* land than we do on land with plenty of water. |
| Comparison: | It was an *arid* land, as dry as any desert I ever saw. |
| Origin: | *Arid* lands developed where rainfall was light and infrequent. |
| General: | We moved from the mountains to an *arid* valley. |

Finally, assessment of the ability to use context can be taken a step further to include assessing the child's ability to use context along with initial or initial and final consonant sound associations to determine the exact word that is missing in context. Such assessments should include the beginning (and ending) consonant letter in the blank, so the child will use the meaning of the other words in the sentence and the sound the consonant letter or letters represent in order to determine the missing word:

Mary used her w_____ to haul the newspapers to school.
Tommy went to the p_____l for a swim.

*Word recognition.* Most reading programs, regardless of philosophy, have to give some attention to word recognition. Even the synthetic and linguistic programs recognize that some words cannot be analyzed through phonics or patterns, whether they call such words "outlaw words" or "circle words." Such words also tend to be high frequency words in English; that is, they are among the most frequently occurring of words because they are structure words: *was, to, of, on, the.*

This author shares the belief of many that learning to read is a matter of developing certain skills (ability to use context, phonics, etc.) and that learning to read is not merely a matter of memorizing words. Nevertheless, we must recognize that the child who has *no* recognition vocabulary (who cannot call a single word in print without analysis) has no context to use in order to unlock other unfamiliar words since all the words in print are unfamiliar. Hence, unless the teacher holds the belief that learning to read is a matter of sounding out each word letter by letter, it is essential that children develop some recognition vocabulary—some words that they can call immediately upon seeing those words and without any kind of analysis.

Informal assessment of children's recognition vocabulary can be made in the process of hearing children read orally, provided the teacher is aware of the high frequency words that are important enough to be recognized instantly. (See "Starter Words" discussed in this chapter.)

More precise and dependable assessment of recognition vocabulary can be made with the important words on flash cards or merely listed randomly on a sheet of paper for the child to read. In making the assessment, teachers must again do the testing on an individual basis: To provide children with the words in sets of three or four other words and have them circle the word spoken by the teacher is not testing for the reading skill. Again, it is a multiple choice spelling activity that is much easier than the reading act where the child must decide what that printed word is without any clues other than recall and phonics and with all of the choices in the English language.

How many words should be in the child's recognition vocabulary? What are the words to check for? First, it is obvious from studies of the language that the number of words worth teaching as whole words is limited. The ten most frequently used words in English account for 25 percent of all words anyone will meet in any English book, from *The Cat in the Hat* to *Jaws*. On the other hand, in reading a typical 200 page book, an individual will see the most frequently used word about 4,000 times and the 100th word in frequency of use (still a rather high frequency word) only about 150 times. Hence, one does reach a point of diminishing returns very soon if one is teaching only words.

As a guide to the "important" words, many people have used the Dolch Basic Sight Vocabulary of 220 words. Without going into detail here in terms of the evidence (7), at least two other lists are probably more useful today for wide reading than the Dolch list. Those lists are Otto's "One Hundred Essential Sight Words" (10) and Hillerich's 190 "Starter" words (6). The list of the starter words reproduced here shows the order of frequency of use and indicates the extent of recognition by typical first, second, and third graders in midyear.

The Otto list is similar to the first hundred of the starter words: seventy-nine of the Otto words are in the first one hundred of the starter list. The starter words are given in order of frequency of use, to enable the teacher to select the first five, ten, fifty, or hundred most important, depending upon the level of development of the child. Building a recognition vocabulary is a matter of adding word by word until the child has enough of the basic structure words to have context when reading.

## What Structural Analysis Skills Does this Student Need?

While phonics deals with the letters and sounds of the language, structural analysis deals with chunks of words and meaning units of the language. Structural analysis includes understanding of what a syllable is, recognition of compound words, recognition of prefixes, suffixes, base (root) words, and common syllables for pronunciation.

*Syllabication.* Undoubtedly, knowing that longer words can be pronounced in chunks is an important understanding for reading success. Therefore, one of the first steps in assessment is to determine if children recognize that words do have parts or syllables. This ability can be assessed by pronouncing a multisyllable word and having the child tell how many syllables or parts that child hears.

Further than this, one might question any attempt to diagnose or to teach rules about the precise point of syllabication. As Wardhaugh (11:788) points out, "Syllabication has no 'truth' value." It is questionable whether one should waste time in a reading class having youngsters find

# The 190 Starred Starter Words in Order of Frequency of Use*

Midyear Norms, based on individual recognition testing in three school districts:

+ = Grade 1 (N=186)—89 words were known by 50 percent or more of pupils.

Grade 2 (N=208)—all words were known by 50 percent except *through* (47 percent).

Grade 3 (N=208)—all known by 75 percent, except *through* (71 percent), *every* (61 percent), *were* (50 percent).

| | | | | |
|---|---|---|---|---|
| + the | from | + down | only | last |
| + and | + up | back | much | away |
| + a | + will | just | + us | each |
| + to | + do | year | + take | never |
| + of | + said | + little | name | while |
| + in | + then | + make | + here | + took |
| + it | what | who | say | men |
| + is | + like | after | got | next |
| + was | her | people | around | may |
| + I | + go | + come | any | + Mr. |
| + he | + them | + no | use | give |
| + you | time | because | place | show |
| + that | + if | first | put | once |
| + for | + some | more | + boy | something |
| + on | about | many | water | + room |
| they | + by | know | also | must |
| + with | + him | made | before | didn't |
| + have | + or | thing | + off | always |
| + are | + can | went | through | + car |
| + had | + me | + man | right | told |
| + we | + your | want | ask | why |
| + be | + an | way | most | small |
| + one | + day | + work | should | children |
| + but | their | which | don't | still |
| + at | other | + good | than | head |
| + when | very | well | three | left |
| + all | could | came | found | white |
| + this | + has | new | these | let |
| + she | + look | + school | saw | world |
| + there | + get | + too | find | under |
| + not | + now | been | tell | same |
| + his | + see | think | + help | kind |
| as | our | + home | every | + keep |
| were | + two | + house | again | + am |
| would | + into | + play | another | best |
| + so | + did | + old | + big | better |
| + my | over | long | night | soon |
| + out | + how | + where | thought | four |

*"Starter Words" ©1973, Robert L. Hillerich.

Hillerich

the precise point of syllabication. Such points are arbitrary, vary in terms of speech and the writing convention, and are usually after-the-fact kinds of reasoning in which the point of syllabication can be determined only *after* the word is named rather than while the child is trying to name it.

Nevertheless, for those people who still believe such machinations are important for children, assessment can begin by giving children collections of words to syllabicate that have two consonants between two vowels (VCCV pattern). Of course, the teacher must also make the arbitrary decision as to how children are to syllabicate these words, according to the writing convention or according to the pronunciation. For example, the word *yellow* would be divided between the two *l*'s (as in the dictionary entry word) for the writing convention; it would be divided after the *l*'s (as in the dictionary pronunciation /yel o/) for pronunciation since there is no /l/ in the final syllable. Further, if the writing convention is the syllabication pattern to be assessed, the test should also include some words where the two consonants are digraphs or clusters, which are not divided (*mother, father*), to be certain children do not automatically divide between consonants every time they see them.

Need one even mention the futility of bothering children with the rule for dividing a VCV pattern (*cabin, baby*)? "Try using the 'short' sound of the vowel before the first consonant and divide after that consonant; if that doesn't sound like a word you know, try using the 'long' sound of the vowel and divide before the first consonant following the first vowel.... And remember, digraphs are treated as single consonants." Why not try that one on *mother* and *father*!

*Compound words.* Teachers may want to construct a brief assessment sheet to determine if youngsters have developed the understanding that some longer words are made up of two known words and that the two known words often give a clue to the meaning of the compound word. Such an assessment should be made of compound words, both parts of which are words the children have been exposed to and would recognize, such as *headlight, windmill, snowshoe, waterfall, highchair, fingernail.*

*Base words and affixes.* Related to the understanding of

compounds is the knowledge that there are times when a prefix or ending is added to a base word that is known. For example, children may recognize the word *play*, but "He'll *replay* the tape" or "Mary *played* the tape" represent entirely new words. In fact, one study indicated that even junior high students may recognize a base word and not recognize that same word when it is affixed. Hence, some assessment of this understanding of base forms when they are affixed can be helpful in instructional planning.

The base or root ought to be a word that children already recognize. Assessment may begin by having them recognize that familiar part with a limited number of common prefixes or suffixes. Initial assessment should include common words with past, plural, and *-ing* endings. Then some of the common prefixes may also be introduced. The assessment is merely a matter of providing a list of such words and having children mark the base word. Follow-up assessment in application requires interpretation of meaning in context.

Incidentally, this is as close as teachers should come to having children find little words in big words. Beyond the separation of base forms from affixes or the recognition of compound words, such a technique will be *mis*leading more often than it is helpful.

*Prefixes and suffixes.* At the elementary level, there are only a few prefixes and suffixes that are consistent enough in meaning and frequently enough used to warrant their assessment and teaching. In terms of prefixes, these are *un-, mis-, re-, mono-, non-* and possibly *in-, inter-, over-,* and *pre-*.

Few suffixes alter the semantic meanings of base forms, since most are inflectional endings, such as past and plural markers, *-ly* for adverbs, *-ion* for nouns, and so on. Nevertheless, such endings should be assessed and taught as meaning units, with the pronunciation becoming a natural outgrowth of recognition of meaning. There is no sense in dealing with these at the phonics level, having children analyze the three sounds of the past or plural marker. What English speaking person will apply the /t/ (as in *trapped*) to the *-ed* ending of *hunted*? Or the /z/ (as in *toys*) to the *-s* ending of *hats*?

Additional suffixes to be assessed might include *-ful* and *-less*, to be assessed for pronunciation and for meaning.

To determine pupil competence in interpreting the meanings of such items, a base word known to them can be affixed and the meaning interpreted by them. Teachers may also design exercises for assessment or for practice that are in the form of charts to be completed by students, where column headings and base forms are supplied. Columns completed by students would appear as follows:

| BASE | un- | re- | mis- | pre- | -less | -ful |
|---|---|---|---|---|---|---|
| lock | unlock | relock | | | | |
| tie | untie | retie | | | | |
| fold | unfold | refold | misfold | prefold | | |
| form | | reform | misform | preform | formless | |
| treat | | | mistreat | pretreat | | |
| word | | reword | misword | | wordless | |
| help | | | | | helpless | helpful |
| hope | | | | | hopeless | hopeful |
| color | | | miscolor | precolor | colorless | colorful |

## What Comprehension Skills Does this Student Need?

While the basic decoding skills previously discussed do form a tentative sequence for the development of reading skill, placement of the comprehension skills after that sequence in no way implies that the latter skills should not be attempted until the decoding skills are accomplished. In fact, reading comprehension skills are really thinking skills applied to reading and as thinking skills they begin before reading instruction starts. The typical preschool child is able to draw conclusions, make judgments, predict outcomes, and so on at the oral level; the one who cannot do these things at the oral level certainly cannot perform the doubly complex task in reading.

Most often the comprehension skills are assessed informally in the process of discussing a selection read. Such a procedure is fine provided the teacher 1) is aware of the variety of comprehension skills, 2) makes certain to range through that variety, and 3) makes certain that the kinds of questions asked are tapping the skills they are supposed to tap.

To give examples of exercises for the assessment of all the comprehension skills would be repetitious. Hence, this section is devoted to the general pattern for assessing any of the comprehension skills and then offers an annotated listing of the major skills.

There are serious pitfalls in attempts to assess comprehension, and teachers once more are cautioned against the use of group tests. Regardless of their claims and clever analyses in terms of skills, group tests are not effective in diagnosing the comprehension skills of an individual (2).

Even on an individual basis, whether in group discussion or in a one-to-one situation, teachers must follow up on answers given to comprehension questions before judgments can be made about the child's skill or lack of skill. Following is a simple paragraph. Assume the teacher asks the child to read the selection and then plans to check if that child can draw conclusions:

> The dilapidated fire truck rumbled to the fire. Its engine was pinging all the way. It was fast as greased lightning bugs and smooth as cobble stone.

An obvious question to check on the ability to draw conclusions would be to ask if the truck was old. Children who answer "yes" might be guessing unless their answer is followed with "Why do you think that?" Worse, children who answer "no" might be quite capable of drawing conclusions and may have done so quite well in this instance. "Johnny, why did you think the truck was not old?" "Because it was 'decorated' (dilapidated), the engine was 'singing' (pinging), and it was fast 'as lightning' and smooth 'as stone.' " In other words, Johnny was good at drawing conclusions, but he was very poor at word identification: The basic skills can alter the reader's comprehension even when the basic comprehension skill is operating.

The procedure for assessing any of the comprehension skills listed below is to provide a selection to be read, to ask a question that requires application of the skill to be assessed, and to ask for justification of the response. This kind of assessment can be part of the regular discussion of material read by the group, provided the teacher takes care that 1) questions range through the skills to be assessed and 2) notes are made of those students who need additional instruction in the specific comprehension skill.

Whether the assessment is handled in a regular reading

group or on a one-to-one basis, if the pupil consistently (over three or four different questions) can answer as expected, one can assume that a pupil can use the particular comprehension skill at that level of reading difficulty. Students who do not give and justify the expected responses must be taught, through examples and demonstrations, how to use that skill.

Assessment must also be continuous from year to year. One cannot assume that the student who can draw conclusions from material written at a fourth grade reading level can also draw conclusions from material at a sixth grade reading level.

Items to be assessed in the area of comprehension include skills of literal comprehension (what the author said), inferential comprehension (what the author meant), and critical reading (what the reader's experience leads him or her to think about what the author said and meant). Also, any of the skills can be asked for on the basis of recognition or of recall. The reading matter may be in front of the reader (recognition) or withdrawn at the time of questioning (recall). Both performances ought to be checked, and the latter—which involves memory as well—is more difficult than the former.

Even in assessing literal comprehension, teachers must be careful to require some translation of the words used in the selection. For example, if the selection is a simple sentence, "Sue fixed her hat," the following exchange would demonstrate nothing about comprehension: "What did Sue fix?" "Her hat." "Who fixed her hat?" "Sue." Such an exchange merely demonstrates structural meaning, which can as well be demonstrated with the nonsense sentence, "The nam pipped a min." (What did the nam pip? A min. What pipped a min? The nam.) Even in the limited sentence above, translation can be accomplished by substituting *girl* for *Sue, clothing* for *hat,* or *repaired/ straightened* for *fixed* in the questions or expected answers.

Following is a listing of some of the major comprehension skills and examples of questions or concerns for teachers to keep in mind in order to assess use of these particular skills in the process of discussing material to read. It should be noted that most responses beyond the literal should be followed with "Why?" or "Why do you think that?" Unless the teacher wants to work on literal comprehension (where too much time is usually spent), that teacher will be inclined to minimize, if not discard, questions beginning with *who, what, when, where.*

*Literal comprehension.* In assessing or in providing practice in literal comprehension, answers to questions asked are stated in so many words in the selection read. Teachers may wish to begin—and it is hoped will choose to focus—on inferential comprehension for two reasons: 1) evidence suggests that too much time and effort are expended on literal skills; 2) success in inferential comprehension presumes understanding of the literal level (6:134). Following are *literal comprehension skills* to be assessed:

| | |
|---|---|
| 1. Word Meaning | (Requires use of decoding skills, context, and/or dictionary.) |
| 2. Pronoun Referents | (Given the sentence *Sue was lucky she found her shoe.*) "To whom does *she* refer?" |
| 3. Detail | "Who?" "What?" "When?" "How many?" |
| 4. Main Idea | "What would be a good title (name) for this story?" |
| 5. Sequence | "What happened first?" "Next?" "Put the following in order the way they appeared in the story." |
| 6. Comparisons | "How were the characters (places, etc.) alike?" "Different?" |
| 7. Cause/Effect Relationships | "Why did...?" "When?" What?" (Check on awareness and use of clue words: *when, because, after, as a result,* etc.) |

*Inferential comprehension.* Questions here deal with understandings that are not stated in the text. The reader must use clues and information from the selection in order to arrive at answers. All answers should be justified: "How do you know?" "What made you think that?"

While Drawing Conclusions is listed as a separate skill, any of the inferential skills require drawing conclusions by requiring use of facts given in order to arrive at an answer not given. Following are *inferential skills* to be assessed:

| | |
|---|---|
| 1. Drawing Conclusions | A great variety of questions is possible; see the example about the fire truck. |
| 2. Main Idea | Same technique as for literal comprehension, except the answer is not given in the selection. |
| 3. Comparisons | Same technique as for literal comprehension, but the comparisons are not overtly stated. |

Hillerich

| | |
|---|---|
| 4. Cause/Effect<br>Relationships | Same technique as literal comprehension, but clue words are not provided in the selection. |
| 5. Making Judgments | "Would you have...?" "Should the character...? |
| 6. Identifying Character<br>Traits | "What kind of person was...?" |
| 7. Predicting Outcomes | "What might have happened if...?" A changed situation or event offers new possibilities. Answers should be based on knowledge of characters/situation, not wild guesses. |
| 8. Interpreting<br>Figurative Language | |
| Simile | This is literal and discussed primarily for appreciation of word choice. |
| Metaphor | "What are being compared?" "How could they be alike?" "How did the author intend for us to consider them alike?" |
| Idioms | Provide examples. If children do not recognize them, have them try context. If that doesn't help, tell them. |

*Critical reading.* Critical reading requires a certain degree of experience with the subject being read or requires reading on that subject in several different sources. The skills can best be assessed and applied with persuasive or factual material as opposed to the fiction and fantasy most often found in basal readers.

Even young children can learn to use many of these skills. However, items 3 and 5 require more maturity in terms of experiential background and logic. Following are *critical reading skills* to be assessed:

| | |
|---|---|
| 1. Distinguishing<br>Reality and Fantasy | "Could this really have happened?" "Is it just make believe?" "Why do you think that?" |
| 2. Distinguishing Fact<br>and Opinion | "Is that a statement of fact or opinion?" "How do you know?" Students should be aware of criteria: fact is evaluated as true/false (objective); opinion is evaluated as agree/disagree (subjective). |
| 3. Determining<br>Adequacy/<br>Completeness | Requires other experience or reading on the same subject. |
| 4. Identifying<br>Slant/Bias | Can pupils identify emotionally loaded word choices of the author? Requires awareness of connotations, e.g., *house: home/hut; mansion/hovel.* |

| | |
|---|---|
| 5. Are Conclusions Based on Evidence? | "What facts were used to get to the conclusion?" "Are other conclusions possible?" "Likely?" Requires awareness of logic; shifts in levels of abstraction. |
| 6. Author's Purpose | "Why do you think the author wrote this?" |
| 7. Author's Competence | "What was the author's background for writing on this subject?" At lower levels children can read or be told an author's background and asked to assess this point. |
| 8. Currency of the Book | "When was the book written?" "Is this a subject in which new things were found recently?" (The date is not always the important point!) |

## What Study Skills Does this Student Need?

The study skills are essential for success in reading in the content areas and are best diagnosed, taught, and practiced with material of a factual or informative nature: Science, social studies, and math provide appropriate material for assessment and for instruction in these skills. In fact, continuous assessment of these skills, like the comprehension skills, can be an informal matter of observation as pupils operate in the content areas, so long as the teacher is aware of the specific skills needed and makes a point to range through all of these skills.

Of course, more formal assessments may be developed on a criterion referenced basis, where the student is presented with the task being tested. For example, when presented with a series of sentences, each of which contains a strange word, can the child use a dictionary effectively in order to determine the meaning of that word in that context? Presented with a selection of several paragraphs, can the child outline the content of that selection?

Then, too, assessments may begin at opposite points, depending upon the level of development presumed in the students. If the teacher has reason to believe most students are fairly competent in a given area, such as outlining, the assessment may require outlining a selection as suggested above. Then, for those who fail to perform that task satisfactorily, the teacher may reassess more specifically to see why they could not outline. Given a paragraph, can such students determine the main idea? Given a main idea, can such students locate supporting details?

In contrast, if the teacher has reason to believe that most students are not competent in the ultimate performance skill, that teacher may prefer to begin assessment with the supporting subskills before moving to assessment of the ultimate skill.

*Dictionary skills.* Certainly basic to any kind of mature reading is the ability to use a dictionary efficiently for pronunciation, meaning, and spelling. At least by the time an individual is reading at the fourth grade level—and from there on—there are times when that person will face a word identification problem where phonics is of no help because the word is not in the oral vocabulary and the context is too weak to help. The only solution is use of a dictionary.

The ultimate skills to be assessed are the ability to use a dictionary for meaning, for pronunciation, and for spelling. All of these presume knowledge of the basic elements of dictionary usage: entry words, alphabetical order of entry words, guide words, pronunciation key, special spelling for pronunciation, and location of meanings.

Of the three uses, use of a dictionary for meaning is the easiest to assess and the easiest in which to diagnose trouble spots. Using a dictionary for pronunciation is usually more difficult for youngsters and requires individual attention in the assessment since the problem is usually an oral/aural one. Presumed in this skill is the ability to isolate the vowel sound indicated in the pronunciation key and to pronounce it in the context of the other letters in the special spelling for pronunciation. Further, if the word is multisyllabic, the pronouncer must demonstrate conscious control of stress. Such skills must be assessed orally, and therefore individually, if the assessment is to be accurate.

The problem spot and subassessments necessary to using a dictionary for spelling are usually in the area of awareness of possible spellings and in the willingness to persist in the educated guessing necessary to find a pronounced word. Pencil and paper activities can be used here if children already know how to use a dictionary for pronunciation. The pronunciations of unknown words can be put on the board or on duplicated sheets and pronounced by youngsters to themselves, with the hunt for spellings (entry words) done independently.

Incidentally, even here, as in the comprehension skills assessment, follow-up questioning can be helpful. Given the pronunciation /mal' stram/ to find a spelling, "What spelling did you check first?" "Next?" Perhaps the first likely spelling checked for the first syllable was *mail*, then *male*, etc. until *mael* was found. Any youngster who begins with *mul* is certainly pretty far afield and needs more education to go with the guessing.

*Locating information.* In this area are three major performances to be assessed: ability to use an index; to use other parts of a book (table of contents, glossary, table of figures); and to locate materials in special aids such as the card catalog, almanacs, encyclopedias, time tables, biographical dictionaries, and so on.

Any of these can be assessed informally through problems to be solved or questions to be answered. Then, with children who have problems in performance of one of the activities, more specific assessment may take the form of checking familiarity with the organization of a card catalog, the information on the cards, or the ability to identify a key word from a question.

*Outlining.* The ability to outline may be checked from two directions. Can the child outline personal thinking? Can the child ferret out the organizational pattern of material someone else has written?

It is wise here to keep the focus of both assessment and instruction on the organization of ideas and not on the mechanics of numbering an outline. Students who have difficulty in any kind of outlining may be having trouble in determining main ideas, recognizing supporting details, or in associating the two. Assessments of the subskills will be necessary to determine where the problem lies, and such assessments may be in the form of oral questions or a worksheet, as indicated in the section on comprehension skills.

*Reading for various purposes.* Assessment in this area will help the teacher determine, either by observation or by criterion referenced testing, whether students vary their rates of reading according to purpose and whether they can skim for

Hillerich

an idea and can scan for a specific item; whether they know how to read a math problem and how to read to follow directions; and whether they know how to read graphs, charts, and tables.

## A Word of Caution

Assessments of any kind present a danger, whether they be criterion referenced or norm referenced, teacher made or commercial. Teachers must always recognize that assessing is not teaching and that time taken for assessment is time taken from teaching.

This is not to say that assessment is unimportant. It is merely to remind one that the task does not stop there. Assessment provides essential guidelines for teaching, but merely to assess a skill is to waste time if teaching does not follow. The assessment is like a practice exercise—it teaches nothing that the student doesn't already know. In other words:

DO assess for those items you know are important to success in reading.

DO NOT assess for items that make no contribution.

FOLLOW the assessment with instruction as indicated by the assessment.

SKIP instruction where the assessment indicates the skill has been mastered.

## The Affective Domain

Whether a teacher is dealing with readers who are bright, average, slow, above level, below level, interested, or disinterested, that teacher is wasting time attempting to develop reading skills if the teacher is not also developing an interest in reading.

Skills instruction in reading must be seen as only one part of the total reading program. In fact, if teachers are looking for a percentage, this author would say that 40 to 50 percent of the time called "reading" ought to be devoted to the enjoyable application and practice of the skills being taught in trade books, magazines, newspapers, or other reading matter.

There are many kinds of activities that teachers can provide to develop an exciting kind of trade book reading program (8). However, since dealing with continuous assessment, it is in this area that the assessment must be turned back on the teacher. Are the children reading independently? Are they seeking out materials to be read? Are such materials easily available to them? Do they seem to be enjoying and sharing the reading that they do?

If not, then the teacher needs to take inventory of the kinds of things being done or not being done in the classroom that are failing to encourage this kind of use of reading skills. Such an inventory might include questions such as the following:

1. Are various kinds and levels of trade books easily accessible in the classroom for students at all times?
2. Are bulletin boards and centers used to stimulate an awareness of the exciting world of children's books?
3. Are records kept to help students see their progress and give them a sense of accomplishment?
4. Are there opportunities for students to share their reading and become motivated through writing, dramatizing, talking, or playing games?

In conclusion, teachers ought to be certain that they continuously assess for reading level and for the important reading skills, that the skills identified are taught as needed, and that practices that make no contribution to reading success are discarded. If these things are done, children will become readers and will enjoy reading!

References
1. Clymer, Theodore. "The Utility of Phonic Generalizations in Primary Grades," *Reading Teacher*, 16 (January 1963), 252-258.
2. Farr, Roger. *Reading: What Can Be Measured?* Newark, Delaware: International Reading Association, 1969.
3. Fry, Edward. "The Orangoutang Score," *Reading Teacher*, 24 (January 1971), 360-364.
4. Hanna, Paul, et al. *Phoneme-Grapheme Correspondences as Cues to Spelling Improvement*. Washington, D.C.: U.S. Office of Health, Education and Welfare, 1966.

5. Hillerich, Robert. *Diagnostic Phonics Test*. Columbus, Ohio: Charles Merrill, 1976.
6. Hillerich, Robert. *Reading Fundamentals for Preschool and Primary Children*. Columbus, Ohio: Charles Merrill, 1977.
7. Hillerich, Robert. "Word Lists—Getting it All Together," *Reading Teacher*, 27 (January 1974), 353-360.
8. Hillerich, Robert. *Fifty Ways to Raise Bookworms*. Boston: Houghton Mifflin, free pamphlet, undated.
9. Hunt, Kellogg. *Grammatical Structures Written at Three Grade Levels*. Urbana, Illinois: National Council of Teachers of English, 1965.
10. Otto, Wayne, and Cathy Stallard. "One Hundred Essential Sight Words," *Visible Language*, 10 (Summer 1976), 247-252.
11. Wardhaugh, Ronald. "Syl-lab-i-ca-tion," *Elementary English*, 43 (November 1966), 785-788.

Memory provides record keeping procedures that enable the teacher to have a continuously accurate knowledge of each student's strengths and needs in any area related to the reading act.

## Chapter Eight    Record Keeping for Effective Reading Instruction

David M. Memory
*Indiana State University*

The numerous pieces of information about the skills, attitudes, and behaviors that go together to produce a good reader at any age level pose a record keeping problem for the most organized teacher. Fortunately, teachers do not have to know the status of every child with respect to all of these components of reading performance. A large percentage of students make entirely satisfactory progress in reading without having their information, skills, attitudes, and behaviors closely monitored from week to week or month to month. Many students, however, fall behind in overall reading development because of specific correctable deficiencies or handicaps. One of the goals of well-managed reading instruction is to prevent these problems or to remediate them when they appear.

## The Importance of Record Keeping

To avoid being overwhelmed by uninterpreted observations of student performance, a teacher needs some organized system for continuously assessing the major components of reading achievement and for recording significant findings. Earlier chapters have dealt with techniques of planning, diagnosis, and ongoing assessment. Those techniques are designed to help the teacher understand student performance and plan effective instruction. If a teacher had only one student with whom to work, it might be possible to combine diagnosis and instruction into one self-guided process. With a group of twenty-five or thirty students, this system is not possible. There is too much variation in the types and magnitudes of deficiencies and handicaps in even a relatively homogeneous class. To use diagnostic information effectively and to carry out instructional plans successfully, a teacher must maintain good records. They are one of the unloved elements of classroom management that turn perceptive diagnosis and inspired teaching into optimal student progress.

Of course, teachers do not need to be informed that record keeping is an unpopular responsibility. For many, the attendance records they must keep could stand alone as a symbol of much of what they dislike about their jobs. Some teachers, however, have not tried to incorporate extensive record keeping into their approaches to organizing instruction in reading. For these teachers, a warning is in order. Trying to do more than can be done successfully is one of the easiest ways to turn oneself completely against a new procedure. This is particularly true of a practice such as record keeping that often does not produce obvious benefits immediately.

An intensive study by the Rand Corporation of six reading projects using diagnostic/prescriptive instruction concludes that the demands of record keeping are one of the main causes of resistance to that instructional approach. The teachers felt that they could not justify taking time away from instruction in order to keep required records (9:358). At least in this respect, there is little doubt that this sample of six projects was representative of programs throughout the country.

If resistance to record keeping is so common, the questions then are how to justify it and how to make it produce the greatest benefits from the least expenditure of teacher time, thought, and effort. This chapter is an attempt to answer those questions. Teachers must understand the functions that records can serve. First in a brief overview and then scattered throughout the discussion of specific practices, this chapter suggests functions that go well beyond the recording of what has happened in the classroom. Most of the chapter, though, is devoted to explaining how a teacher can make record keeping procedures as efficient and beneficial as possible. It is hoped that these suggestions will make the initial efforts of teachers rewarding. Then there is a good chance they will not forsake the whole notion of record keeping but will experiment further until they have found the optimal balance in their roles as motivators and managers of learning.

## Functions of Records Kept by the Teacher and Students

Though the word *record* implies it, record keeping does not serve only to keep track of what has occurred in a classroom. When used efficiently and effectively, records have functions that make them an important part of almost all elements of successful instruction.

1. One obvious function of records is to indicate what has been attempted in the classroom. When starting out, many teachers assume that outsiders will accept their word that student time is being used in justifiable ways in their classrooms. Less and less, though, is the teacher's assurance alone being accepted as evidence that schools are at least attempting to fulfill their responsibilities as educators of youth. With recent discussions of accountability, minimal competency testing, basic skills instruction, and competency-based teacher evaluation has come an increasing demand that teachers be able to prove that they have been doing educationally defensible things in their classrooms. If those activities are instructionally sound, then one possible form of proof is the records that teachers and students maintain. This chapter suggests specific ways in which teachers can produce and use records for that purpose.

2. Related to what has been attempted in the classroom is how successful those activities were. If instruction is effective, then most teachers will want to have evidence of success for themselves and their students. Good records can serve that function and can help teachers respond to public demands for proof of educator performance. More important educationally, though, are the day-to-day uses of records which show the effectiveness of activities. Some of these records involve test results and other, objective measures. Others should be based on student evaluations of their own performances and of the materials and activities used in their reading instruction. Both objective and subjective measures help teachers know what instructional approaches work best

with specific students, and they guide teachers in planning group and individual instruction. With this information available, teachers can also conduct student-teacher and parent-teacher conferences that go beyond preconceptions and deal with the realities of what actually works.

3. When records are maintained to chart student progress, it is usually easy at the same time to develop profiles of the strengths and weaknesses of both individuals and whole classes. With this information available on student status, it is easier for the teacher to insure that specific instruction is provided when it is needed. Using individual student profiles, the teacher can plan instruction to correct the deficiencies and handicaps that might otherwise retard overall progress in reading. With this information about the skill levels of students, the teacher is also better able to insure that each one is performing tasks that are neither so difficult as to be frustrating nor so easy as to be boring. When instruction is focused in areas of need and is geared to appropriate skill levels, alert students are more likely to feel that their teachers deserve cooperation and hard work. Another perspective in the analysis of student status involves class profiles. The teacher can study the scores of whole classes and determine whether adjustments are needed in group instruction and identify the areas toward which those adjustments should be directed.

4. Because of this close relationship between record keeping and good instructional planning, it is possible for the same efforts to serve both functions. Good plans describe the instruction that will take place. By adding informal observations and statements of results, the teacher can transform these plans into comprehensive descriptions of the instruction that occurred and how effective it was. When a teacher intends to use plans in this way, there is often a greater willingness to use the time and effort needed to produce plans that will facilitate effective instruction.

5. If instruction is effective, then the results are likely to be something that will please the students who have made progress. Records that show these results are evidence of what these students have accomplished. By using records of success and progress in this way with students, the teacher rewards past effort, builds confidence, and motivates continued cooperation and initiative.

6. Even in a well-organized classroom, much instruction and even some assignments are not previously planned. They are formulated during interaction with students and are immediate responses to observed student performance. Since they are based on direct observation of student responses and behaviors, these activities are potentially effective. To insure maximum success, though, the teacher needs to provide follow-up evaluation, discussion, or practice based upon these special activities and assignments. Therefore, the teacher needs to have a record of what has been done or assigned. When this follow-up is provided, the students are more likely to feel that what the teacher has assigned is important and what they as students have done is viewed in that way, too.

7. Frequently in an effectively managed classroom, many students will be doing different things at the same time. This condition necessitates careful planning and the use of posted or distributed schedules and plans. Of course, it is possible for many students to make responsible decisions about where they will work and what they will do. However, when the teacher has to ask a student what he is doing or is supposed to be doing, much of the potential impact of individual attention is lost. Therefore, the time is well spent in making master schedules and plans or records of what individual students or small groups will be doing. It enables the teacher to give the type of individual attention that demonstrates the concern and awareness that encourage students to work.

## Characteristics of Good Record Keeping

To increase the chances that a record keeping procedure or system will survive the demands placed upon a teacher and help the teacher provide effective instruction, there are certain characteristics that the system should have. The specific information that is retained and the actual forms on which it is recorded can and should vary depending upon circumstances and upon the objectives of instruction. However, teachers who keep these general characteristics in mind are more likely to devise record keeping schemes that will produce desired results with minimal expenditure of teacher time and effort.

1. One of the most important characteristics of efficient and effective record keeping is that it is integrated with diagnosis, prescriptive planning, and assessment, as well as with the materials and activities used in instruction. It is not a self-contained procedure or system existing in isolation.

To make this integration possible, it is important that the teacher think through sequential instructional and management procedures before devising forms to be used in record keeping. These forms should not dictate what is done in the classroom. Rather, they should reflect the well-reasoned decisions and intentions of the teacher. As the standard procedures used in a classroom change, the record forms should be revised to keep them relevant to those procedures. If increased individualization is a goal, though, the teacher should not wait to see what procedures will evolve before setting up a record keeping system. As has been emphasized, good records serve essential functions in individualizing reading instruction and, therefore, should be a planned feature of classroom management.

Related to the importance of thinking through instructional and management procedures is the need to relate records kept to the specific objectives of instruction. One situation in which a teacher needs to analyze the relationship between records and objectives is when preexisting record forms are used. Many of the record forms provided with basal series and with published skills management systems deal with objectives that some teachers may consider unimportant. If a teacher does not plan to provide instruction in certain skills, there is no need to maintain records related to those skills. On the other hand, if important objectives are not adequately represented in existing forms, additions should be made to insure that the intended emphasis is placed on these objectives. In general then, the teacher should make certain that the information recorded in the published or teacher-made forms in use does in fact reflect the objectives toward which instruction is directed.

Another element in the integration of record keeping into the overall process of classroom organization involves the use of test booklets, protocols, and test sheets used in initial diagnosis and continuing assessment. Though tests may be administered with specific limited objectives in mind, they usually contain additional information that may later prove of value in diagnosis and assessment. Therefore, it is wise to save them for possible later reference. Knowing that the original testing instruments will remain available, the teacher can then transfer to class lists or other record forms only the information that is necessary for prescriptive planning or for reporting progress or that will be helpful in motivating the students.

Planning is another management activity that can be combined with record keeping. Whole-class lesson plans, small-group plans, and individual plans should be designed so that they become records as the plans are carried out by the teacher or the students. Of course, some information may need to be compiled and transferred from the completed plans. By using plans as records, the teacher avoids having to devise and complete separate forms that would probably lose much of the information contained in the original plans.

Another important part of the coordination of record keeping with other elements of reading instruction relates to materials and other instructional resources. As management systems in basals and self-contained management systems become more comprehensive, there is a greater possibility that teachers will find themselves with record forms keyed to reading materials and other resources to which they do not have access. To avoid needless expenditure of time and effort, the teacher should study existing record forms carefully to insure that the information to be retained can in fact be used in conjunction with available instructional resources.

2. If record keeping is well integrated with other management and instructional procedures, it is usually both possible and beneficial to let students participate in maintaining records.

One advantage of student participation in record keeping is that it leaves the teacher with more time to devote to tasks for which students cannot be responsible. Students can check their own work; they can record their results; and they can write comments evaluating materials they have used and activities in which they have participated. Another advantage is that participation in record keeping can generate in students the feeling that they are responsible for what they are learning and can motivate them to work harder, partly because they see the results of progress made but also because they know that they will not get as much from their efforts if they do not perform their record keeping duties well.

To maintain a positive attitude among students toward participation in record keeping, there are several things the teacher should do. Through comments and assignments, the teacher should make it obvious to students that their record keeping efforts are being used to their benefit. The teacher's use of recorded information should convince students that maintaining records is not just busywork. For instance, the teacher should monitor student records regularly and should assign supplementary materials and activities when these records indicate that the students have not achieved the objectives of the initial instruction or practice. Similarly, if students make evaluative comments about materials and activities in their records, the teacher should be prompt in making changes that seem appropriate. Though these actions by the teacher will have powerful effects, complimentary words are needed, too. When records indicate that a student has performed well on an activity, the teacher should take the opportunity to comment in writing on the records or directly to the student about the quality of work.

There are other characteristics of good record keeping, but these two—integration with other management and instructional procedures and student participation—are ones that are most important for efficiency and effectiveness in most of the varied situations in which records are needed. Therefore, these characteristics should be kept in mind as the teacher plans the record forms and record keeping schemes to meet classroom needs.

## General Procedures for Good Record Keeping

Regardless of the teaching approaches used in a classroom, there are several general record keeping procedures that are essential for well-managed instruction.

1. One procedure which is helpful in any classroom where reading is taught is use of a summary form onto which

pertinent information from a student's permanent record folder is transferred. In the rare cases in which a teacher can keep permanent folders in the classroom, it is not essential that summary forms be maintained. Much more common are the situations in which permanent records are officially kept in a central location but are often unavailable because they are being used by counselors, psychologists, or other support personnel in the school. In these situations it is important that the teacher have immediate access to test scores and background information that might be helpful in making diagnostic and instructional decisions. Even if permanent records are accessible, they are often difficult to use. Important information is often hidden among irrelevant forms and comments. Moreover, the recording schemes used from one teacher to the next often vary so much that the scores and other information a teacher might need are not readily interpreted. A summary form such as the one shown can be used to compile important information in a location and format that would permit easy reference and use. Similar information on this topic may be found in Chapter Six.

### Summary of Permanent Records

Name _____ Address _____

Vision _____ Hearing _____ Date of Birth _____

Medical Problems _____

Unusual Environmental Conditions _____

Interests and Hobbies _____

Attitudes toward School _____

Attitudes toward Reading _____

|       | Name | Age | Marital Status | Education | Occupation |
|-------|------|-----|----------------|-----------|------------|
| Mother |     |     |                |           |            |
| Father |     |     |                |           |            |

|       | Address | Phone Number | Attitude toward School |
|-------|---------|--------------|------------------------|
| Mother |        |              |                        |
| Father |        |              |                        |

## Siblings

| | | | | | | |
|-----------|--|--|--|--|--|--|
| Name | | | | | | |
| Age | | | | | | |
| Grade in School | | | | | | |
| School Grades | | | | | | |
| Physical Problems | | | | | | |

### Grades in School

| | | | | | | | | | |
|-----------|--------|--|--|--|--|--|--|--|--|
| Reading | Period | | | | | | | | |
|  | Grade | | | | | | | | |
| Language Arts | Period | | | | | | | | |
|  | Grade | | | | | | | | |
| Math | Period | | | | | | | | |
|  | Grade | | | | | | | | |
| Social Studies | Period | | | | | | | | |
|  | Grade | | | | | | | | |
| Science | Period | | | | | | | | |
|  | Grade | | | | | | | | |

## Standardized Test Results

**Reading**

| Test/Form | | | | | |
|---|---|---|---|---|---|
| Date | | | | | |

**Scores**

| Vocab | | | | | |
|---|---|---|---|---|---|
| Comp | | | | | |
| Sight Voc | | | | | |
| Word Att | | | | | |
| Rate | | | | | |

**Language**

| Test/Form | | | | | |
|---|---|---|---|---|---|
| Date | | | | | |
| Score | | | | | |

**Math**

| Test/Form | | | | | |
|---|---|---|---|---|---|
| Date | | | | | |
| Score | | | | | |

**Social Studies**

| Test/Form | | | | | |
|---|---|---|---|---|---|
| Date | | | | | |
| Score | | | | | |

**Science**

| Test/Form | | | | | |
|---|---|---|---|---|---|
| Date | | | | | |
| Score | | | | | |

| Type | | | | | |
|---|---|---|---|---|---|
| Dates | | | | | |
| Results | | | | | |

For each student, this form should include the information considered most important for diagnosis and prescriptive planning. For example, only the most recent and most trusted standardized test scores need be transferred from permanent records. Of course, if sets of scores in one area show significant patterns of increased or slowed progress, it is worthwhile to record all of those scores. Though norm referenced reading test scores are of limited diagnostic value, low scores on such tests relative to classroom assessment can indicate the need for instruction in test taking. Scores on standardized tests in the content areas can also be helpful. For instance, confident readers can be given supplementary materials on topics in areas of weakness as indicated by test scores to help increase their general knowledge in those areas. In contrast, reluctant readers and poor readers who need to build confidence can be given supplementary materials on topics in content areas in which they have scored relatively high.

The same type of information can be gained from analysis of grades in school. Subjects in which a student is weak can be identified so that relatively easy supplementary materials can be provided in those areas. If complex comprehension and critical reading skills are to be taught or practiced, materials from areas of strength can be used. As with standardized test scores, only recent grades and sets of grades reflecting significant changes in performance need to be transferred to this summary form.

Some of the remaining information that can be recorded on this form can be found in most permanent folders. Some of it, though, would have to come from observations, from informal interviews, or from special data forms completed by the students or their parents. All of this information can help guide the teacher in diagnosis and prescriptive planning and should be collected if possible. However, the teacher may choose to gather some of the less accessible information on those students only whose performance is least satisfactory or most puzzling. By having such a form on hand, the teacher will find it easier to record new information as it becomes available either through informal conversation with students or through planned efforts. Moreover, when the teacher wants to use some of that information, it will be readily accessible in a location and format of the teacher's choosing.

2. Another general record keeping procedure that can be helpful in any classroom in which reading is taught is the practice of having each student keep a folder for his record forms, individual plans, contracts, and other reading-related papers. With young students, thin expansion or accordion files can be used. The closed ends of this type of file prevent papers from falling out when children are carrying their folders. An adequate alternative for expansion files is a simple manila folder stapled or taped at one end to help keep the papers in the folder. These folders should be kept in an open file box or in the students' desks so that the teacher can use them when necessary. The teacher will need to have access to these folders to keep some teacher records up-to-date and to organize information for parent-teacher conferences.

The contents of this folder—the record forms, individual plans, and so on—are tangible evidence to each student of success in reading. The folder can play a motivational role with parents as well. The whole folder or recently completed materials in it can be sent home periodically for parents to see. This practice gives the parents a chance to praise their children for the work they are doing. Seeing the completed work and other materials in the folder also can make parents stronger supporters of a reading program.

3. Though most of the important information about each student can logically be recorded on one planned form or another, some of it will not fit into the categories represented in these forms. Therefore, it is important that a teacher have a notebook readily available or set of cards for maintaining anecdotal records. The easiest way to keep anecdotal information organized is probably to use a notebook. A separate page or set of pages in an inexpensive loose-leaf binder could be

designated for each student. When a student says or does something that should be recorded for possible later reference, the teacher can quickly turn to the student's page, jot down a note, and record the date.

These recorded comments can, for example, be helpful in assessing changes in a student's attitude and work habits. In the absence of formal instruments, anecdotal information is the best basis for assessing effective instruction. Since attitude and behavior changes are often more impressive than test score results, these anecdotal records can be used as evidence. For these reasons, the recorded comments can be used in parent-teacher conferences; in diagnostic conferences with counselors, school psychologists, and other support personnel; and in student-teacher conferences when the teacher wants to point out things a student needs to know about personal performance in class.

4. Some of the types of observations needed in diagnosing reading problems are not efficiently recorded in anecdotal form. Often a more suitable format is a checklist. The list can remind the teacher of the behaviors to observe and can greatly reduce the time for recording pertinent information. Checklists illustrated throughout this text are examples of the types a teacher should have available. It is not necessary to maintain a set of lists on each student. These lists should simply be available so that when a teacher decides to start diagnosing a problem, it will be easy to gather relevant information. For example, the teacher might record dates on these lists to keep track of the times a student exhibits behaviors considered to be of diagnostic significance. For difficult cases, these lists can be studied by a reading specialist or school psychologist. Records of this type can also provide support when difficult decisions have to be made about changes in a student's instructional program.

## Record Keeping in a Basal Centered Program

Most reading instruction is centered around a basal reader, and most current basal programs include record forms and instructions to the teacher on ways of charting student status and progress in reading. The record keeping aids in some basal programs, in fact, constitute complete manage-

## Checklists of Significant Behaviors Related to Reading

Seems to have visual difficulties:

_____ Squints, blinks, frowns, and contorts face in other ways
_____ Holds book close to face
_____ Is tense during visual word
_____ Thrusts head forward
_____ Moves head excessively during reading
_____ Loses place while reading
_____ Rubs eyes
_____ Reports headaches

Seems to have hearing difficulties:
_____ Asks to have statements repeated
_____ Misunderstands directions
_____ Seems inattentive during discussions and presentations
_____ Turns one ear toward the speaker
_____ Cups a hand behind the ear
_____ Reports earaches
_____ Reports buzzing or ringing in the head
_____ Pronounces words poorly
_____ Has monotonous pitch

Seems to have an oral language deficit:
_____ Phrases improperly during oral reading
_____ Ignores punctuation
_____ Shows improper inflection
_____ Misunderstands simple directions and questions presented clearly
_____ Makes poor use of context clues

Seems to be anxious in oral reading (or silent reading or nonreading) situations:
_____ Has trouble concentrating
_____ Bites nails
_____ Stutters
_____ Is disruptive
_____ Shies away from tasks
_____ Gives up easily
_____ Seeks approval

Seems to have general health problems:
_____ Does not participate actively in sports and other physical activities
_____ Sleeps or seems sleepy in class
_____ Moves sluggishly
_____ Slouches at desk
_____ Reports headaches or dizziness
_____ Is easily distracted
_____ Has poor eating habits
_____ Breathes in a labored manner
_____ Reports stomach aches or nausea
_____ Is irritable at end of day or after exertion
_____ Has poor small muscle coordination

Memory

ment systems. Therefore, most teachers of reading already have record keeping systems provided for them. Since these systems reflect careful thought and planning, it is usually wise for teachers to at least try to use them in the ways intended by the publishers.

Even the most complete basal program does not, however, include every feature of a good record keeping system. Moreover, some of the forms provided in a program and some of the suggestions made in the teacher's manual may not be appropriate for some teaching situations. Teachers should study carefully what is available in the programs they use and should make the changes and additions that will make the record keeping systems appropriate for their instructional objectives and the circumstances in their classrooms.

Two procedures not usually built into basal programs which should be considered by all teachers using basal centered instruction are discussed below.

1. The teacher should keep a notebook that parallels each teacher's manual used. In this notebook the teacher can describe supplementary activities and materials to be used with each lesson suggested in the teacher's manual. After a lesson has been completed, the teacher should record in the notebook comments about how well both the suggested activities and the supplementary ones worked. If there have been problems, the teacher can make notes of changes needed in future activities, either later with the same students or in subsequent years. At the beginning of a school year, the teacher can glance through the notebook from the preceding year and get an idea of the types of changes that should be planned for that year.

This notebook is also a convenient place to list the names of students identified as needing supplementary work in small groups or individually to extend the teaching of skills introduced in a basal lesson. If special assignments are instantaneously formulated and given to certain students, this notebook is a good place to keep that information as well. When such assignments are recorded in one central location, it is easier for the teacher to keep track of them and provide the follow-up discussion and evaluation necessary to make the assignments effective.

2. Another record keeping procedure not often suggested in basal programs is one that involves the use of periodic tests on comprehension of the story read and on vocabulary and sight word knowledge. Tests of this type are usually provided at the end of each level, but rarely are they available at frequent intervals within a level. Testing every day obviously would be unwise, particularly in the lower primary grades. Nevertheless, there are important benefits that can come from the use of written tests once a week or so if the tests are well designed. To be effective, the tests should give the students practice in answering varied types of questions, and they should assess recognition of important sight words and understanding of new vocabulary. The tests should be difficult only for students who should not be placed in material at that level. If the tests are relatively easy, most students will feel good about their performances and can keep a chart of their successes. This charting of progress will help motivate future student effort.

Students whose results on these tests are consistently poor or exceedingly good will need closer assessment for possible shifts to other levels. Of course, informal observations can and should be used in determining which students may be inappropriately placed. However, some students are so quiet and cooperative that a teacher can go for weeks unaware that changes are needed. Written tests of this type can provide the hard evidence that is often needed to supplement the useful but not infallible observations of teachers. The tests themselves or scores from them are, also, records of performance that are much easier to maintain than notes about teacher observations.

## Keeping Records of Skills Development

As has been mentioned, many new basal programs have record forms and other management aids for keeping track of the development of reading skills. In addition, several published skills management systems can be purchased separately. For teachers who want to create their own record keeping systems for skills development, there are helpful guides such as Duffy and Sherman's *Systematic Reading Instruction* (3) and *Focused Reading Instruction* by Otto and others (7). There is something available by which to build or support almost any kind of skills program, no matter how structured or flexible the teacher wants it to be. Among these many possibilities are two basic patterns. Either the teacher can use or adapt a published skills management system, or the teacher can devise a system to meet the needs in his classroom. Which approach a teacher takes, determines the kinds of record keeping tasks that he will face.

1. If a separately published skills management system or a system within a basal program is used, one of the first jobs of the teacher should be to study the system thoroughly and critically. Many of these systems have been field tested, and the obvious problems in record keeping have been worked out. Weaknesses remain, however. In some for instance, there is only one space in the records for indicating mastery of a set of twenty or so initial consonant sounds. If a teacher has to wait until a student has mastered all of those sound-symbol relationships before recording any information, then the records are not an aid in teaching the relationships.

An unfortunate characteristic of many skills management systems is that some complex reading processes are treated as groups of isolated skills in which a student can supposedly demonstrate mastery. Having a management system that reminds a teacher, for example, to ask cause-effect questions is certainly worthwhile. On the other hand, records that indicate a student has mastered cause-effect relationships if he passes an assessment test are at best misleading and could be detrimental when used unquestioningly by teachers. In general, the types of problems that appear to varying extents in the record keeping components of published skills programs involve 1) the absence of detail where it is needed to accurately describe student knowledge and abilities and guide skills instruction, 2) the presence of detail where it does not reflect the indivisibility of some reading processes and misrepresents what can actually be taught and mastered as distinct skills, 3) the absence of provisions for keeping track of skills which the teacher considers important and able to teach, 4) the presence of provisions for keeping track of skills which the teacher considers unimportant or is unable to teach, and 5) the presence of provisions for keeping track of skills which the program claims to test but actually does not.

Of course, even the most knowledgeable scholar of reading processes and of skills instruction does not have the expertise to pass judgment on every feature of available skills management systems. Too little is known about reading and reading instruction. Nevertheless, to avoid needless record keeping, the teacher must go ahead and decide which listed skills to keep track of, which to ignore, and which unlisted skills to add. In making such decisions about the management of instruction in word recognition skills, it helps to be familiar with the content of books like Heilman's *Phonics in Proper Perspective* (6) and Durkin's *Phonics, Linguistics, and Reading* (4). A good reference for vocabulary skills development is *Techniques of Teaching Vocabulary* by Dale, O'Rourke, and Bamman (2). No comparable book exists in the area of comprehension, partly because helping students improve their comprehension abilities is not nearly so straightforward a process as teaching word recognition and vocabulary skills. As a result of the complexity of comprehension processes, there is considerable disagreement among professionals in reading about what should be done in this area of instruction. Few would dispute the importance of asking varied questions, such as the types described in Barrett's Taxonomy of Reading Comprehension (8). In other respects, however, the views of reading educators about comprehension differ substantially in both theoretical assumptions and instructional recommendations. Therefore, the teacher must read widely to get a comprehensive view of possible approaches to use in this area. The final decisions about what comprehension skills or abilities to keep track of should reflect both this wide reading in professional literature and a thorough awareness of the types of reading tasks that students face in school and others that they will have to deal with as adults.

Assuming the teacher has adapted the published management system to personal views and classroom needs, then the next major job is to use the tailored record keeping components in the most efficient ways possible. Few specific suggestions apply for all such systems. Rather, the teacher should study carefully the record keeping procedures described in the program manual and should examine the forms supplied with the system. Then the teacher should try to envision how those procedures and forms will fit into the established instructional and management routines and should formulate new routines that will avoid duplication of effort and allow the teacher to spend as much time as possible actually working with students in instructional activities. In other words, paraprofessional, parent, and student aides should be used whenever possible to grade assessment tests and record results. When looking over those results in order to plan instruction, the teacher should doublecheck at least part of the work of the aides and give them feedback about the quality of their efforts. Where aides are not available, the teacher is likely to find that periodic updates of records during planning periods or after school are necessary. If this approach is used, it is important that the teacher keep together the test sheets and other student work from which information to be recorded is taken.

Since many of the procedures for maintaining records are basically mechanical, it can often be helpful to ask someone unfamiliar with existing classroom routines to come in and observe or study the procedures that are used. A fresh perspective, particularly if it is from someone who is regularly concerned about the efficiency of operations, can often reveal duplications of effort, needlessly cumbersome procedures, and practices that do not do what is intended. Suggestions from such an outsider can lead to changes that free the teacher for greater attention to tasks that are best performed by a perceptive, creative educator of children.

Even after a skills management program has been well adapted to a specific classroom, there is the continuing need to make students aware of their progress. Most students respond well to posted charts that let them see when they have mastered a skill. Transferring information from teacher records to such a chart takes time but can be worth the effort, particularly if the teacher is selective in what is posted. Too much detail in skills listings can make this charting of progress cumbersome, but not enough results are shown in charts that record changes in status only every month or so. For students who can be expected to make slow progress with skills posted, it is even possible to have separate charts which reflect the number of lessons or activities completed, rather than the number of skills mastered.

2. Many of the suggestions made regarding published skills management systems also apply to skills programs organized by the teacher. Nevertheless, there are special tasks that a teacher must face who decides to create a system for keeping track of the reading skills mastered or not yet learned by students.

One of the first jobs is to devise a useful skills listing. Even if the basal series in use does not have a comprehensive skills management system, it probably has a scope and sequence chart of skills taught in the program which can serve as the foundation for the skills listing. Items from the Barbe Reading Skills Check List (1) might be added, as could skills from published systems such as the Fountain Valley Teacher Support System. In any case, the listing should reflect what the teacher has the assessment instruments to test and the materials and activities to teach. This listing should then be the guide for devising the forms and checklists that the teacher will use for record keeping and prescriptive planning.

One type of record that a teacher should consider maintaining is an individual skills profile. This form should list the skills or groups of skills which can actually be mastered permanently. For example, most students can truly learn the sound-symbol relationships of the initial consonants, consonant blends, and consonant digraphs. Therefore, it is reasonable to have a space on a skills profile to indicate mastery of the initial consonant sounds, a space for two-letter blends, one for three-letter blends, and one for the consonant digraphs. With younger students, the same is true about knowledge of letter names. If the teacher is trying to keep track of sight word knowledge, information about basic words mastered can also be maintained on the form. One convenient way to do this would be to group the words according to the basal reader level in which they are first introduced. There could be a space for first level words, one for second level words, one for third level words, and so on. If the basal series in use does not have a good listing of words taught at each level, then the Harris-Jacobson list (5) or a similar core vocabulary listing could be divided and used for keeping records of sight word learning. The teacher might want to keep track of knowledge of word families, as well, since knowing two or three words in a family usually means that the student can identify the other ones in that family by initial sound substitution. As with sight words, it would be convenient to divide these word families into groups based upon the order in which they are introduced in the basal series or in the supplementary word recognition program in which they are taught. Then a space should be provided on the skills profile for each of those groups of word families. Another bit of knowledge that can be learned permanently is the short and long sounds of vowels. A space could be included on the form for the set of short vowel sounds and one for the set of long sounds. Related to this knowledge are the single vowel, closed syllable principle, and the final silent *e* rule. If students know the vowel sounds, they can usually master these phonics principles and apply them successfully in identifying one-syllable words in actual reading. Some other skills that can probably be mastered involve the inflectional endings. Therefore, a space could be provided for each of them on the form. A portion of a sample individual skills profile is shown.

## Individual Skills Profile
(Enter date when skill group is mastered.)

Knows the sound-symbol relationships of the following groups of letters and letter clusters:

| | | | |
|---|---|---|---|
| Initial Consonants | _____ | Final Consonants | _____ |
| Initial Consonant Blends | _____ | Final Consonant Blends | _____ |
| Initial Consonant Digraphs | _____ | Final Consonant Digraphs | _____ |

Recognizes the following groups of words:

| | | |
|---|---|---|
| Level 1 Words _____ | Level 5 Words _____ | Level  9 Words _____ |
| Level 2 Words _____ | Level 6 Words _____ | Level 10 Words _____ |
| Level 3 Words _____ | Level 7 Words _____ | Level 11 Words _____ |
| Level 4 Words _____ | Level 8 Words _____ | Level 12 Words _____ |

Uses initial sound substitution with the following groups of word families:

| | | |
|---|---|---|
| Group 1 _____ | Group 4 _____ | Group 7 _____ |
| Group 2 _____ | Group 5 _____ | Group 8 _____ |
| Group 3 _____ | Group 6 _____ | Group 9 _____ |

Many other skills listed on scope and sequence charts and on published skills checklists, however, are not truly mastered by most students. Some of those skills are rarely used in reading and, therefore, are learned slowly. Others are based on principles that are not consistently applicable, and, as a result, the skills are not reinforced by actual reading. A disconcertingly large number are not truly distinct, unitary skills; rather, they are each a group of abilities or bits of knowledge that are not usually learned together. For example, the ability to identify words which have been formed by combining two or more smaller words is not truly a single skill of recognizing compound words. The most important step in recognizing a compound word is knowing the words that compose it. Therefore, it is of no practical value and may even be misleading to record that a student has mastered the skill of recognizing compound words. For similar reasons, most comprehension skills should be left off of this individual skills profile. Whether, for example, a student demonstrates the ability to recall a sequence of events in a story depends on a complex combination of abilities and bits of knowledge, including the ability to recognize certain key words, knowledge of the meanings of those words, and the presence of background knowledge and experiences to draw upon or to relate to the story. Recalling a sequence of events in a story, as well as most other comprehension skills, is simply not a distinct, unitary skill that can be mastered. Therefore, this record form should not even allow the teacher to hint that those skills have been learned on a long term basis.

If the individual skills profile is constructed in the manner suggested, it can be referred to with confidence that it reflects abilities and knowledge that the student actually possesses. Therefore, within a school or district, it could be standardized and passed from one teacher to another as part of a student's permanent records.

Another type of form that the teacher should maintain is a detailed class record of skills that are currently being taught and that can actually be mastered. This form can be called the *class record of skills mastery*. For example, with first graders one record might list the names of all students in the class down the side and the initial consonants across the top. A plus mark can be put in the appropriate space when a student demonstrates competence in a certain sound-symbol relationship. With a student who has trouble, a minus mark should be put in the space for the consonant if it is not learned when it is first introduced. Additional minuses can be used when students fail on subsequent assessments. When the relationship is eventually mastered, the minus can be changed to a plus. By looking at the pluses and minuses in the columns of interest, the teacher can use the class record in identifying students who need to be grouped together for supplementary skills instruction. Similar records could be prepared for consonant blends, consonant digraphs, and vowel sounds. Some teachers might even want to keep detailed records on knowledge of common word families. In general, this type of record should be maintained for the types of skills described earlier that can actually be mastered. When a student, for example, has learned all of the two-letter consonant blends, the space for them on the individual skills profile can be checked off. A portion of a sample class record of skills mastery is shown.

This type of record can also be posted as a progress chart. For example, with one group of first graders, a chart can be prepared to show mastery of the initial consonants. If this is done, only the plus for mastery should be used. The minus indicating a problem area should be marked only on the teacher's record. Depending on what students are working on and what they are learning reasonably well, other charts could be posted to let them see the results of their efforts.

A third type of skills record form that a teacher should maintain can be called the *class record of skill weaknesses*. This record deals with skills that should be taught and practiced but that are never truly mastered. Virtually all of the comprehension skills are of this nature. In addition, most oral reading skills are not learned once and for all. Rather, the quality of a student's oral reading depends on the difficulty of the vocabulary and syntax in the material being read. To an extent, the student has to comprehend the material in order to demonstrate appropriate phrasing and intonation. Therefore, it is senseless to maintain records which can imply that certain oral reading skills have been mastered. The use of context clues is another skill of this nature. It is never mastered. A student can develop the habit of studying the context in which an unrecognized word appears in order to figure out what the word or its meaning may be. The student, however, has not mastered the use of context clues.

For skills such as these, a different type of form is

## Class Record of Skills Mastery

(A plus indicates mastery. Each minus indicates a failure to demonstrate mastery.)

| Student | Verbs | | | | | | | Nouns | | | | | Modifiers | | | | | | |
|---|---|---|---|---|---|---|---|---|---|---|---|---|---|---|---|---|---|---|---|
| | ed | ied | d | ing | s | es | ies | s | es | ies | er | is | er | ier | est | iest | y | ly | ily |
| Mary C. | + | + | + | + | + | + | + | + | + | + | + | | + | | + | | | | |
| Jose R. | + | + | − | + | + | + | + | + | + | + | − | | + | | + | | | | |
| Jerry W. | # | = | − | + | + | + | − | + | − | − | − | | − | | − | | | | |
| Audrey F. | # | = | + | + | + | − | − | + | − | − | − | | − | | − | | | | |
| Frank S. | + | # | + | + | + | + | − | + | + | − | − | | − | | + | | | | |
| Phil W. | # | = | − | − | − | − | − | + | − | + | − | | − | | − | | | | |
| Marie H. | + | + | + | + | + | + | + | + | + | + | + | | + | | + | | | | |
| Denise D. | = | − | − | − | + | − | | + | − | | | | | | | | | | |
| Helen B. | = | − | − | − | − | − | | = | − | | | | | | | | | | |

needed. It should be designed so that the teacher can record several instances of failure or success in demonstrating a certain skill. For example, the teacher should have a class record that lists the names of the students down the side and the most important types of comprehension questions across the top. The spaces on this record should be large enough for several marks. If a student, for example, misses a main idea question in a directed reading lesson, the teacher should put a minus in that space. If the student later misses another main idea question in a supplementary comprehension exercise, another minus should be recorded. On the other hand, if the student later gets a main idea question right, perhaps on a written check list, then a vertical mark should be put in the space. The teacher should continue recording this information until a decision has been reached about whether there should be a special emphasis on main idea questions for that student. A shift toward vertical marks lets the teacher know, for example, that the student is probably beginning to read effectively for the main idea and does not need extra work in that area.

A similar record can be maintained for use of context clues, for recognition of compound words composed of known small words, for use of prefix and word root knowledge when analyzing unfamiliar words, and for other skills that can and should become habits but are never truly mastered. It is even helpful to have a place to keep a record of the actual use of known phonics elements, such as initial consonants, consonant blends, and consonant digraphs, when analyzing unrecognized words. Some students may have knowledge of this type but not use it in actual reading. When keeping track of this information, the teacher may want to use a separate space on the form for each sound-symbol relationship. Part of a sample class record of skill weaknesses is shown.

## Record Keeping for Language Experience Activities

A good reading program will certainly include much more than managed skills instruction. In the lower primary grades and with poor readers in upper grades, a teacher is likely to use language experience activities as one supplemen-

## Class Record of Skill Weaknesses

(Each horizontal mark represents an instance of failure to use a skill or group of subskills that are assumed to be known by the student. Vertical marks indicate evidence that the student is beginning to use a skill successfully.)

| Student | Initial Consonants | Initial Clusters | Final Consonants | Final Clusters | Syntactic Context | Semantic Context | Inflectional Endings | Compound Words | Word Families |
|---|---|---|---|---|---|---|---|---|---|
| Maurice F. | | | | | | | ⦀⦀ (5) | | |
| Anna P. | | | | | | | | ⦀⦀ (5) | |
| Ernestine S. | | | | | | | | | ⦀⦀ (5) |
| Fred R. | ‖ | ‖‖‖‖‖ | ‖‖‖‖‖ | | | | | | |
| Nan T. | | | | | | | | | |

| Name | | | | | | | | |
|---|---|---|---|---|---|---|---|---|
| Joe L. | ‖ | ∣ | | | ▦ | | | |
| Marcia T. | | | ‖‖ | ‖‖‖‖‖ | | | | |
| Sheila F. | | | | | | | | |
| Tommy W. | ‖ | ‖‖ | ‖‖‖ | | | | | |

Key to skill headings

1. Fails to use initial consonant clues
2. Fails to use initial consonant cluster clues
3. Fails to use final consonant clues
4. Fails to use final consonant cluster clues
5. Substitutes words that do not fit the syntactic context
6. Substitutes words that do not fit the semantic context
7. Fails to recognize known words with inflectional endings
8. Fails to recognize compounds composed of known words
9. Fails to recognize members of known word families

tary technique. This approach can be so effective that even a poorly organized use of it can produce dramatic improvements in interest, in self-confidence, and in overall reading achievement. To get maximum results from language experience activities, however, a teacher needs a system for keeping track of the efforts of students. There are two record keeping procedures that are particularly well suited for this instructional approach.

1. The teacher should have each student keep a notebook of stories dictated or written. Such a notebook provides evidence to the student that he is making progress because of improvements in the stories. Particularly with younger students there can be obvious increases in the maturity level of the vocabulary and sentence patterns used. If the stories have been dictated, students can make copies directly from the teacher-written versions and can see improvements in their printing or writing as well.

The teacher-written version of a dictated story can also be used to keep track of the words the student knows. The student can underline the familiar words in the story. Seeing the number of underlined words increase is motivating. Even after stories have been placed in the notebook, they can continue to help the student in mastering unrecognized words. These stories will provide known context by which the student can isolate unfamiliar words.

2. Another way of using language experience activities for sight word improvement is by having each student keep a word bank, usually in the form of a card file. On one side of each card is a word, and on the other may be a picture illustrating the word, the definition or definitions, or simple sentences which are examples of how the word is often used. By alphabetizing a word bank, a student gets practice in spelling and alphabetizing.

More importantly, such a file is a good way to keep track of words that a student knows in stories the student has dictated. When a word is mastered, the student moves it to a special part of the file. Seeing the known words increase in number motivates most students. As an additional incentive, the teacher can put a star on the card file for every ten words that a student has studied and mastered. For instructional purposes the mastered words can be used by the teacher to illustrate phonics principles and other clues to word recognition.

The words that have not yet been learned are usually kept in the front of the word bank. They are in a convenient place for the student to study them, and the teacher can check through them to see which words need to be emphasized in other activities. By using word banks in conjunction with language experience activities, the teacher can concentrate efforts on words that students use in their own speech and, therefore, ones that students are likely to consider important and are likely to learn quickly.

## Record Keeping for Individualized Reading

Another approach to reading improvement that can be built into almost any instructional program is individualized reading. As at least a part of a reading program, a teacher can emphasize the self-selection of books and other materials and can stress wide reading to build vocabulary, broaden interests, and practice skills introduced in other elements of the program. In other words, a teacher can create an atmosphere that encourages independent reading and still not practice in all details every suggestion offered in the books and articles which originally popularized individualized reading.

If some form of individualized reading is used, part of the structure that can characterize basal centered instruction or skills management programs can be lost. For many students this change can lead to increased interest in reading and to more rapid improvement in word recognition and comprehension. With other students, however, the decreased structure can become detrimental. To maintain some of the monitoring that is possible in more structured programs, a teacher using individualized reading should plan a record keeping system to keep track of what students are doing and learning. Two types of records can help a teacher.

1. The teacher should have the students themselves keep records on their own reading. Among these records should be a list of the titles of books each student has read. The topic of each book should be recorded to give a profile of the student's interests. Most students enjoy seeing a list of book titles grow,

and many are even motivated to read more than they would otherwise in order to see it grow. Of course, the teacher should emphasize the fun of reading and what can be learned from books and should not let list building become an end in itself. However, the motivational effects of such lists and the information about student interests that can be gained from them make this procedure one worth trying.

Another type of record that students can keep is their impressions of books they have read. A student feeling strongly about a book should complete a card with the title, the author, and any comments that might guide other students who are considering reading the book. These cards should be filed by author name for easy reference by students deciding what they will read next. It would be worthwhile to keep these cards from one year to the next since young students often respect the views of their older friends and might be convinced by comments recorded in earlier years.

Particularly with less able readers, another helpful type of record is a list of unfamiliar words encountered. This list can be in the form of a looseleaf notebook with a sheet for each letter of the alphabet, or it can be a card file maintained like a word bank. Along with each word should be the sentence context in which it was found and the definition. By checking off each word mastered, a student can see evidence of progress. Words found by students and listed for further study can then be selected by the teacher to illustrate the use of structural analysis and other clues to pronunciation and word meaning.

2. If students spend a considerable part of class time reading independently, the teacher will probably decide to have occasional conferences with individual students to discuss what they have read. For these conferences to be effective, it is important that the teacher maintain several types of records.

The teacher should have a separate notebook for use in these conferences, or the one for anecdotal records can include a special page for each student for this purpose. When the teacher meets with a student, the title of the book being discussed, the author, and the pages read should be recorded so that the teacher can be aware of what each student is reading.

Having this information available enables the teacher later to ask motivating questions, make knowledgeable comments, and in other ways let the students know of teacher interest in their reading. Comments by the student during a conference should also be recorded as evidence of interests and attitudes toward the book being discussed and toward reading in general. This type of information can be helpful in guiding students to books they might enjoy and in planning instructional activities.

Another part of an individual conference is likely to be oral reading. This is a good time for the teacher to identify basic sight words with which a student is having trouble. Important words that the student misses during oral reading can be recorded so that follow-up activities can be planned to provide help. If a student has a special problem with, for instance, essential function words, the teacher should file a prime frequency list, such as the A&P list (7) or a basal vocabulary list, to keep track of the words missed by the student and the ones studied and mastered. To do this, the teacher could put a minus beside each word mispronounced or substituted for in oral reading. Supplementary activities should be planned to help the student learn these words. Then when a word is mastered, the minus could be changed to a plus. The teacher could purposely keep the number of words marked with a minus at an appropriately low level to avoid discouraging the student. As minuses are changed to pluses, the teacher can point out other target words for study and still keep the student primarily impressed with what is being learned and not with the number of words that are still not known. The oral reading done during these conferences is also a good time for the teacher to record observations about the use of word recognition skills on the class records of skill weaknesses discussed earlier.

From questions following the oral reading, the teacher should note problems in comprehension. These observations can be recorded in the notebook or can be tallied on the class record of comprehension skill weaknesses. A pattern of problems observed over time can serve as the basis for making special assignments. If supplementary activities or materials are assigned, the teacher should make a record of these in the notebook so that there can be follow-up discussion and evaluation of what the student has done.

## Record Keeping for Learning Centers

Regardless of the overall approach to reading instruction that a teacher chooses, there are always opportunities to use learning centers. The chance for students to work independently at their own pace can make centers popular, particularly if they contain materials at a range of difficulty levels. In some classrooms containing a wide variety of centers, it sometimes even appears that the teacher does not have to do much of anything. Despite this appearance, careful planning and record keeping are essential in order for centers to be effective instructionally. Most of the records can be maintained by the students, but this practice will work well only if the teacher has organized the centers well and keeps some records, too.

1. One form that the teacher should prepare and then have the students maintain individually is a record of centers completed. This form should list all available centers and should have a "Date Started" column and a "Date Completed" column. It should also contain columns for recording results of any check tests used at the centers and space for comments by the students about centers completed. Each student's folder should contain a copy of this form to keep track of what has been done and to see the resulting efforts.

The comments that students make on their individual record forms will give the teacher information about how the centers might be changed to work better in the future. However, some students may be afraid to put critical comments on their own forms. Therefore, it is a good idea to keep an evaluation form available at each center for students to complete anonymously if they choose.

If the reading program in a classroom includes extensive use of centers, it is important to have an "In Use" chart. There should be a block or a hook on the chart for each available center. Before students start to work, they put their name tags in the block or on the hook for the center where they will be. This policy helps the teacher keep track of where the students are working and what centers are open for use.

It is also helpful to have a class list posted at each center. As students complete the work at the center, they can write the date when they complete the center and make comments. From these lists, the teacher can know immediately when the activities at a center have been completed by all students and, therefore, when it is time to put out different activities.

2. To coordinate student use of the centers it is helpful for the teacher to have a master listing with the names of all students in the class down the side and with all centers across the top. A code can be used to show successful completion, unsuccessful completion with a need for additional work, and successful completion of that additional work. This information can be compiled from the individual record forms maintained by the students. Of course, if students do not keep these records well, the teacher may have to get this information directly by checking tests completed by the students at the centers.

## Record Keeping for Independent Learning

Most of the instructional activities and related record keeping procedures discussed so far require considerable teacher involvement. Of course, learning centers are intended to allow students to work independently, but they are most often used simply to supplement basal programs and other teacher centered instructional approaches. It is possible, though, to structure major components of a reading program so that students can work independently on tasks designed to meet their individual needs. Successful use of independent learning does not just happen, however. The more individualization a teacher attempts, the more complex is the job of record keeping. At least three major approaches are now being used to meet individual needs through independent learning. The descriptions of these approaches that follow will be based on the assumption that individual students are working alone, but it is possible to adapt the first two approaches for use with small groups of students who have similar needs.

1. In one approach to independent learning, each student is given a separate activity schedule each day. This approach necessitates careful planning by the teacher but has advantages which many teachers feel outweigh the demands

placed on their time. Receiving an individual schedule is likely to heighten the student's feeling of worth and sense of responsibility, particularly if the schedules are written to include the personal feeling that general plans and skills management devices usually lack.

To be efficient, individual schedules should simply direct students to learning centers, kits, and other independent activities to avoid scheduling conflicts. The centers and kits themselves should have the detailed directions and provisions for record keeping. To get feedback about the appropriateness of the scheduling, the teacher should encourage students to jot down comments about such concerns as the amount of time allotted for each activity and the variety or monotony in the work done. The schedules should be saved long enough for the teacher to read these comments and make appropriate adjustments in future schedules.

When individual schedules are used, the teacher also needs to maintain a master schedule with information condensed from the individual schedules. This master schedule enables the teacher to know at a glance what each student is supposed to be doing. It is possible to use a weekly rotation scheme or some other systematic procedure for keeping track of what each individual is to do each day. However, if there is an emphasis on diagnosis and prescription, such standardized schemes for scheduling are not appropriate. Instead, the teacher needs to keep a file of completed master schedules to refer to as new individual schedules are being made up. On the master schedules the teacher should also record observations about the appropriateness of the scheduling. Some of these observations will be based on comments the students have made on their individual schedules. Others will come from observing how well the students work on the assigned activities and how organized is the movement of students from one activity to another. The master schedule should also be used for keeping track of students who need to repeat or continue activities assigned but not completed satisfactorily.

2. Rather than tell a student what to do each day, it is possible to let the students do their own scheduling within a standard weekly plan formulated by the teacher. This approach is suitable for comprehension improvement, vocabu-

lary development, and other types of learning which do not require sequential instruction. When this approach is used, work on word recognition skills can either be organized separately or the student can be allowed to decide when to fit skills work into the schedule. The teacher has to insure that the appropriate sequence of skills activities is followed.

In this approach to independent learning, each student is given a listing of the recommended or required minimal number of lessons or activities to be completed in each type of material each week. Within these guidelines, the student should be allowed to decide which material to use during any certain period.

For this approach to work effectively, each student needs a copy of a standard record form and a list of names and abbreviations of all available kits, supplementary series, and other materials designed for improvement of comprehension and vocabulary. This form should include spaces for the student to record the abbreviation of the material used, the lesson or pages completed, the results of any test involved, the date completed, and comments about the activity.

The minimal number of lessons or activities to be completed in each type of material each week can be included as part of the record form, and the form can become a contract by which the student and the teacher signify what they can expect from each other.

There are at least two potential problems in an approach such as this which requires the students to take the initiative in deciding what they will do at any certain time and keep records of their work. There are ways to minimize these problems, however.

One of these problems can result when a teacher tries to introduce a lot of new materials and activities at the same time that the new management approach is being started. This procedure often results in mass confusion with students trying to figure out how to use the materials and activities while they are also learning how to keep track of what they are doing. To increase the chance that the students will do a good job of record keeping, the teacher should make certain that they have been well instructed in use of the materials and activities before they are put on their own as independent learners; that is, activities which have been well integrated into classroom routines should be the first activities transferred into plans for independent learning. Then unfamiliar materials and activities can be introduced gradually.

Another potential problem is that the routine of doing lessons and recording results may soon become monotonous or unmotivating. Of course, the best way to prevent this condition is to use interesting materials at the appropriate difficulty levels and to have other types of instructional activities, including group activities, built into the reading program. These intrinsically motivating qualities of instruction can fail, however. For that reason, progress charts are often a helpful feature of approaches to independent learning. For example, with young students a chart might list the names of all students in a class down the side and, across the top, the various types of materials included on the standard record form. As students complete a specified number of lessons or activities in a type of material during a one week period, they get a star in the column for that material. To be effective, the minimal level for success should be low enough to not penalize students for being slow readers but high enough to avoid rewarding less than acceptable effort. These stars can be evidence to the student that his hard work is not going unnoticed. For older children, posters displaying the quantity of student work might not be motivating. Instead, students might have personal charts. Then the teacher should make a point of examining the student record forms at least once a week and filling in the charts to let the students know that their efforts are recognized and appreciated.

3. When levels of performance rather than quantity of work completed are the concern, then standard weekly plans are not suitable. For example, with the learning of word recognition skills, the varied patterns of strengths and weaknesses and different learning rates of students make it inefficient to assign the same activities to everyone. The same objectives might apply for all students, but how they reach those objectives and how long it takes can vary. Tasks for the teacher include identifying the desired objectives, planning several means by which students might attain them, and devising ways to know when those objectives have been

reached. One of the best approaches for accomplishing these tasks within the framework of independent learning is through use of contracts. In addition to work on word recognition skills, contracts can be used to motivate the learning of sight words and to organize independent study on extended topics.

The first step in using contracts is for the teacher and the student to settle on certain objectives. They may involve mastery of several related skills or mastery of a specified number of sight words. The student is then given several activities to carry out in order to accomplish the objectives. The activities can be teacher prepared; they can be part of a skills management program, or they can be in basal or supplementary workbooks. When the student has completed several of the activities and feels ready, efforts are evaluated. By this evaluation the teacher determines whether the student has attained mastery or whether additional work related to the objectives is needed.

The contract should include the name of the student, the date of the agreement, the objectives of the contract, methods and materials that can be used, means of demonstrating accomplishment of the objectives, the contracted date of completion, signatures of the student and the teacher, and spaces for comments by the student and the teacher after the contract is completed. In addition, the student should have a way to indicate which activities or materials were used in accomplishing the objectives.

The teacher should have a running record of pretests, contracts, and posttests. Therefore, two copies should be made of each individualized contract. In addition, a master form can be kept on each student to record the abbreviated title of each contract used, the contracted date of completion, the pretest and materials chosen. This information is needed in deciding whether to adjust the time periods for future contracts. Also, this information helps the teacher know which activities and materials students like and which work well.

If contracts are used extensively in a classroom, the teacher may not have time to prepare a lot of individualized forms. In this situation several standard contracts with time periods left open can be kept on file. Only one copy needs to be completed when these standard contracts are used. The student would keep this copy. The information that the teacher needs to keep track of can be recorded on the master record form for later reference.

With younger students the teacher might consider putting a star on completed contracts as an acknowledgment of good work. Even with older classes it can be effective to let students display fulfilled contracts on bulletin boards. The greatest impact for the students, however, is likely to come from knowing that they have agreed to do something and have honored that agreement.

## Record Keeping with Assessment Activities

Since tests are formalized information gathering instruments, it is easy to assume that they will do the rest of the work if the teacher only administers them, scores them, and reports the results. Of course, that is not true. A lot can be done with tests and other assessment devices that goes well beyond the formalized procedures for obtaining scores.

1. One part of making full use of assessment activities involves the interpretation of test results. When standardized test scores are received, the teacher should jot down on the forms any remediation or instruction that the results suggest. Insights into the meanings and implications of score patterns do not come easily. When they occur, they should be recorded carefully so that they can be referred to later when needed. The same applies to thoughts about results from teacher made tests. Before filing or discarding score profiles and tests, the teacher should incorporate thoughts about interpretation and prescription into individual and group plans for instruction. For example, information about problems can be recorded on the class records of skill weaknesses.

2. From assessment activities it is also possible to get important information that is not conveyed by scores themselves. When standardized or teacher made tests are administered in the classroom, the teacher should record observations about the behavior of the students. It helps to note signs of anxiety, pleasure, frustration, and other reactions to tests. The teacher should also take note of unusual approaches that students take in completing tests and other assessment tasks.

How a student does something is often as important as the answers he gets and the responses he gives. Significant observations can be recorded in the notebook of anecdotal records or on a special checklist of behaviors similar to those described earlier.

## References

1. Barbe, Walter, and Jerry Abbott. *Personalized Reading Instruction: New Techniques that Increase Reading Skill and Comprehension.* West Nyack, New York: Parker, 1975.
2. Dale, Edgar, Joseph O'Rourke, and Henry Bamman. *Techniques of Teaching Vocabulary.* Reading, Massachusetts: Addison-Wesley.
3. Duffy, Gerald, and George Sherman. *Systematic Reading Instruction.* New York: Harper and Row, 1977.
4. Durkin, Dolores. *Phonics, Linguistics, and Reading.* New York: Teachers College Press, Columbia University, 1972.
5. Harris, Albert, and Milton Jacobson. *Basic Elementary Reading Vocabularies.* New York: Macmillan, 1972.
6. Heilman, Arthur. *Phonics in Proper Perspective.* Columbus, Ohio: Charles E. Merrill, 1976.
7. Otto, Wayne, et al. *Focused Reading Instruction.* Reading, Massachusetts: Addison-Wesley, 1974.
8. Smith, Richard, and Thomas Barrett. *Teaching Reading in the Middle Grades.* Reading, Massachusetts: Addison-Wesley, 1976.
9. Wirt, John. "Implementing Diagnostic-Prescriptive Reading Innovations." *Teachers College Record,* 77 (February 1976), 352-365.

O'Donnell and Moore explore the issues that frequently interfere with the implementation of an effectively organized classroom and bring to this discussion their background of experience in the development and implementation of goals and programs designed to articulate national reading literacy goals.

## Chapter Nine  Eliminating Common Stumbling Blocks to Organizational Change

Michael P. O'Donnell
*University of Southern Maine*

Beth Moore
*Southern Methodist University*

There are many forces for educational change. Initiation for change may come from teachers who are dissatisfied with existing approaches and materials for teaching reading. Another incentive for change is administrative. Many superintendents and principals attend conferences and workshops in which current practices are questioned in view of the development of newer and supposedly more effective approaches. When standardized test scores highlight and suggest a general lack of reading accomplishment in the schools, pressure to do something about it comes from the community and parents. How can the administrator or teacher who is genuinely concerned with change succeed? What are the most propitious strategies, and how can obstacles to change be removed or diminished?

The obstacles which confront the innovative educator seeking to design and institute organizational changes are not unique to certain staffs, to school districts, or to particular geographical regions. Nor are they implicit or explicit in any one organizational or grouping plan. They represent common expressions of concern which may be real or imagined, justifiable in terms of local resistance to change, or merely excuses for inaction. These stumbling blocks can be encountered at virtually any professional level. In every instance, however, they tend to stimulate negative attitudes and create a climate that makes objective self-introspection, an essential ingredient for fostering educational progress, difficult if not impossible to achieve.

There are no uniform approaches for change which can be applied to most situations. Innovation can be fostered, however, with an awareness of the influences which regulate change and with knowledge of some basic theoretical and practical principles regarding the nature of individual differences. The writers surveyed literally thousands of teachers in an attempt to identify typical stumbling blocks to organizational change. The reader is cautioned that these surveys were nonscientific and included schools located mostly in the Southwest and Northeast. However, striking similarities were apparent in regard to the obstacles to organizational change. The responses were placed in seven categories: 1) administration, 2) parents, 3) community, 4) resources, 5) assessment and evaluation, 6) willingness to change, and 7) the problem of working with large numbers of students. Perhaps the most pervasive and obvious stumbling block was the self-fulfilling prophecy: "But our school just doesn't have the staff or resources to do it; therefore, I can't do it."

Traditionally, educators attempt to deal with problems by seeking relevant information. Specifically, what help can potential innovative educators obtain from a survey of the literature and research relating to classroom organization? A serious search will reveal striking inconsistencies and disparate recommendations for altering organizational schemes, often without documentable evidence regarding the effectiveness of specific plans. Many articles on classroom organization are simply personal exhortations by writers on "what should be." The suggestions and even the topics covered are as diverse as the target populations that they purport to serve. The current literature provides the reader with blueprints which may have been successful in one situation; however, they are not exportable because they require unique staffing patterns and special resources. Realizing these problems, it is still possible to evolve some generic principles which are workable in most instances.

Common stumbling blocks to organizational change can be classified and analyzed according to two major categories: *institutional* and *instructional*. Although some overlap is unavoidable, institutional conditions usually include administrative backing, administrative leadership, resources which are available or which may be reliably anticipated, and the support from the community. Instructional conditions are managed primarily by teachers and nonadministrative staff and are involved directly with services for the clients of the school. The instructional dimension of change includes factors such as the readiness level of the staff, an awareness of the need to provide more adequately for individual differences, and a commitment to change as a vehicle for improving the quality and the level of existing services. This chapter is organized around these topics and provides an integration of both theoretical and practical considerations.

## Institutional

*Administrative.* Change must be perceived as a process which occurs within the organizational structure of the school. O'Donnell (*11*) investigated internal conditions which contributed to change in nine highly innovative projects identified by state departments of education in New England schools. Contrary to what may be popularly thought, an absolute requisite for change in all instances was the involvement and unaltering support of the building principal. Although many administrators were not familiar with the precise operational details of the project, they all verbalized total support and commitment for the enterprise. Other studies have reported similar conclusions.

Optimally, change in organization should proceed with enlightened and progressive administrative support. Organizational change can be accomplished by recognizing that principals do have a genuine concern for students and an extreme sensitivity to public reaction. Despite some feelings to the contrary, most administrators are managers who have high regard for the harmonious orchestration of every aspect of the school operation. Precipitous action, without involvement and consultation, can suppress even the most worthy innovation. Change is most likely to occur in school situations where channels of communication are established and utilized, where the roles of teachers are defined, and when collective involvement in decision making is solicited. The administrator must be involved from the beginning as a franchised member of the conceptual planning and process.

Unfortunately educators may perceive themselves as islands within the school structure, often with exaggerated feelings about having to deal with unsympathetic and hostile forces. A genuine willingness to involve others and to become involved fosters change and creates acceptable levels of risk taking for both change agents and administrators. Managing the changing process requires skill in human relations and utilizing these interactions positively. Administrators can become effective allies and vocal advocates of change. They want to identify with an enterprise which promises better quality education. The change agents offer the principal or reading consultant an opportunity to get involved in a good thing. Everyone, including students, can benefit from this collaboration.

The involvement of administrators in systematic program planning has become a major concern of many professional organizations and funding sources. For example, the *National Right to Read Effort* has committed itself to viable staff development programs as the primary strategy for improving the quality of reading instruction. Inherent in this approach is the design and administration of a comprehensive needs assessment instrument and organization of local inservice activities according to precisely focused objectives. So crucial is the administrator's participation in this process that a guide, *The Assessment and Planning Handbook* (15), was developed to direct reading consultants and principals. These methods and techniques for facilitating program planning can be modified by innovators to identify current strengths and weaknesses within the school and evolve acceptable long range implementation plans.

*Community.* Instituting a major organizational change can be a complex and frustrating process. Frustration is particularly evident if the school's constituency, the community, and parents are not informed and involved from the beginning. Research and experience reinforce an obvious conclusion: the successful implementation of educational innovation requires the support of parents. Most schools have devised practical and effective strategies for obtaining community involvement, including: orientation meetings, advisory councils, inviting parents to respond to a needs assessment, enlisting volunteer assistance, organizing community curriculum committees, and launching public relations programs. The closer an activity is to the children, the greater the need for parental involvement.

Parents perceive the school from their own personal experiences. Generally, they expect their children to be exposed to traditional and conventional aspects of instruction, including teacher control, established grouping patterns, competition for grades, recognition of individual achievement, emphasis on the basics, and liberal doses of seatwork to take home. Significant deviations in these expectations usually cause concern and a qualitative judgment of the shcool program. Since the parents' contact with teachers is usually through their children's eyes, parents are susceptible to rumors and hearsay. Students have the ability to interpret and relate school incidents in a perspective which does not entirely conform to the context.

Parental and community support for change resides with the staff. The teacher assumes a vital role in developing and sustaining a positive image of the school and its enterprises within the community. No public relations campaign can counteract the impact of negative comments made about the school by teachers. Unguarded remarks about the principal or the quality of the reading program expressed at a party often find their ways back to the superintendent and board of education in a much more expanded and uncomplimentary context. Teachers underestimate the impact of their personal opinions and the counterproductive nature of criticism. The need for participatory membership in the change process assumes even greater significance for the innovative educator's peers.

Parents and the community, whose ideas and concerns must be examined and addressed before change is proposed, should always be represented on curriculum advisory and schoolwide reading committees. The educator uses this opportunity to relate the program planning process and explain how modifications in the reading program can improve the quality of existing services. These sessions should be carefully planned so that educational jargon is minimized and the major ideas are clear and apparent to everyone. The composition of the committee should be representative of the clientele of the school. Decisions must reflect a consensus of the group and should never be ignored.

Parental involvement should continue concurrently during all phases of the implementation of specific organizational plans. For example, the writers worked in a small college on a project to reorganize the structure and focus of the reading program in the kindergarten. Initially, there was considerable hostility toward the proposal. Parents were invited to attend several orientation sessions and to interact with members of the staff. Reading readiness and initial reading instruction were explained nontechnically and related to the school program. This kind of functional participation continued throughout the adoption cycle. Parents were able to experience a feeling of ownership in the project and testified to the positive change that occurred in the attitudes of their children toward school.

An effective program of parental and community involvement requires good public relations skills. The emphasis must be on establishing an open, nondefensive dialogue, not justifying or selling the position of the school on some particular issue. Periodic opinion surveys can provide a plethora of information which can be used to guide proposals for change. There are virtually no limitations on the kinds of information which can be derived. The innovative educator is able to analyze, anticipate, and address potential sources of opposition long before the intricacies of a new organizational scheme are unveiled. Public reaction is encouraged and developed.

*Resources.* Speculating on resources necessary for effecting organizational change is almost analogous to classifying the designs of a kaleidoscope. The need for resources will vary depending on the nature and magnitude of the enterprise. For example, consideration of an individualized reading program immediately raises questions concerning the availability of a variety of independent reading fare, teacher's skills, and manageable pupil-teacher ratios. Generally, decisions relating to resources include four categories: 1) instructional materials, 2) class size, 3) inservice activities, and 4) financial support.

The principle concern of many educators is obtaining adequate supplies of reading and instructional material. Although the lack of adequate supplies and materials is cited frequently as an obstacle for change, most teachers are able to suggest creative solutions for solving the problem. In many instances, resources can be reallocated. For example, paperback book purchases may be substituted for workbooks. The creative educator can always find a way.

Perhaps no other topic has received more attention or has generated more speculation than what constitutes an appropriate pupil-teacher ratio. The surplus of teachers has led many professional organizations to recommend optimum class sizes. The question of size is viewed simply by schools as a matter of economics. Lower pupil enrollments have been matched in many areas by school closings, consolidations, and teacher transfers. The present public feeling about property taxes makes it unlikely that this situation will be altered. Most innovators will have to operate within the context of already established pupil-teacher ratios.

Most individual schools have no control over budgeting except in situations where federal project monies are available. Absence of additional or supplemental funds is often cited as a stumbling block for change. Pupil expenditures vary widely from community to community. Barbe (1) examined successful implementation of classroom organizational plans in monetary terms. He emphasizes that individualized instruction would be prohibitively expensive if executed in literal terms. The study also cited by O'Donnell (11) reveals that alterations in school organizational plans do not necessarily cause an immediate need for new or additional resources. Many changes can occur and prosper within the structure of an existing organization.

There is little empirical research to support the reduction of class enrollments when reading achievement is used as the primary variable. A study by Greaney and Kelly (5) reported at the annual Reading Association in Dublin, Ireland, gives no justification for small classes. The national pupil-teacher ratio in Ireland is thirty to one. In fact, variations in reading achievement seem to favor students in larger classes, particularly when the interaction effects of verbal ability are analyzed. Most comparative studies do not differentiate the proportion of students failing and achieving in small and large classes. Spitzer (14) reviewed the reading achievement of 5,000 third and sixth graders and concludes that there are no significant differences between students instructed in large and small classes.

How can the innovative teacher plan to manage and accommodate large classes? Obviously, experience dictates that fewer students make it *easier* to provide more individual attention, develop suitable materials, and encourage more involvement in learning activities. The same kinds of opportunities can be offered to students in larger classes if the teacher plans well and schedules time effectively. Successful classroom management depends on a number of competencies. Teachers must be conversant with the reading process, knowledgeable about books and instructional materials, and be able to utilize support systems. Given these abilities, the teacher deals with problems associated with instruction and is not preoccupied with the constraints of class size.

There are many ways to augment the efforts of classroom teachers. Some schools encourage parent volunteers. However, a volunteer program requires careful planning and appropriate assignment. Still others make use of pupil tutors either within the class or from another classroom. Some teachers design independent activities systematically so that self-direction is maximized. An approach which maximizes self-direction requires precise explanation, direction, and an efficient record keeping system. In schools where additional resources are available, teacher aides and assistants may be employed. Implementing any or all of these suggestions depends on a well-developed organizational plan.

Instituting change requires some alteration in the way students are instructed for reading. Retraining in the form of staff development and inservice programs is receiving major emphasis, particularly because of low staff attrition in most school districts. The educator has an array of resources to draw upon for conducting training activities. Perhaps the most available and least expensive consultants are successful practioners and program specialists from the county and state departments of education. Many universities have organized departments especially to provide staff development to local school districts at a modest cost. Regardless of the source, resource persons should be given specific assignments/roles which have evolved from the objectives of the project.

State departments of education may have staff development monies available through reading improvement projects. Many states encourage schools to develop mini training proposals which may include the cost of instruction and materials. Mini training proposals are an appropriate and effective use of limited funds. The writers have worked in many schools which have used small grants ranging from less than $1,000 to $1,500 in order to organize specifically focused staff development workshops which made a difference in the quality of reading instruction. The innovator is well advised to investigate inexpensive resources which are available at the local and state levels.

A significant stumbling block for many innovators is the lack of support materials for conducting inservice training. This problem has been recognized as a major obstacle by professionals responsible for preservice and inservice training. Possible sources for materials include 1) regional service agencies, 2) publishing companies, 3) state departments of education, 4) U.S. Office of Education, 5) local universities, and 6) local school district curriculum services.

## Instructional

Many of the stumbling blocks which have been discussed thus far are only peripherally related to instruction. In this section those aspects of organization which are directly concerned with the services rendered by teachers are examined. These factors have been arranged according to three categories: *Staff*, professional expectations and willingness to accept change; *Program*, soundness, philosophy of the school, and pupil management; and *Preparation*, the competency levels of teachers. These considerations, seldom singly but always collectively, exert tremendous influence on the atmosphere of the school and the quality of reading instruction.

*Staff.* Working out difficulties inherent in any new organizational plan depends upon the willingness of teachers to cooperate. The *Twenty-Seven Cooperative First Grade Studies* (2) clearly demonstrate that teachers' skill in presenting subject matter, their enthusiasm, and their professional commitment make the selection of a particular approach for teaching reading or an organizational design a secondary consideration. Simply stated, an effective teacher can make any approach for teaching reading work. No innovative plan for teaching reading or method for instructing students can succeed unless the staff is professionally and personally committed to change.

Winning the approval and support of the staff begins by involving them. O'Donnell (*11*) discovered that innovative teachers often ignore this important consideration; consequently, the change had little, if any, impact on the total school. Being able to predict the outcome of a particular instructional mode or organizational design is a major source of security. If teachers are not conversant with the proposed change, their suspicion and resistance can be anticipated. Overcoming this potential stumbling block begins by establishing channels of communication which allow the staff to interact nondefensively and to participate in the decision making process. The magnitude of the proposed change will determine how often the staff should be consulted. For example, shifting from a departmentalized reading program to an open concept classroom will require frequent and long term dialogue among all those concerned.

The most insignificant occurrences are usually the most significant in maintaining openness and communication between the staff and the innovator. Disapproval of a proposed practice, expressed even covertly, can undermine the influence of even the most effective human relations effort. Sincere recognition of individual efforts must be dispensed liberally. The staff must be allowed to uncover even the unsatisfactory elements of the program. Communication must be continuous and deliberate. The educator should be an expert in diffusing potentially troublesome situations as well as being a sympathetic listener who can be counted on not to take sides. Human relations skills involve compromise not surrender. The staff's perception of the proposal is crucial for successfully effecting change.

The reward system of the school should be utilized liberally. Honest praise for a significant contribution in the form of a letter with appropriate carbon copies to administrative staff, personal invitations to attend a training program, and/or mention in a newspaper release can boost support and magnify ego involvement in a project. Well-distributed recognition dissipates opposition and allows everyone to experience a feeling of ownership. A deliberate effort should be made to acknowledge the administration and allow them to assume credit for many of the positive aspects of the program. After all, they provided the backing from the beginning. Parity of recognition should not concern the innovative educator; it is the consequence which matters.

*Program.* No other discipline seems to be more susceptible to fads and the prevailing philosophies than reading. Advocacy of approaches and programs often reaches evangelical proportions. The innovator should recognize and avoid these pitfalls. The remnants of ill-conceived educational changes still inhibit progress in many schools. The implications of change must be considered in terms of the orientation and training of the staff, traditional expectations, alterations which will be necessary at preceding and following grade levels, and the community.

A school philosophy should be more than a written exercise to impress the citizenry and satisfy the board of education. It should be the benchmark for all program development and a pivotal point which can be used to align and direct change according to expectations recognized as promising and significant. If the school is really committed to individual differences, an organizational scheme should incorporate this commitment.

Teachers frequently cite the way students are assigned for reading instruction as a stumbling block for change. Many schools are concerned with grouping plans that promise to reduce variability within classes. Perhaps no other issue has caused more controversy than whether students should be instructed according to homogeneous or heterogeneous grouping patterns. The critics of ability grouping are quick to emphasize that homogeneous groups cannot possibly be constituted. There are too many variables which escape control. Conversely, the advocates of such schemes stress the value of allowing teachers more time to work with limited and carefully focused levels of achievement.

The innovator will have considerable difficulty justifying either a homogeneous or heterogeneous group by drawing upon contemporary literature and research. Neither approach has been demonstrated to be clearly superior. There are many factors which cannot be controlled including the motivation and readiness of teachers. However, some general observations of teachers can be made from comparative studies. Homogeneous grouping may be slightly advantageous for high ability students. This homogeneous grouping seems much more apparent at the secondary and college levels, particularly in specialized and technical subjects. Deploying students by mental ability or reading achievement often reduces competition among members of the group and tends to have deleterious effects on less able students. One might infer that this self-fulfilling prophesy is evident: "When pupils are expected to function inadequately, they don't disappoint the perceiver."

The interaction effects of motivation, the approach for teaching reading, the grouping plans, and reading accomplishments are beginning to receive attention in the literature. Williams (17) explored the relationship between grouping patterns and the motivation of students in Lincoln, Nebraska. Her motivation scale reveals that ability grouping creates snobbishness among bright students and feelings of inferiority among less capable pupils. Motivation is only one aspect of a student's self-concept; however, it is an important ingredient for school success. It would be advisable for schools to evaluate the benefits of homogeneous versus heterogeneous grouping in terms of how responsive the grouping makes pupils for learning.

Considerable work focuses on the virtues of departmentalization. A study by Lamme (9) reveals that teaching reading as a separate subject through organizational plans which emphasize departmentalization tends to negate the development of independent reading habits of students. Pupils who are segregated by reading ability read fewer books, make less use of the library as a resource, and are not influenced as greatly by the teacher. Departmentalization emphasizes achievement of the group and does less to foster conditions which encourage students to read independently. Teachers are perceived as specialists often with little if any inclination to communicate individual pupil progress. The content for reading instruction follows a rigid pattern and most groups cover the same objectives.

The limitations of ability grouping must be understood and incorporated in plans to instruct students. Organizational schemes which consign students according to reading achievement may not be articulated and ignore real individual differences. Teachers who work with pupils at specific ability levels seldom have the inclination to communicate reading progress to other members of the staff. Reading is treated as a discrete subject and is divorced from reading in the content areas. In most instances, pupils are assigned a common text in the content areas. Grouping students solely by reading level does not account for variations in learning rate and the wide range of specific reading proficiencies which are typical within reading instructional levels.

The popularity of ability grouping can be attributed to teacher acceptance of the concept. Reading instruction is conceived generically, and objectives are evolved which reflect group rather than individual needs. The notion that homogeneity is possible allows for one kind of instruction, despite the range in reading accomplishment among pupils as they progress through school. The primary concern is not the assignment of students but is the attainment of competencies which enable teachers to manipulate discrepant instructional needs successfully. The outcome of any new organizational plan depends on diagnostic and adaptive teaching skills.

The research and literature dealing with grouping organizational plans can be summarized as follows: 1) homogeneous grouping has not been demonstrated to be an effective method for raising the reading achievement levels of students; 2) ability grouping tends to result in a hardening of the categories, especially among low achieving students; 3) interaction among students of different achievement levels tends to stimulate less able students; 5) criteria for composing groups has to be carefully examined; and 6) grouping plans should include an analysis of strengths and weaknesses within groups.

Most of the stumbling blocks regarding grouping plans can be resolved by the teacher. Classroom organizational plans emphasize management of the class—not specific grouping schemes. Students are involved as they relate personally to the teacher; opportunities for demonstrated success are apparent; individual differences are appreciated and understood; many learning options are provided; and instruction proceeds with methods and materials which reflect and incorporate different interests and ability levels. These attributes underlie the success of any grouping strategy.

*Preparation.* When confronted with a new approach for teaching reading, the staff may complain: "But they didn't teach me that in college." For any number of reasons, inability to implement some different grouping organizational schemes may be the justifiable absence of skill. Speculation concerning why these deficiencies occurred can serve no good purpose. The situation can be effectively ameliorated by providing a viable and relevant staff development program. The quality of training exercises is directly proportional to the amount of time which is given to planning and organizing. The objectives must be linked specifically to data derived from a needs assessment. Suggestions for designing such an instrument using *The Assessment and Planning Handbook* (15) have already been cited. Planning a successful staff development program involves specifying the skills and competencies necessary for implementing the proposal.

A well-designed needs assessment can be translated into statements which allow teachers to assess their present skills nondefensively. Individual responses are carefully tabulated and scrutinized to identify potential concerns and to formulate a training agenda. Generally, the most effective kinds of staff development experiences are those which allow participants opportunities to apply concepts in classroom situations or to participate in simulation exercises. The importance of relating training activities to the perceived needs of the staff cannot be overstated. The needs assessment can be administered at the end of the workshop experiences and used to evaluate outcomes.

The expectations that teachers establish for teaching reading may create real or imagined stumbling blocks for organizational change. It is not uncommon to hear the staff complain: "But I have to cover all the material assigned to my grade." This complaint is usually the result of strict (and unnecessary) adherence to a teacher's training manual. In some instances, principals may use this directive to guarantee that all of the skills prescribed by the reading experts are being presented and mastered. No empirical research exists to support one scope and sequence approach for teaching reading. Well-executed staff development programs can help teachers extricate themselves from grade level and program constraints and deal with teaching reading as a process.

Staff time, especially for staff development programs, is negotiated by most teacher organizations; consequently, involvement in training exercises is a formidable problem. Teacher contracts often stipulate how much and what kind of inservice will be provided. In some school districts, workshop leaders must be drawn from the ranks of existing staff. In these circumstances, the change agents may feel that they are the only ones with a professional commitment to the project. Developing interest and commitment may mean employing some of the incentives already mentioned—recognition for training in the form of certification, receiving university credit, or granting professional leave. In other situations, recognition dispensed within the school district for attending staff development sessions may promote involvement.

Staff development is educational renewal. The staff development activities should contain the elements necessary to successfully realize organizational change, irrespective of the setting. The competencies of the staff need to be systematically assessed and incorporated into the activities. Established practitioners and consultants from a state department of education or a university may provide resources for the staff development training. Training is competency based, bonding practical applications with theoretical foundations.

Planning is the most crucial consideration in formulating and implementing staff development programs. The fate of a proposal is often decided by the quality and relevance of the training exercises. A successful program presumes that specific needs have been identified and substantiated, program goals address these concerns, the presenter is grounded in both the theoretical and practical applications of the material, opportunities are provided for participants to manipulate and apply the important skills, and an evaluation system is used for continuous feedback. An array of staff development resources has already been indicated which may assist the change agent in planning and implementing a staff development program.

The remaining part of this chapter highlights three possible organizational strategies: the classical classroom, the transitional classroom (using grouping), and the classroom organized for individualized reading instruction. The first two approaches are briefly summarized as it is likely that the reader has had opportunities to observe these patterns of instruction in classroom settings. A fuller treatment of individualized reading instruction is included to provide a detailed example for educators wishing to alter the more traditional grouping and teaching strategies widely used at present.

## Classical Classroom

The classical classroom organization was the format most often used through 1970. The model has the teacher's desk up front, student desks in rows, and a basal reader plus a skill book with the teacher directing all learning activities in the classroom. Many basal reader programs suggest using three reading groups, and most teachers adhere to this suggestion. Teachers find a broad span of abilities within each reading group; thus, they experience the same difficulties that their predecessors encountered when reading was taught from a single book to the entire class. This type of arrangement provides little flexibility. There are limited opportunities for students to gather in a quiet corner and read just for fun. The program is planned and managed by the teacher with little input from the students.

## Transitional Classroom

An alternate to the classical approach is a grouping or transitional classroom. Students are assigned to groups of four to six pupils according to reading group placement. The teacher still directs as students start on their way to independent learning. They respond more positively to small group instruction rather than the structured, classical classroom. Interest areas in art or math, for example, and a center where students have a rug and floor cushions adjacent to a bookcase containing appropriate books are part of the transitional approach. This approach is a popular and effective teaching design for beginning individualized instruction. The basal reader is used as the backbone of the reading program and provides a sequence of skill development, a step-by-step formula for presenting each lesson, and an assortment of enrichment activities to assure acquisition of specific skills as well as reading tests and skillbooks. Figure 1 shows this plan.

## Individualized Reading

At the opposite end of the management continuum is individualized reading instruction. Individualized reading embraces three premises: self-seeking, self-selection, and self-pacing. Reading activities flow spontaneously from topics and materials which have been identified by students as relevant and personally appealing. Self-selection of materials is an integral program component. Teaching integrates all the language-communication arts: listening, speaking, reading, and writing. Students progress according to schedules that they have helped to establish. Reading always leads to an opportunity for a summarizing activity. In some instances, small groups may be convened; however, group structure is flexible and temporary, and it evolves from specific and immediate needs.

Figure 1

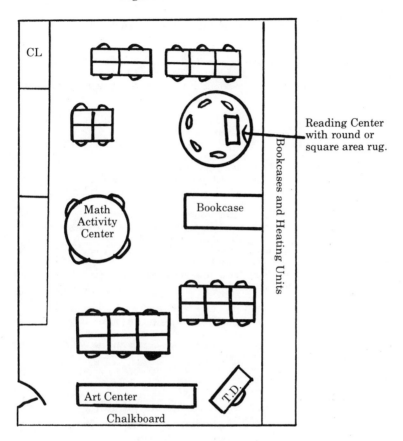

Reading Center with round or square area rug.

Some of the ways one can individualize learning are 1) programmed learning materials such as kits, worktexts, etc.; 2) instructional packages designed by the teacher to supplement and reinforce curriculum items; 3) contracts made by mutual agreement between teacher and learner; 4) work-study experiences (the opportunity to practice what has been taught); and 5) community involvement (resource persons).

The following questions provide a schema for an individualized reading program.

*Diagnosis*
1. What facts, concepts, and skills does the student know?
2. What degree of proficiency has been attained, and at what level is he functioning?
3. What are the students' specific interests, skills, abilities, aptitudes, and degrees of maturity and motivation?
4. What are the best learning experiences for various school or self-selected tasks?

*Self-selection*
1. How will the student plan his own progress?
2. What alternatives will the student be permitted to use, e.g., additional media resources, learning activity alternatives, and human or environmental resources?
3. How can the student modify or apply his objectives?
4. How will the student interact with others in the learning process?

*Assessment by teacher and/or student*
1. How will the teacher and the student assess and redesign new objectives based on the individualized evaluation?
2. Which objectives and procedures may the student design in the interest of his own self-fulfillment?
3. How will the new, individualized experiences aid in additional diagnosis and prescriptions?

*Prescription*
1. What are the jointly determined objectives to be achieved by the student?
2. What are the alternative learning resources and activities available to reach those objectives?
3. What are the optional methods by which the student may demonstrate that he has attained the objectives?

The basic characteristics of individualization are 1) teacher and student diagnosis; 2) teacher and student prescription; 3) student selection or goals, learning materials, activities, and instructional techniques; 4) self-pacing; 5) self-leveling; 6) self-assessment followed by cooperative assessment; 7) self-selection of learning process determined by learning style; 8) objectives and prescription based on student interest; and 9) student creativity incorporated into self-selection aspects.

Schedules for individualized reading vary. Most students receive one and a half hours of instruction, two or three times a week. Resource teachers provide daily activities for shorter periods of time. The plans suggested by the writers may be changed to fit any of these variations. Reading instruction at the initial stage of reading has unique characteristics which dictate certain management considerations.

Students require direct interaction with the teacher and are not capable of extended independent work. However, it is possible to organize small groups of beginning readers and design activities which involve students working together on

**Figure 2**

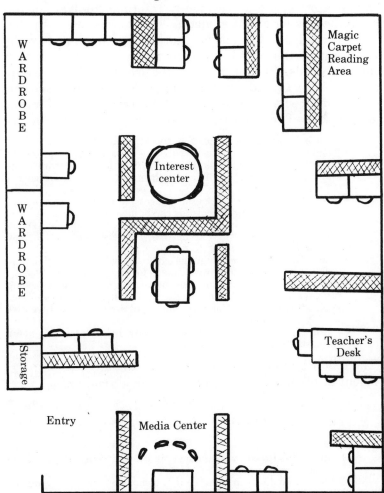

similar projects. The provision of interest centers in the classroom facilitates this kind of individual and group involvement. Classroom arrangement is most important in the individualized program. One type of room arrangement is shown in Figure 2.

*Sample schedules for the initial stage of reading.* Most readers at the initial stage of reading have successfully completed the readiness tasks. At this point it is generally advisable to establish the student's level of accomplishment through appropriate assessments. Informal analysis of the transcribed materials of students is one assessment. In this informal analysis, the teacher may assess familiarity with word forms, letters, and ability to discern initial and final sounds of words. Students do not have to be taught these skills before learning to read. The language experience approach can be utilized for simultaneously teaching readiness and initial reading skills. The following is a representative schedule:

- Establishing rapport/discussion (five minutes).
- Silent reading of the language experience episode dictated during the preceding session. Students are asked to underline all the words they know. This work may be followed with an oral reading by the teacher (10-15 minutes).
- Silent reading of words from the students' word bank or vocabulary notebook. A list of problem words can be identified and students are instructed to turn their word cards over and read the sentences silently in which the words appear. The teacher directs attention to the sentence and initial letters (10-15 minutes).
- Motivation for another language experience episode, dictation and writing (10 minutes). Copies are made for students to take home.
- Follow-up activities: auditory and visual integration practices, word recognition exercises created by the teacher, stressing the combined application of context, phonics and word structures, and creative writing discussion (10-15 minutes).
- Closing/suggestions for independent work, use of language experience, word cards, etc. (10 minutes).

The following is an example of a typical daily log for a student at the initial or beginning stage of reading.

**Daily Log**

Tutor_____Margo Wood_____ Student___Kevin, Age 7, Initial___

*Objectives*
1. Student will read own language, in context, using a language experience episode.
2. Identify (auditory to visual) initial blends and digraphs, using new and old language experience episodes.

O'Donnell and Moore

3. Practice and reinforce sight vocabulary by using sight words in a new context.

*Specific activities*

1. Discuss "Loch Ness Monster" filmstrip seen yesterday. Student will dictate as tutor records whatever he wishes on this topic. They then read back the story together. Type and give student a copy to take home.
2. Word Hunt. Student will find words that begin or end like stimulus words pronounced by tutor. (Find me a word that begins like "play," etc.)
3. Spread all sight word cards out on table. Have student compose sentences using the sight words by picking out cards and placing them in front of him in sentence form. Read each sentence. Tutor records and saves for later reading practice.

*Materials*

1. Paper, pencils, typewriter, carbon paper.
2. Typed language experience episodes.
3. Word box of sight word cards.

*Evaluation*

1. K dictated a four-sentence episode, mostly about the speed-boat race incident on TV. Read back with me—read back alone, easily.
2. Very successful. Getting much better on ending sounds—only problem was with final one. K distinguished "sh, ch" with no problem.
3. He really enjoyed this—scanned cards quickly to find the one he wanted each time—composed original sentences and enjoyed reading them—tutor made him a copy to take home (at his request). Next time try having *him* write the sentences.

Raymond (*13*) suggests 100 activities for helping students summarize reading at the different stages of reading progress. Her reaction and a sample of activities appropriate for students at the initial stage of reading follow.

In an individualized reading program, the main emphasis should be on reading. Everyone reads something every day. In the primary grades, children often read more than one book a day. The students take a few minutes to react to each book—draw a picture of their favorite part, write about the part they like best, tell what happened first, second, third, fourth and last in the story, etc. The child may do this on one of the prepared forms from a table or one that is self-devised. Suggested activities include:

- Draw pictures to illustrate the story.
- Make a book jacket and write something about the book on the inside.
- Make a poster to advertise your book.
- Make a miniature stage set of a scene from your book.
- Make a model of one of the characters from clay or other material.
- Make a diorama.
- Make a mobile.
- Make a mural.
- Organize a book fair or display several books about one topic.
- Make a map or diagram to illustrate the setting of the story.

- Make a three dimensional scene in a shoe box.
- Collect objects that would remind one of the story. (The piece of jigsaw puzzle that was swallowed by Curious George, for example.)
- Make a filmstrip to illustrate the book.
- Make a display of objects or pictures of objects associated with your book.
- If more pictures were to be added to your book, what would you suggest?
- If your book is about a family, make a family picture album by drawing pictures of the family members and writing something about each one.
- Draw or paint a picture to illustrate a scene from your book. Tell why you chose that scene.
- Make a roller movie or TV show using a box and two sticks or do it in miniature.
- Dress dolls to represent your favorite characters.
- Copy a good description from your book and then paint or draw a picture to illustrate it.
- Make some puppets and put on a puppet show.
- If someone in your book made something, you make one too.
- Draw or paint pictures to show how you think the characters looked or how you imagine a scene in the story.

*Sample schedules for the upper stages of reading.* As soon as students have advanced to the rapid development stage of reading, independent reading should receive major emphasis. The teacher monitors each student's progress through reading conferences which are an essential part of an individualized reading program. The teacher's purposes in conducting the conferences are to check students' comprehension, to evaluate their choices and use of reading material, to listen to them read orally if they choose to share a favorite part of their selection, and to learn more about them, their preferences, opinions, and ideas. The organization of the individualized conference is unlike the fomat of the directed reading lesson in which teaching strategies are derived from the reading material. In a conference, the teacher takes cues from the students and their interaction with the material. In some instances, a conference may include two or three students who have read the same material. The conference will require approximately ten minutes. The steps for conducting a reading conference are as follows:

*Preparation by the student and teacher:* The student is told that independent reading will be discussed, difficult words examined, and some selective oral reading shared. Teachers may provide forms on which students list the number of pages

O'Donnell and Moore

they have read, record difficult words, and complete some form of summarizing activity, such as those suggested by Raymond (*13*). The teacher needs to be aware of good questioning strategies, so that appropriate questions can be framed, regardless of the extent of the teacher's familiarity with the student's reading selection.

An individual conference may be framed as follows:

*Comprehension check.* Students should be encouraged to react to the book in terms of their own backgrounds and experiences. Hunt (*7*) emphasizes that the success of an individualized conference depends primarily on the quality of questioning. He suggests three major themes:

1. *Appropriateness*
   Why did you select this story book?
   What did you particularly like about it?
   Was it hard or easy to read?
   If you met the author, what would you say about the book?
2. *Appreciation*
   What part was the most interesting?
   Why do you think the writer wrote this?
   Do you usually like material of this nature?
   How did it make you feel?
3. *Values*
   What new ideas did you learn?
   What happened that you wanted to happen?
   What happened that you did not want to happen?
   What was the most important part?
   Would you recommend it to a friend?

The following is a transcript of a conference on *The Emperor's New Clothes*, by Hans Christian Anderson, conducted with a seventh grade student who entered the reading clinic with an extremely negative attitude toward reading. This transcript incorporated the three major themes suggested by Hunt (*7*).

T: Why did you choose this book?
S: 'cause I saw the movie and I thought I'd like to read about it.
T: Did you enjoy the book as much as the movie?
S: Yeah, I guess so.
T: Why?
S: Because it was about the same thing, and it showed most of the stuff it showed in the movie.
T: If you had to choose between the book and the movie, which would you choose?
S: The movie, because in the book they didn't move around.
T: Did you enjoy the art work in the book as well as in the movie?

S: Sort of; the art work in the movie was movable; in the book they just stand there.
T: Which part of the book did you like best?
S: When he walked into town naked.
T: Why did you like that part best?
S: It was the most funniest and embarrassing.
T: Would you liked to have been there in the story?
S: Yeah, when the little kid jumped out and said he doesn't have any clothes on at all.

Teachers need to keep conference records which include dates, titles of books read, and brief notes on the quality of comprehension and follow-up work of each student.

*Vocabulary check.* The student is encouraged to maintain in a separate vocabulary notebook a record of unfamiliar words encountered while reading. These words are presented in context. The teacher may suggest word recognition or study strategies to aid in deriving pronunciations and meanings. Students may use the words in different contexts or incorporate them in writing activities. Vocabulary development is functional and should always result in utilization of newly acquired word meanings.

*Oral reading.* An oral reading check is an optional part of the individual reading conference. The teacher may invite students to reread a selection that they particularly enjoyed. Oral reading is undertaken for a pupose in a meaningful audience situation. The objectives include natural expression, tempo, and tone. The teacher uses the occasion to make a general observation of overall reading performance. Specific problems become the focus of subsequent exercises.

*Follow-up activities.* Careful relation to individual instructional objectives should be considered in the follow-up activities in order to determine the value and usefulness of reading exercises. What specific kinds of practice would be the most appropriate? This judgment is based upon an awareness of the instructional characteristics of the stages of reading. Activities are carefully delimited and spaced over several sessions until mastery is determined. Follow-up activities may be related to the book which was discussed in the conference.

Raymond (*13*) makes the following additional suggestions for creative dramatic and oral activities which can be used at the upper stages of reading progress:

O'Donnell and Moore

Dramatize a scene from your book or put on a puppet or marionette show.

Present your story in pantomime.

Dress up like one of the characters.

Select a part to read aloud. Tell why you chose it.

Read parts of your book to a friend. Then listen to your friend read parts of his book to you.

Find a story suitable for a younger child and read it to him.

Invite a speaker to talk about a topic related to your book.

Using the setting for your book, make believe you have just returned from a trip there and give a travel talk.

Tape parts of your book. As you listen to the tape, decide how you could have read it better. Try again.

Tell about the funniest, saddest or most exciting part.

Join with others who have read the same book and present it as a play.

After reading a number of books on the same subject, give a short talk while displaying the books.

Present your book as a radio book talk.

Demonstrate how to make or do something described in your book.

Present the story as a TV drama.

Have a panel discussion about books relative to one topic.

Record parts of your story with sound effects and musical background.

Organize a quiz show featuring questions about books and authors. (Adapt the format of popular TV shows.)

Give an illustrated lecture about your book using a flannel board.

The successful management of an individualized reading program involves good record keeping procedures. An effective technique is to have students keep personal records of their own independent reading. Reading diaries vary but most include the book title, author, number of pages read, and difficult words encountered.

DAILY READING RECORD

NAME _____

AUTHOR _____

TITLE _____

FICTION OR NONFICTION _____

| DATE | PAGE STARTED | PAGE ENDED | VOCABULARY PROBLEMS | PAGE # |
|------|--------------|------------|---------------------|--------|
|      |              |            |                     |        |

The following log was planned for a student working at the upper stage of reading progress.

## Daily Log

Tutor     Barbara Jenkins       Student    Brian

Date     7/18

*Objectives*

1. To improve organization and comprehension of written material.
2. To engage in sustained silent reading for 15-20 minutes.
3. To discuss report based upon organization, content, and writing style.
4. To increase vocabulary through specific word study.
5. To choose an appropriate follow-up activity.

*Specific Activities*

1. Written Report—appropriate heading, title, paragraph formation and content; stress organization as related to prepared outline.
2. Silent Reading—continue reading *Frederick Douglas*; discuss material read thus far—summarize events, note troublesome vocabulary, relate to previous study of the underground railroad movement; add vocabulary words to notebook if necessary.
3. Review Report on Porcupines—check grammar, spelling, sentence structure, organization, paragraph development as related to outline; give suggestions for improvement.
4. Vocabulary Notebook—review previous entries made, and add at least two new words from research materials for specific word study; use words in sentences and make vocabulary slips.
5. Follow-up Activity—suggest possible hands-on experiences such as making a clay model, a crossword puzzle using research and vocabulary, making a soap carving, etc.

*Materials*

Research books *Nature's Pincushion*
                   *The World of the Porcupine*
                   *Frederick Douglas*
Vocabulary notebook
List of possible follow-up activities

*Evaluation*

From his previously prepared outline, Brian was able to write a well-organized, descriptive paragraph about porcupines. He used major topics from his outline to develop paragraphs, and incorporated numerous new vocabulry words which will be used in his notebook for specific word study. Brian made a number of spelling errors; he was concerned about his mistakes since most of the words missed had been copied directly from his outline. I praised Brian for his organization and paragraph development, which were major objectives, and told him that we would work on spelling tomorrow while we planned his crossword puzzle, which he chose to develop for a follow-up activity. Brian chose the words "timberline" and "albino" for vocabulary entries. These will be used in his crossword puzzle.

The key to a successful individualized reading program lies in the organization of the classroom. Veatch and her associates (*16*) provide an excellent review of interest centers which can be readily adapted in most self-contained classrooms.

Interest areas provide opportunities for structuring independent activities which may be teacher-pupil planned or initiated by students independently. These activities are pursued by the students as the teacher works with other pupils. The creation of centers is not dependent upon elaborate resources but rather on the teacher's ability to innovate. The following centers can be used by students with a minimum of supervision:

*Library center.* Essential to the success of an individualized reading program is the availability of a variety of reading matter. The reading material should include group and individually dictated stories which have been typed and illustrated, expository prose, reference materials representing many publishers and reading levels, well-selected narrative books, magazines for different age levels, and newspapers and informational brochures.

*Writing centers.* Writing centers should be located in a quiet place and may be divided into small areas. They should contain a supply of paper, pencils, and typewriters. Even students in the initial reading level can use their word boxes or vocabulary notebooks for writing.

*Math and science center.* The math and science area should contain manipulative materials, objects, measuring devices, microscopes, plants, and other observational tools. Activities should include opportunities to experiment.

*Communications center.* The communications part of the room provides an opportunity for groups of students to meet and confer. Spontaneous sharing of experiences, developing ideas for projects, and meaningful audience centered oral reading can be promoted. Reticent pupils can be encouraged to converse in an informal and relaxed atmosphere.

The innovative teacher can be successful in a classical classroom, a transitional classroom, or a classroom organized for individualized reading instruction. If the reading program is to be successful in any type of setting, it is necessary to assess the student's reading program, to design reading program goals and objectives based on the instructional needs of the pupil, and to implement an instructional program to meet these objectives.

## Summary

This discussion of stumbling blocks to both schoolwide and individual classroom organizational change is not inclusive. Innovative educators differ in the weight that they assign to certain problems. In all instances, however, success depends on how well the change is planned and the strength of the commitment on the part of all persons involved. These two factors are dynamic forces that when activated can help overcome any obstacle.

### References

1. Barbe, Walter B. *Educator's Guide to Personalized Reading Instruction.* Englewood Cliffs, New Jersey: Prentice-Hall, 1961.
2. Bond, G.L., and R. Dykstra. *Coordinating Center for First Grade Reading Instruction Programs.* Final Report of Project No. X-001, Contract No. OE-5-10-264. Minneapolis: University of Minnesota, 1967.
3. Dallman, Martha, and others. *The Teaching of Reading.* New York: Holt, Rinehart and Winston, 1974.
4. Durr, Rita, and Kenneth Durr. *Educator's Self-Teaching Guide to Individualized Instruction.* West Nyack, New York: Parker, 1975, 50-73, 112-156.
5. Greaney, Vincent, and Paul Kelly. "Reading Standards in Irish Post Primary Schools," *Studies in Reading.* Republic of Ireland: Education Company, 1977.
6. Hawkins, Michael L. "Mobility of Students in Reading Groups," *Reading Teacher,* 20 (1966), 136-140.
7. Hunt, Lyman (Ed.). *The Individualized Reading Program: A Guide for Classroom Teaching.* Newark, Delaware: International Reading Association, 1967.
8. Indrisano, Roselmina. "Reading-Managing the Classroom Reading Program," *Instructor,* January 1978, 117-120.
9. Lamme, L.L. "Self-Contained to Departmentalized: How Reading Habits Change," *Elementary School Journal,* 76 (1976), 208-218.
10. Nichols, Nancy J. "Interclass Grouping for Reading Instruction: Who Makes the Decisions and Why?" *Educational Leadership,* 26 (1969), 588-592.
11. O'Donnell, Michael P. "Innovation in New England's Schools," *Educational Technology,* 13 (1971), 131-135.
12. O'Donnell, Michael P. *Teaching the Stages of Reading Progress.* Dubuque, Iowa: Kendall-Hunt, 1979.
13. Raymond, Dorothy. *Individualized Reading in the Elementary School.* West Nyack, New York: Parker, 1973.

O'Donnell and Moore

14. Spitzer, Herbert F. "Class Size and Pupil Achievement in Elementary Schools," *Elementary School Journal*, 55 (1954).
15. U.S. Office of Education. *The Assessment and Planning Handbook*, National Right to Read Project. Washington, D.C.: U.S. Government Printing Office, 1974.
16. Veatch, Jeannette, and others. *Key Words to Reading: The Language Experience Approach Begins*. Columbus, Ohio: Charles E. Merrill, 1979.
17. Williams, Mary Heard. "Does Grouping Affect Motivation?" *Elementary School Journal*, 73 (December 1972), 130-137.

Curry presents the reader with evaluative scales which may be used to determine the effectiveness of several dimensions of the managed curriculum.

## Chapter Ten   How Am I Doing? Assessing the Components of a Managed Curriculum

Joan F. Curry
*San Diego State University*

The organization of the reading program is the responsibility of the teacher. In the process of organizing a classroom for reading, the teacher may want to assess each component of the program. As suggested throughout this text these components are 1) the teacher, 2) the structure of the learning environment, 3) the students (their attitudes, interests, abilities), and 4) materials. This chapter presents some checklists and inventories which the teacher may use to evaluate the many aspects of a reading program. The checklists and inventories are guides so that when the teacher asks, "How am I doing?" there may be data on which to base conclusions.

## The Teacher

The dynamic practices of teachers and the ways in which they interact with students have lasting effects on student achievement. Much research today indicates that the teacher is the one who can determine the success or failure of a reading program.

The task of classroom or special reading teachers is multidimensional. They must determine their most effective teaching style; they must develop effective teacher-student rapport; they must be knowledgeable about the field of reading, and they must understand their roles as facilitators of learning. To help teachers assess where they are at this point in their roles as teachers of reading, the "Self-evaluation

Checklist" is presented in Figure 1. Upon its completion, teachers may have a better picture of their strengths, needs, and explicit areas in which they may wish to obtain more information.

## The Learning Environment

Teachers have the challenge and the responsibility to create an environment for the learner that is conducive to the learning process. This environment includes not only the appropriate use of space, of bulletin boards, and interest centers but also the skill utilized by the teacher in making available audiovisual equipment and whatever else the students may need to positively affect their learning abilities.

The "Learning Environment Checklist" will quickly assess the teacher's success in providing an environment conducive to learning (see Figure 2).

Since Learning Centers are becoming increasingly apparent in classrooms, a checklist for assessing this part of the learning environment is included in Figure 3.

## Student Attitudes, Interests, Abilities

### Attitudes

Attitudes toward reading play a most important role in a child's desire to learn to read. It would be helpful for the classroom teacher of reading to determine those attitudes her students hold. To assist the teacher in doing this, Campbell's "Reading Attitude Inventory" (Figure 4) is presented. It can be used with the very young child as well as with the older one. The questions may be read aloud.

The "Reading Attitude Inventory" by Molly Ransbury is included in Figure 5 as another means of evaluation. Again, the questions can be read aloud.

### Interests

Talking to students about what they enjoy doing and what they do in their free time may be useful ways to gather data which might influence the implementation of the reading program. Another useful procedure is to assess student reading interests by using an informal survey. A sentence completion type of survey (Figure 6) may give the teacher a more complete understanding of students' individual personalities.

## Learning Style

Each person has a preferred learning style for every task undertaken. The "Learning Style Indicator" by Lapp and Flood (3) will help the teacher assess students' perceptions of their own best styles. The teacher can then decide whether to teach to this style or to help students build a variety of effective styles (Figure 7).

## Readiness

Reading readiness activities are usually an integral part of the total first grade program. Standardized tests may highlight factors that are important in deciding whether a child should be taught to read. However, informal checklists can help the teacher decide if a particular program and approach are conducive to learning and if the students have the necessary background to begin to learn to read.

The "Barbe Reading Skills Checklist - Readiness Level" (Figure 8) may quickly assess a student's readiness level. In checking the child's abilities, the teacher may discover those areas where instruction is particularly strong or where instructional techniques may need some improvement. This is not to say that one student's checklist will yield this information. Rather, the overall class data may produce patterns and tendencies which will assist the teacher in making future decisions about the program based on past performances.

A more informal type of readiness checklist can also help the teacher assess a program. By completing the columns, the teacher can quickly determine those areas where more work is needed and also which children need work in which particular skills. Again, the teacher can make some decisions based on data obtained as to which areas of the curriculum may require more instruction and/or a different organizational pattern to help the students achieve competency at the readiness level (Figure 9).

## Oral Reading

Oral reading can communicate ideas and provide enjoyment for others. It can also be used as a diagnostic tool. Some difficulties revealed in oral reading *may* also be extant in silent reading. As such, the teacher may wish to assess the oral reading of her students not only to improve their oral reading competency but also to help them improve in their silent reading skill. The "Oral Reading Checklist" will be useful in analyzing oral reading performance (Figure 10).

## Silent Reading

Fluent and accurate silent reading is essential for success in school. Instruction in silent reading begins in the first grade at the same time as instruction in oral reading begins. As students progress in mastery of their reading skills, they can comprehend more difficult reading materials. As in oral reading, it behooves the teacher, from time to time, to informally analyze a student's silent reading skills. The "Silent Reading Checklist" may be a useful instrument for this analysis (Figure 11).

## Vocabulary

Vocabulary development is concept development and develops from a variety of experiences. A program of vocabulary development is essential in improving the reading and comprehension skills of children. To this end, the skills needed for vocabulary acquisition and application need to be surveyed. This "Survey of Vocabulary Skills" may give information which will assist the teacher in organizing her classroom for reading instruction (Figure 12).

## The Materials

Selecting appropriate materials is crucial to the success

of a reading program. With the plethora of reading materials on the market, it becomes increasingly time consuming to select those materials which seem best for a particular class of children. The "Materials Selection Checklist" (shown in the Appendix) may help to crystallize teachers' thinking as they review materials for possible use in the reading program (Figure 13).

This chapter is designed to aid you in assessing the components of a managed curriculum which are addressed throughout this text. If further information is needed, the following references may be of assistance.

### References
1. Goldbecker, Sheralyn S. *Reading: Instructional Approaches.* Washington, D.C.: National Education Association, 1975.
2. Johnson, L.V., and M.A. Bany. *Classroom Management: Theory and Skill Training.* New York: Macmillan, 1970.
3. Lapp, Diane, and James Flood. *Teaching Reading to Every Child.* New York: Macmillan, 1978, 146.
4. Wallen, C.J., and L.L. Wallen. *Effective Classroom Management.* Boston: Allyn and Bacon, 1978.

APPENDIX

## Figure 1

Self-Evaluation Checklist for Classroom Reading Teachers

Rate your present skill or knowledge for each of the following aspects of teaching reading.

| | Yes | Somewhat, but I Need More Information | No |
|---|---|---|---|
| 1. I understand the processes involved in reading comprehension. | | | |
| 2. I know a variety of methods of reading instruction—the strengths and needs of each method. | | | |
| 3. I know my role as teacher in the learning process. | | | |
| 4. I understand the sensory and perceptual factors that affect the reading ability of the child. | | | |
| 5. I understand the cognitive factors that affect the reading ability of the child. | | | |
| 6. I understand the language factors that affect the reading ability of the child. | | | |
| 7. I understand the socioeconomic factors that affect the reading ability of the child. | | | |
| 8. I know the prereading skills. | | | |
| 9. I understand the concept of readiness at all levels. | | | |
| 10. I understand the importance of motivation in helping children learn to read. | | | |
| 11. I know books that should be read to children. | | | |
| 12. I know how to share a picture book with children. | | | |
| 13. I know the Newbery and Caldecott Awards. | | | |
| 14. I know how to read aloud well. | | | |
| 15. I have enough knowledge about children's literature to be able to buy appropriate books for my classroom. | | | |
| 16. I know how to establish a reading center or corner. | | | |
| 17. I read aloud to my students every day. | | | |
| 18. I know how to assess my students' attitudes toward reading. | | | |

**Figure 1** - *continued*

| | Yes | Somewhat, but I Need More Information | No |
|---|---|---|---|
| 19. I know many ways that children can share books with one another. | | | |
| 20. I know how to involve children in dramatic play. | | | |
| 21. I know the processes involved in developing listening skills. | | | |
| 22. I understand the interrelatedness of the language arts. | | | |
| 23. I know the processes involved in developing speaking skills. | | | |
| 24. I understand the use of graphophonic cues to help children decode words. | | | |
| 25. I understand the use of syntactic cues which allow children to understand word arrangements. | | | |
| 26. I understand the use of semantic cues which enable students to understand the meaning of texts. | | | |
| 27. I know sight word strategies for analyzing unknown words. | | | |
| 28. I understand the role of structural analysis strategies in word recognition. | | | |
| 29. I understand the role of contextual analysis strategies in word recognition. | | | |
| 30. I understand the role of questioning in the development of reading comprehension. | | | |
| 31. I understand comprehension as a thinking process. | | | |
| 32. I know the study skills. | | | |
| 33. I can help children learn to use study skills effectively. | | | |
| 34. I know the skills common to reading in any content area. | | | |
| 35. I understand the interrelatedness of reading and mathematics, reading and social studies, reading and science, and reading and music and art. | | | |
| 36. I know the historical overview of reading instruction in the United States. | | | |
| 37. I understand the special needs of bilingual and English-as-a-second-language students. | | | |
| 38. I understand the linguistic influences in second language teaching. | | | |

| Figure 1 - *continued* | Yes | Somewhat, but I Need More Information | No |
|---|---|---|---|
| 39. I know the most appropriate methods of diagnosing the reading ability of bilingual and second language speakers. | | | |
| 40. I know methods to teach reading in the native language as well as reading in English. | | | |
| 41. I know how to determine the readability of printed material. | | | |
| 42. I know how to informally assess a student's achievement. | | | |
| 43. I know the differences between criterion and norm referenced testing. | | | |
| 44. I know how to compute the reading expectancy levels of my students. | | | |
| 45. I understand the concept of thematic teaching. | | | |
| 46. I understand the techniques of grouping. | | | |
| 47. I know how to write behavioral objectives. | | | |
| 48. I understand the value of classroom management. | | | |
| 49. I can use a process of continuous evaluation. | | | |
| 50. I understand the value of sequencing instruction. | | | |
| 51. I know what the International Reading Association is and have read the publications of the organization. | | | |

**Figure 2**

Learning Environment Checklist

Rank yourself on a 1-5 continuum, 5 being the highest ranking.

| | 1 | 2 | 3 | 4 | 5 |
|---|---|---|---|---|---|
| In my classroom: | | | | | |
| 1. Many types of books are available for browsing and reading—fiction and non-fiction. | | | | | |
| 2. Interest centers are available. | | | | | |
| 3. A library corner is provided. | | | | | |
| 4. Children have access to tapes and records that accompany books. | | | | | |
| 5. Reading material other than books is provided. | | | | | |
| 6. Films and filmstrips are available. | | | | | |
| 7. Creative materials are available for personal interpretation. | | | | | |
| 8. Research opportunities are provided. | | | | | |
| 9. Space is allocated for oral activities (readers' theatre, choral speaking, play acting) so as not to interfere with silent reading or listening activities. | | | | | |
| 10. Tapes are provided so that students may listen to their own stories or their oral reading experiences. | | | | | |
| 11. A quiet corner is established where students may write, read, dream, think. | | | | | |
| 12. Bulletin boards enhance the learning environment. | | | | | |
| 13. Charts are used both as a means of improving the classroom living and also as a vehicle to improve reading skills. | | | | | |
| 14. Space is available for creative sharing of books. | | | | | |
| 15. Learning centers provide reinforcement of learned activities through independent work. | | | | | |

## Figure 3

### A Quick Checklist for Learning Centers

| Do the Learning Centers | Yes | No |
|---|---|---|
| 1. Provide activities to develop and enhance motor and reading skills? | | |
| 2. Provide opportunities for the students to reinforce a previously presented skill? | | |
| 3. Provide opportunities to listen to material being read aloud? | | |
| 4. Provide the students with activities that will allow them to practice their writing skills? | | |
| 5. Provide the students with activities that will allow them to respond creatively? | | |
| 6. Provide opportunities for children to share their work with their peers? | | |
| 7. Provide activities which the students can do alone, in pairs, in small groups? | | |
| 8. Provide games which will reinforce formerly presented reading skills? | | |
| 9. Provide complete directions and materials so that confusion and noise are kept to a minimum? | | |

**Figure 4**

Reading Attitude Inventory

Paul Campbell, 1966

Name _____ Grade _____ Teacher _____

1. How do you feel when your teacher reads a story out loud?

2. How do you feel when someone gives you a book for a present?

3. How do you feel about reading books for fun at home?

4. How do you feel when you are asked to read out loud to your group?

Curry

5. How do you feel when you are asked to read out loud to the teacher?

6. How do you feel when you come to a new word while reading?

7. How do you feel when it is time to do your worksheet?

8. How do you feel about going to school?

9. How do you feel about how well you can read?

10. How do you think your friends feel about reading?

11. How do you think your teacher feels when you read?

12. How do you think your friends feel when you read out loud?

13. How do you feel about the reading group you are in?

14. How do you think you'll feel about reading when you're bigger?

Curry

## Figure 5

### Reading Attitude Inventory

#### by Molly Ransbury, 1971

Yes    No

1. I visit the library to find books I might enjoy reading.

2. I would like to read a magazine in my free time.

3. I cannot pay attention to my reading when there is even a little noise or movement nearby.

4. I enjoy reading extra books about topics we study in school.

5. I would like to read newspaper articles about my favorite hobbies or interests.

6. I feel I know the characters in some of the comic books I read.

7. My best friend would tell you that I enjoy reading very much.

8. I would like to belong to a group that discusses many kinds of reading.

9. I would enjoy spending some time during my summer vacation reading to children in a summer library program.

10. My ideas are changed by the books I read.

11. Reading is a very important part of my life. Every day I read many different types of materials.

12. I read magazines for many different reasons.

13. My friends would tell you that I'd much rather watch TV than read.

14. When I listen to someone read out loud, certain words or sentences might attract my attention.

15. I would only read a book if my teacher or my parents said I had to.

16. Magazines, comic books, and newspapers do not interest me.

17. I do not enjoy reading in my free time.

18. I would enjoy talking with someone else about one of my favorite books.

19. I might go to the library several times to see if a special book had been returned.

20. I am too busy during vacations to plan a reading program for myself.

21. Sometimes the book that I'm reading will remind me of ideas from another book that I've read.

22. If my only reading was for school assignments, I would be very unhappy.

23. Reading is not a very good way for me to learn new things.

**Figure 5** - *continued*

_____  _____    24. I think reading is boring.

_____  _____    25. If I see a comic book or magazine, I would usually just look at the pictures.

_____  _____    26. I sometimes read extra books or articles about something that we have discussed in school.

_____  _____    27. I enjoy going to the library and choosing special books.

_____  _____    28. I do not read during any of my vacations from school.

_____  _____    29. I would not want to help set up a book exhibit.

_____  _____    30. It would be very, very nice for me to have my own library of books.

_____  _____    31. I don't try to read many different kinds of books.

_____  _____    32. If I do not read many things when I'm an adult, I will miss many important ideas about life.

_____  _____    33. I read because the teacher tells me to.

_____  _____    34. I read only because people force me to.

_____  _____    35. I must shut myself in a quiet room in order to read almost anything.

_____  _____    36. I never do extra reading outside of school work because reading is so dull.

_____  _____    37. I only read extra books if my parents say I have to.

_____  _____    38. Reading certain newspaper articles might make me happy, or sad, or even angry.

_____  _____    39. I should spend some of my time each day reading so that I can learn about the world.

_____  _____    40. Before I make up my mind about something, I try to read more than one writer's ideas.

_____  _____    41. When I read, I sometimes understand myself a little better.

_____  _____    42. Some characters I have read about help me to better understand people I know.

_____  _____    43. Reading is a very important part of my life. I read nearly every day in books or newspapers and I enjoy doing so.

_____  _____    44. I would like to read some of the novels my teacher reads to the class.

_____  _____    45. I would like to read more books if I had the time.

_____  _____    46. I might keep a list of the books that I wish to read during the next few months.

_____  _____    47. My parents force me to read.

_____  _____    48. If people didn't tell me that I had to read, I would probably never pick up a book.

_____  _____    49. Sometimes I think ahead in my reading and imagine what the characters might do.

Curry

**Figure 5** - *continued*

_____ _____ 50. I wish I could buy more books for myself.

_____ _____ 51. Sometimes I wish the author of the book had written the story in a different way.

_____ _____ 52. Much of my free time is spent in reading, library browsing, and discussing books.

_____ _____ 53. I read lots of different newspaper articles so that I can learn more about the world.

_____ _____ 54. Reading is as much a part of my life as eating, sleeping, and playing.

_____ _____ 55. A story that I see on television might also be interesting to read in a book.

_____ _____ 56. Even a little reading makes me feel tired and restless.

_____ _____ 57. I try to read many different types of materials in my free time.

_____ _____ 58. I would always rather talk about things, than to read about them.

_____ _____ 59. I have never wanted to read a book twice.

_____ _____ 60. When I am an adult and work all day, I will not read.

_____ _____ 61. I would feel disappointed if I could not find a book that I was very interested in reading.

_____ _____ 62. I have sometimes told my friends about a really good book that they might like to read.

_____ _____ 63. I look for some main ideas that the writer presents when I read a magazine article.

_____ _____ 64. Reading is a very important part of my life when I am not in school.

## Figure 6

### Interest Inventory

Name _____     Date _____

1. My favorite animal is _____ because _____.
2. My favorite color is _____.
3. The best book I ever read is _____.
4. My brothers and sisters _____.
5. My favorite sport is _____.
6. When I have free time, I _____.
7. My favorite television program is _____.
8. The movie I enjoyed most is _____.
9. The day of the week I like most is _____ because _____.
10. The person I admire most is _____ because _____ _____.
11. Reading is _____.
12. I like to read stories about _____.
13. The subject in school I like best is _____ because _____ _____.
14. The subject in school I don't like is _____ because _____ _____.
15. When it rains, I _____.
16. My hobbies are _____.
17. I am going to be a _____ when I grow up because _____ _____.
18. Poetry makes me _____.
19. I wish my teacher would _____.
20. My parents _____.
21. Libraries are _____.
22. If I had three wishes, they would be
    1. _____.
    2. _____.
    3. _____.
23. My favorite food is _____.
24. I'd like to visit _____
    because _____.
25. If I could be anywhere in the world right now I would be in _____ _____ because _____.
26. If I could do anything I wanted to do I would _____ _____.

**Figure 7***

Learning Style Indicator

DIRECTIONS: Read each pair of statements and mark the box next to the statement that *most closely* describes you.

1. I understand things better from a picture. ☐ ☐ I understand things better from someone telling me or reading about them.

2. I look at charts and diagrams before I read the written part. ☐ ☐ I read the written part before I look at the charts and diagrams.

3. I memorize things by writing them out. ☐ ☐ I memorize things by repeating them aloud.

4. I like examples first, rules later ☐ ☐ I like rules first, examples later.

5. I usually get more done when I work alone. ☐ ☐ I usually get more done when I work with others.

6. I enjoy doing a number of things at the same time. ☐ ☐ I prefer doing things one at a time.

7. I usually ask "why" questions. ☐ ☐ I usually ask about facts.

8. I prefer working quickly. ☐ ☐ I prefer to work slowly.

9. I answer questions quickly. ☐ ☐ I answer questions carefully and slowly.

10. I take chances at making mistakes. ☐ ☐ I try to avoid making mistakes.

---

*From Diane Lapp and James Flood, *Teaching Reading to Every Child*. New York: Macmillan, 1978, 146.

## Figure 8

Barbe Reading Skills Checklist

Readiness Level

| (Last Name) | (First Name) | (Name of School) |

| (Age) | (Grade Placement) | (Name of Teacher) |

I. Vocabulary
   A. Word Recognition
      1. Interested in words and symbols     _____
      2. Recognizes own name in print     _____
      3. Names upper case letters     _____
      4. Names lower case letters     _____
      5. Matches upper case and lower case letters     _____
      6. Identifies numerals 1-10     _____

   B. Word Meaning
      1. Listening vocabulary adequate to understand ideas     _____
      2. Speaking vocabulary adequate to convey ideas     _____
      3. Comprehends meaning of:

| Place words | | Quantitative words | Descriptive words |
|---|---|---|---|
| \_\_ here | \_\_ there | \_\_ number words 1-10 | \_\_ color words |
| \_\_ under | \_\_ over | \_\_ many | \_\_ size words |
| \_\_ in | \_\_ out | \_\_ more | \_\_ shape words |
| \_\_ near | \_\_ far | \_\_ much | \_\_ same |
| \_\_ up | \_\_ down | \_\_ some | \_\_ different |
| \_\_ right | \_\_ left | \_\_ all | \_\_ alike |
| \_\_ front | \_\_ back | \_\_ none | |
| \_\_ top | \_\_ bottom | \_\_ most | |
| \_\_ beside | \_\_ next to | \_\_ few | |
| \_\_ above | \_\_ below | \_\_ whole | |
| \_\_ inside | \_\_ outside | \_\_ part | |
| \_\_ middle | \_\_ between | \_\_ half | |
| \_\_ beginning | \_\_ end | | |
| \_\_ on | \_\_ through | | |
| \_\_ first | \_\_ last | | |
| \_\_ second | \_\_ third | | |
| \_\_ around | \_\_ behind | | |
| \_\_ before | | | |

      4. Classifies objects and pictures into logical categories     _____
      5. Aware that printed words represent spoken words     _____

## II. Perceptive Skills

### A. Auditory
    1. Reproduces pronounced two and three syllable words     _____

    2. Hears minimal differences in words (Are these the same or different? hat-hit, pot-cot, cat-cap)     _____

    3. Able to hear word length (Which is the shorter word? boy-elephant)     _____

    4. Recognizes spoken words with same initial sound     _____

    5. Recognizes spoken words with same final sound     _____

    6. Hears rhyming words     _____

### B. Visual
    1. Sees likenesses and differences in

      colors     _____

      shapes and designs     _____

      directionality and size     _____

      letters     _____

      words     _____

    2. Recognizes word boundaries     _____

    3. Visualizes part-to-whole by assembling seven piece puzzle     _____

    4. Left to right eye movement     _____

## III. Comprehension

### A. Interest
    1. Wants to learn to read     _____

    2. Enjoys being read to     _____

    3. Shows interest in books and other printed materials     _____

### B. Ability
    1. Adequate attention span     _____

    2. Remembers from stories read aloud

      main ideas     _____

      names of characters     _____

      some major details     _____

    3. Can sequence events logically     _____

    4. Follows oral directions     _____

    5. Looks at books

      from front to back     _____

      from left hand page to right hand page     _____

    6. Aware of usual text progression

      from left to right     _____

      from top to bottom     _____

## IV. Oral Expression

    A. Expresses self spontaneously     _____

    B. Expresses complete thoughts (sentences)     _____

    C. Able to remember and reproduce a five word sentence     _____

    D. Can retell a story in his own words     _____

---

Teacher's Notes

*Assessing a Managed Curriculum*     235

**Figure 9**

Informal Teacher Checklist

Student's Name _____ Date _____

| Skill | Yes | No | Has Some Ability | Comments |
|---|---|---|---|---|
| 1. Can identify letters named | | | | |
| 2. Can give the names of letters | | | | |
| 3. Can match upper and lower case letters | | | | |
| 4. Can write letters of the alphabet | | | | |
| 5. Can hear sounds in words | | | | |
| 6. Can identify numerals | | | | |
| 7. Has adequate oral language vocabulary | | | | |
| 8. Has adequate listening vocabulary | | | | |
| 9. Can classify objects | | | | |
| 10. Can rhyme words | | | | |
| 11. Can recognize words | | | | |
| 12. Can differentiate between same and different objects | | | | |
| 13. Can sequence pictures | | | | |
| 14. Can tell a story about a picture or sequenced pictures | | | | |
| 15. Exhibits an interest in words | | | | |
| 16. Is alert to task at hand | | | | |
| 17. Enjoys being read to | | | | |
| 18. Can follow oral directions | | | | |

**Figure 10**

An Oral Reading Checklist

Child's Name _____ Date _____

Material Read _____

Grade Level of Material Read _____

I. Fluency

_____ 1. Word-by-word reading

_____ 2. Incorrect phrasing

_____ 3. Monotonous tone

_____ 4. Ignores punctuation

_____ 5. Repeats words

_____ 6. Adds words

_____ 7. Omits words

_____ 8. Substitutes words

II. Word Skills

_____ 1. Errors on easy words

_____ 2. Limited sight vocabulary

_____ 3. Ignores errors

_____ 4. No system of word attack

_____ 5. Guesses constantly

_____ 6. Makes no use of context clues

_____ 7. Uses configuration

_____ 8. Unable to blend

_____ 9. Auditory discrimination poor

_____ 10. Tends to reverse letters

III. Enunciation

_____ 1. Poor enunciation in all reading

_____ 2. Stutters

_____ 3. Voice strained

_____ 4. Voice too loud

_____ 5. Voice too soft

IV. Posture

_____ 1. Holds book too close

_____ 2. Moves head while reading

_____ 3. Points with finger

_____ 4. Lays book flat on desk to read

_____ 5. Squints

V. Comprehension

_____ 1. Oral reading comprehension better than silent reading comprehension

_____ 2. Oral reading comprehension poorer than silent reading comprehension

**Figure 11**

A Silent Reading Checklist

Child's Name _____ Date _____

Material Read _____

Grade Level of Material Read _____

| When reading silently, the child | Never | Sometimes | Always |
|---|---|---|---|
| _____ 1. Is distracted. | | | |
| _____ 2. Persists in endeavors. | | | |
| _____ 3. Moves lips. | | | |
| _____ 4. Reads at a rate commensurate with the purpose of reading. | | | |
| _____ 5. Exhibits smooth left-to-right eye movements. | | | |
| _____ 6. Exhibits effective eye hand coordination. | | | |
| _____ 7. Uses hand as a marker. | | | |
| _____ 8. Assumes a proper reading posture. | | | |
| _____ 9. Comprehends recall type questions. | | | |
| _____ 10. Displays adequate vocabulary skills. | | | |
| _____ 11. Can find the main idea. | | | |
| _____ 12. Can skim to locate details. | | | |
| _____ 13. Can scan for particular items of information. | | | |
| _____ 14. Can follow the sequence of the story. | | | |
| _____ 15. Can follow directions. | | | |
| _____ 16. Exhibits competence in critical and creative thinking. | | | |

## Figure 12

### Survey of Vocabulary Skills

Name of Child _____ Date _____

| The student | Usually | Rarely | Never |
|---|---|---|---|
| 1. Can define a word by example. | | | |
| 2. Can define a word by description. | | | |
| 3. Can define a word through comparison and contrast. | | | |
| 4. Can define a word by using a synonym or antonym. | | | |
| 5. Can define a word by apposition. | | | |
| 6. Can develop meanings for new words through experiences. | | | |
| 7. Can develop new meanings for known words through experiences. | | | |
| 8. Understands the connotation of words. | | | |
| 9. Understands idiomatic expressions. | | | |
| 10. Can use figurative language (similies, analogies, metaphors). | | | |
| 11. Makes use of context clues. | | | |
| 12. Understands compound words. | | | |
| 13. Can discriminate between/among homonyms. | | | |
| 14. Understands and can use prefixes. | | | |
| 15. Understands and can use suffixes. | | | |
| 16. Understands the root meaning of words. | | | |
| 17. Is aware of multiple meanings of words. | | | |
| 18. Understands concept of acronyms. | | | |
| 19. Can use the dictionary competently. | | | |
| 20. Can use a thesaurus. | | | |

## Figure 13

### Materials Selection Checklist*

| Material Being Reviewed _____ | Yes | To Some Degree | No |
|---|---|---|---|
| 1. Do you, as the teacher, understand the philosophy behind the material? | | | |
| 2. Does the material teach the skills the children need? | | | |
| 3. Is the material appropriate for the children who will be using it? | | | |
| 4. Is the material interesting to children? | | | |
| 5. Are readiness materials available at all levels? | | | |
| 6. Will the activities motivate the children to learn? | | | |
| 7. Are the skills taught by the material applicable to reading situations outside reading class? | | | |
| 8. Is the material so organized that the skills learned may be applied to reading in the content area? | | | |
| 9. Is the material free from sex, ethnic, racial stereotypes? | | | |
| 10. Do you understand *how* the vocabulary is controlled if the material claims to have a controlled vocabulary? | | | |
| 11. Is the material up-to-date? | | | |
| 12. Are all areas of the reading process treated adequately? | | | |
| 13. Does the material allow for ongoing diagnosis and evaluation? | | | |
| 14. Is the material comprised of all areas of literature—poetry, prose, fiction, nonfiction? | | | |
| 15. Is the teacher's manual adequate? | | | |
| 16. Will the format of the material be appropriate for those children who will be using it? | | | |
| 17. Do the authors of the material provide any research relative to the efficacy of their material? | | | |
| 18. Is the cost of the material reasonable? | | | |

*Adapted from *Preparing to Teach Reading,* Grayce Ransom. Boston: Little Brown, 1978, 93-94.

Curry